The Spirit Life &
3-Books of Evelyn

by

Evelyn Adams

Concerning the Three books, all names and places have been changed to protect the privacy of those individuals whose stories and experiences appear in these books.

Medical Disclaimer: The information in these books is not intended or implied to be a substitute for professional medical advice, diagnosis, or treatment. All content is for general information purposes only.

To Evelyn: A Simple Invocation

"Open my Eyes to help me See. Open my Ears to help me Hear and Open my Heart to help me Feel. Grant that I be able to be used as a Channel whereby I can help the person coming to me for help and advice, and to those I come into contact with each day and Grant that I may be a Channel whereby I can impart Peace unto the one who I am trying to help, as well as those God brings me into contact with."

"The Rising of the Sun and the Setting of the Sun are the two times of the Day when you can feel closer to the Presence of God. Try watching both often as you can and opening yourself to the Oneness of God and to his Energies."

Smenkhare (Evelyn's Master Teacher)

Message from Master Smenkhare

There is One God, The Creator of all that is in The Heavens and on The Earth. All are created equal regardless of Race, Nationality, Religion or Station in Life. The Belief in That One God is what is important. He breathed The Breath of Life into all Living Things and thus so, All Creatures of God are to be appreciated and respected because, they too, are Living Souls. Look to Nature to see The Wonders of God's Creations, even a common blade of grass is created so perfect that no Scientist can possibly re-create what God has made. When we can allow ourselves to open up to those Creations and feel the Oneness of God, we can find Peace within ourselves. Without our having this, we cannot expect to be able to help or guide others on the Path of Life.

About the Author

This is the mediumistic journey my life has taken thus far in this physical world. The 'illusion and physical human body' are necessary if we are to fulfill our inner desires to learn and experience what we cannot receive in our true dimensional home world. One incarnation here equals ten lifetimes of lessons and experiences on planet earth, it is that hard. That is why 'Billions' of Energy Beings come here to work on their spiritual advancement.

Love and Blessings,
Evelyn Adams

___Dedication___

To Alexander and my Inner-Band members, and to all the other energy companions, teachers and friends who have come at different times to assist me in becoming the Medium I am today.

For without their 'Energy, Wisdom and Love' I would still be wandering in the darkness; I give my most heartfelt gratitude and love!

You bring enlightenment to a world in great need; let your light continue to shine ever so brightly that others may find their way out of the darkness of the Devine Illusion!

Index

Evelyn's Mediumship Development.......... **(7)**

Personal readings given to Evelyn by Alexander...................................... **(20)**

Annoying Dead People Book #1... **(58)**

More Annoying Dead People Book #2.. **(156)**

Really Annoying Dead People Book #3.. **(263)**

Parting Words............................... **(377)**

Evelyn's Mediumship Development

****

As a child and teenager, I had no special ability as a Medium or Psychic. I never had any interest in the 'New Age' stuff, what little I had seen on the subject. I had heard other people speak of gypsies and fortune tellers who cheated gullible people out of their hard-earned money.

I would be around age thirty-two before I got my first experience of anything occult or psychic as it were. There was a Psychic Fair being organized just down the street from my apartment at a little church that had been rented out by some spiritualist group.

Being bored on a Saturday afternoon, I went in to see what it was all about. There were different speakers in the main floor area giving talks on Karma, Auras, Reincarnation, Chakras, Crystal Stones, and other such stuff, most of which I had never heard of.

There was a sign which said 'Spirit Readings' were being conducted in the basement of the church. So, I ventured down the stairs and came upon an older woman who sat at a small table. She gave me a little tutorial on what was going on.

For a love donation of five-dollars you could sign up for a fifteen-minute reading with one of the four psychics whose names were listed on a chalkboard that stood next to the small table.

Not knowing who any of the psychics were I just chose a name at random. His name was Richard

Blake. I chose a time he was open, and the nice lady wrote my name in that slot. Every fifteen minutes or so she would ring a small brass bell to alert the psychics to finish up and be ready for the next person.

There were maybe fifteen people who were waiting for a spirit reading. The bell rang, and at my appointed time I headed for Richard Blakes table. The four psychics were all sitting at fold-out individual card tables that were separated by gray curtains to offer some privacy.

Richard Blake was a man who looked to be in his mid-forties I figured and was very pleasant. He asked if I had any questions and I said 'not really' so he gave me what he said his guide wanted me to know.

He told me, which came as a total shock to me, that I had a tremendous power in what he called the 'spiritual arts.' That if I wished to pursue my abilities in that direction, he would be glad to have me join a mediumship development class he was mentoring for several others at his home.

Richard said there was no charge, his services were free to those who were invited to attend his development class.

I must admit, I was afraid that this was some type of scam. I had heard some people talk about phony psychics charging big sums of money to bilk old widows with promises of letting them speak to their dear departed husbands and whatnot.

The fifteen-minutes went by very quickly, and I thanked Mr. Blake for the reading. He handed me his card with his address and phone number.

It would be several weeks before I worked up the courage to attend a development class at Richard Blakes home, my curiosity finally got the better of me.

My first class started with Richard Blake, his wife Edna, their friends Nathan, Barbara and Conny. All were working on some type of mediumship, except for Richard, who was a trance (direct voice) medium and our development teacher.

The following are the dates I attended Richard's development classes and a little bit of what transpired:

01/19/1988

Richard would go into a trance state and different entities would bring greetings and information to the group through him.

I was first given the names of my inner band who would be working with me on developing my abilities. My Master Teacher is Smenkhare, he was Egyptian, a Pharaonic King in the 18th Dynasty of his last lifetime upon the Earth. My Spirit Doctor was Alexander, the guide I would work closely with. My Chemist was Dr. Lyndall Rice, his last lifetime was as an Englishman, he was an archaeologist in the Sudan region of Africa. My gate keeper (joy guide) is called Priscilla. I have three Native Americans (Apaches). Chief Red Bird, my shaman medicine man. Chief Red Blanket, my protector, and Chief Grey Horse, who will assist the others in bringing energy. They said more guides will be coming to join my inner band as needed.

It was explained to me how to have a private class (by myself) at my home. To start off, I was to say the Lord's Prayer out loud, then call all my inner band members by name out loud. I was to breathe in/out slowly (7) seven times to relax.

I was to close my eyes and clear my mind (meditate) for 15-30 minutes, three times a week. If I had trouble clearing my mind, I was to listen to soft, meditative music.

Sitting in a straight-backed chair with feet flat on floor and legs not crossed. Hands to be placed on my thighs, palms facing down. I was to sit in a quiet, darkened room and wear comfortable loose-fitting clothing.

Once I got the basics learned, I was to start sitting with the lights on; said I would not be giving readings in the dark.

The development class was held once a week on the same day of the week, same exact start time and the class lasted about 45 minutes. The group would say the lord's prayer out loud together then take turns calling our inner bands to come join us. Then we would meditate for about 30 minutes and spend the last 15 minutes listening to messages from different entities (guides) who came through Richard while in a trance.

01/21/1988

In trance speaking, voice comes from the Medium's voice box (vocal cords). In Trumpet Séance, voice of spirit comes from trumpet, not from the Medium. Vocal cords are created (so-to-speak) from inside the trumpet. A materialized spirit can speak with its own voice box (vocal cords).

01/26/1988

Priscilla (Evelyn's joy guide), Virginia (Edna's joy guide) and Pansy (Richard's joy guide) came in to speak. Said can live on 800 calories a day when working with your guides. They (guides) can enhance the 800 calories to 2 or 3 times for the physical body. Said Evelyn would be moving in 60 days.

02/02/1988

Pansy, Grey Wolf (Barbara's Native American), Dr. Morton (Conny's Spirit Doctor), Dr. Kelly (Edna's Spirit Doctor) and Ralph (Barbara's younger brother, who was in the Navy, who died at age 19 when a plane crashed on the deck of an aircraft carrier he was assigned to) came in to speak. Ralph sang a short song of 'I'm Alive.' Conny was given the name of her Master Teacher, JA-ZARR, each letter is the first letter of each of his full name's. JA-ZARR is close to going over the 7th Level.

02/09/1988

Evelyn received her 'Health Guides' name, her name is Betty Amarillo, she was from France in her last lifetime. Betty will advise on what food, drink, rest, and exercise will be needed for spiritual and physical development. Conny received the name of her new chemist, Dr. Thomas Parker. Edna's great grandfather came in to say 'Hi' to the group.

02/16/1988

Grizzly Bear (Richard's Native American), Pansy, Dwight Eisenhower (former President) and Beth Ann (Edna's sister who died at birth) came in to speak. Said Conny had something to go through in next 48 hours. Wouldn't say what, but she's getting a private reading after class about it.

*Note to Reader: Conny's ex-husband said if she didn't return to him, he would kill their three small children and then commit suicide and that it would be all her fault. Her guides said it was an empty threat, that he had no true intention of harming his children or himself, he was acting out because of his alcoholism. Advised her to notify authorities of threat and not to speak or meet with him.

03/01/1988

Dr. Charles Tree (Richard's Spirit Doctor) told Conny to rest, relax, seek new adventures before age 40. At that age she will be doing what was programmed for her to do in this lifetime. For at age 40, she will not have the time to play, as it were, for she will be doing spiritual work and it will be all-consuming. Dr. Charles Tree told Evelyn to use her basic instinct and that she is number one (#1). No one else is to run her life, she is the boss of herself. Not to follow friends or co-worker's advice when situations arise, she will make the decision what needs to be done concerning her life, no one else.

03/15/1988

Dr. Charles Tree told group, once you start on path of mediumship development, it is always moving forward. Spiritual development continues even into the spirit dimension after one dies, and crosses over.

03/29/1988

Pansy came in to speak, said all would be fine now with Conny's problem (ex-husband). Evelyn's chemist, Dr. Lyndall Rice performed a procedure on her. She said it felt like needle pricks on top and left side of her head. Pain ran from top of head to lower neck. Lasted only three seconds.

*Note to reader: Conny got full custody of all three children.

04/05/1988

Dr. Charles Tree came in, told Evelyn to seek an apartment, not a house to rent at this time. Evelyn was shown a face during development class in her mind's eye. It was a black and white picture of a female. Dr. Charles Tree told her if see or hear something, mentally tell her guides. Let them know what I'm receiving from them so they can make adjustments. For example, they may have shown a picture in color, but she only received it in black and white, so they know what needs work to bring about desired result in her development.

04/12/1988

Conny has another new member to her inner band, a 'Sister Ti Sung' of the 'White Order of

Sister's.' She was the first daughter of the very first Emperor of China in her last earth lifetime.

05/10/88

Mary Jane (Mae) West, American actress, came in to speak to group. Said love is 90% in the mind and 10% sex. Said her favorite movie line was "Save your nickels, and save your dimes, and when you get a dollar…come up and see me sometime." Pansy said for everyone to stay on same vibrational level, if change, vibration will go into another direction.

05/24/1988

Dr. Charles Tree said, more energy is present if two or more people meditate together. For example, if two people meditate together, you have person one's energy plus person's two energy plus combined energy of both people which brings three times the energy.

06/07/1988

Evelyn asked about the Higher Self. Dr. Meadows (Chemist for Richard) spoke, said the Spirit (true you) are encased in the ethereal body which is encased in the physical human body. Barbara was advised not to crack her knuckles, because it can cause arthritis down the road, same with falls. Dr. Meadows said the chemicals they put into our bodies for development are based in part on our physical weight. If lose weight too fast, it can bring on illness.

06/14/1988

Dr. Charles Tree explained to Edna how for her, not everyone, that certain foods give off vibrations which have an adverse effect on her nervous system.

06/21/1988

Beth Ann said Spirit Doctors sometimes make it sound like the Spirit World is less appealing, so we won't want to return home too soon before our lessons are learned, but she said it's Fantastic! Christa McAuliffe (American Teacher and Astronaut who perished in the space shuttle Challenger disaster) came in to say 'Hi' to group. Said after explosion she (soul) went to a spirit hospital for a while to re-orientate herself back to her home dimension due to the abruptness of her death.

07/05/1988

Dr. Kelly spoke, said when they work on Evelyn's crown chakra, it causes the memory loss she sometimes experiences. Dr. Karris (Barbara's Spirit Doctor) talked to Barbara about sitting for development. He advised Conny to file for bankruptcy and talked to her about a rare form of mediumship she would be doing around her 40th birthday.

07/12/1988

Barbara's Master Teacher (SA-ZARRA) came through and told her to shield herself from those who are not in harmony with her.

07/26/1988

Pansy came in to speak, said Barbara needed to put more effort into her development and remove herself from the 'mind games' she plays and release her mind set on having so much in the way of material things, which does nothing to help humanity.

08/02/1988

Dr. Charles Tree said to Evelyn, after a period of time, guides don't need for her to sit in a straight-backed chair. She can lay on her bed or in a recliner chair, as long as she doesn't fall asleep. If her guides need to move her body for a particular procedure, they will give thought energy to it. Her Native American Indians (extremely high spiritual beings) will then generate the energy necessary to reposition her body.

08/23/1988

Chief Red Bird (Evelyn's Shaman Medicine Man) told Evelyn to view things in her life from a larger perspective. Said things seem less important when look at overall picture, instead of focusing in on one little event. Chief Red Bird told Evelyn she and him were, in a previous life, 'Blood Brothers' and they remain blood brothers now and forevermore. She was called in that lifetime, 'Running Buffalo.'

09/06/1988

This would be Evelyn's last visit to Richard Blake. Instead of a development class Richard gave her a trance reading in which her guide Alexander came in to speak with her. Alexander told her to exercise, reduce salt intake, no added sugar or pepper to her diet. No fried foods, no grease. Can have ice cream and cake, but not every day. Take vitamins C and A, also take B-complex, it will help her to not feel nervous. Starting next week, sit for development each night for one-hour. Sit at the same time every night and all her guides will be there. Reason for this, the procedures her guides are going to perform on her take 2 or 3 weeks to prepare in advance and it takes an hour to administer it to her physical body. Also want her to expand her mind. Alexander told her this will be her last life experience on the earth plane, so enjoy it to the fullest.

The following are some of Evelyn's experiences from her private development classes sitting by herself:

October-1988

My guides showed me what looked like a radio clock with the following numbers in red – 1209.

I was shown four words but could only make out the first word – YOU – the rest flashed too fast to read. They were black letters on a white background.

Saw the face of a female who had brown hair and brown eyes.

November-1988

Guides flashed – ARE YOU – could not make out the last word, flashed so fast. Last word started with a 'D.' Letters were reddish-purple on white background.

December-1988

Flashed face of a male, red beard, glasses, and an old hat which looked to be from the eighteen hundred period.

January-1990

Shown – TALD – which was printed on the back of a red-brick house.

Guides said they were working on me to develop, clairvoyance, clairaudience, and trance speaking.

February-1990

Became ill during class, just chemicals guides were pumping into my body. Ill sensation passed after about two minutes.

Sitting every day made me too sensitive, would start crying for no reason it seemed. Guides said they had finished doing the procedures on me, so told me to stop sitting for thirty days, then sit only three times a week for thirty minutes from now on.

March-1990

I was shown two male faces and one female face. I described what I saw in detail and color wise to my guides so they would know how much I was receiving and therefore what I needed to work on.

In healing process, key element is to forgive. To forgive yourself, as well as forgiving all others.

Napping replenishes energy, guides can commune with us while resting, not sleeping.

I see purple and white energy clouds when meditating. These colors deal with purification and change into higher spiritual form.

April-1990

When my guides worked on my chakra's, it felt like I was paralyzed and couldn't move, then like bed was spinning around and floating up into the air. Guides said it was just my brain trying to make sense of what was being done to my body.

I felt like needle pricks were sticking me in my head and had the sensation that something was being pumped into my head, yet no pain was observed.

I heard a loud vibrational explosion from my Native American Indians, who wanted to show how much power they were generating.

During one procedure, I felt like something seized my body, I was paralyzed, it felt like something was mashing in my front teeth and I could taste the blood in my mouth. It lasted less than a minute and I was released. My guides said it was the only way my brain could make any sense of what was taking place. Simply a procedure my guides were doing to prepare my body for mediumship.

The following are 'personal' readings given to Evelyn over the years from her guide Alexander:

****

Evelyn's Body Weight:

What body weight level should Evelyn maintain for optimal physical health and for her Mediumship abilities?

Her weight is not detrimental for her abilities at its current level (125 lbs.), nor is it interfering with her development and mediumship. There is a weight level that should be maintained for influence at a later time, and this can fluctuate between 120 and 135 pounds as she finds it comfortable. There is no detriment within this level because it does not interfere with the physical and energy-based process that have direct influence over the areas that serve medium and communication abilities. It is more important to maintain the consistency at a weight setting more than it is important to set a weight goal at this time. There is no problem for you caused by health which impacts your breathing or chest cavity for the flow of breath and energy. Focusing on your diet to maintain the weight with your physical exercise should be the focus. Maintaining a weight at which you feel comfortable within this range. If you enjoy 120 pounds, it is acceptable, if you enjoy 135 pounds, it is acceptable. It is important that you do what feels comfortable with you but continue your diet in the manner that you have been recently. These create balance and health for you and serve the energetic purposes on a physical level which build the basis for development and implementation of the skills and abilities on which you are working. Maintain, do not overindulge, or starve yourself at any point. Maintain. You can weigh less but dropping your body to a physical weight below 100 will not cause greater comfort for you and will have an impact on the energy stores for your communication channels. For, it is necessary, there must be some fat, not to detrimental levels, but it must be maintained in small amounts in the body to retrieve and access it during the production of spirit communication and physical apparitions, much in the same way the physical body accesses stored energy during exercise. What you eat is important but maintaining a specified weight within a few pounds at all times is far more important. Doing this will provide consistency in the level and amount of energy and other forms that are delivered to you at times of producing an ability or strengthening it. Losing weight does not change our work level or our desire to work with you, there is only difference in the type and level of energy and chemicals sent to you or reworked within your body to allow for this difference, you can proceed as you have been should you wish. Your diet and exercise are what, within your current weight zone, is providing the health that you desire.

Garlic Capsules:

Are garlic gel capsules bad for Evelyn Adams or for those seeking to develop any form of mediumship?

It is important to know that no matter what pill you allow to enter your body, that you do so, on a regular basis, so that the chemical formulation of that which is used within your body during the mediumship is balanced and regulated. It is possible to take any form of pill consistently or to take it only when the need for that specific pill should arise, but you should not take the pill, or any pill, sporadically, as it becomes more difficult to regulate the chemical and energetic make-up of the entire body as it relates to any form of spirit communication or phenomenon. For you, these can be beneficial. For heart and blood, they are a purifier. They serve to clear away the problems that certain medical doctors issue antibiotics for. There is a strong odor from these and will impact the body adversely until it acclimates to it. It is important to take these, if you will do so, only once per day no matter what the label advises and do so routinely if you wish. You may take them only in time of illness if that is what you feel you are more comfortable with. In a time of sickness, it is the dis-ease that often adversely affects any skill or ability you possess more than that of which you consume in order to rebalance your body. They are not negative simply because when they become routine the balancing process can be made to establish care and order within the body. It is necessary for you to take these but only do so if you believe that there is something within you that is causing a need for it. For, general maintenance with pills often prevents the body from producing its own chemicals for the body to get rid of certain problems and may interfere with certain healing processes. It is important to know that there is no direct reason for you, specifically, Evelyn Adams, to take these though they will contribute to overall health that is missed by the absence of certain vegetables within the diet. Though it is not any specific one that will offer the same specific satisfaction and purpose as garlic, they all, in combination, serve these purposes. It is acceptable to take this. It will not interfere with your goals or objectives. Maintain a balance and routine in what you do that regularly impacts the physical body and the energy radiating from it and that which is sent to it will find harmony. Seek balance in the level of carbohydrates that energize the body in relation to meat or protein, these should be in equal portion to fruit and vegetable. It is important for you to eat what comes from the ground, from your earth, directly. You are making progress on this. It is coming through now that you are. These subtle changes improve the clarity of your energy, the means you will use to communicate. The slow paced and small changes that take place serve to keep your chemical balance from altering drastically so that your balance is not offset and detriment, so that mediumship, any physical mediumship, or communication of any kind will not be hindered.

Egyptian Lifetime:

I lived a lifetime in Egypt where I was taken into the Great Pyramid. I was led up to the sarcophagus and laid inside while undergoing some type of initiation or training.

Neurologist:

What should Evelyn know about going to see a neurologist (nerve trouble in lower back)?

Evelyn Adams needs to realize that there isn't much standing in her way. She can go to the doctor, but we know she won't agree with much they have to offer her or have to say. There is much more she can do herself than what they provide. A pill is what they will offer you. Exercise is what you need to do. You may go but it will provide you confirmation of what you already know. A doctor cannot peer inside your body in the way that you want them to. They do not consider anything that does not come from their education, learning, knowledge, or textbook. Please be patient with them. All you need is love.

What should Evelyn do to keep every level of her being healthy at this time?

She needs to do more than just walk; walking is great for emotions but does nothing for the mind.

Exercise it (mind) too. There is much work to be done, she should not make excuses for lacking physical effort. Evelyn is a strong woman when she wants to be. Ask us, we will provide. Stop doubting, just do. So many are limited because of the thoughts they have of themselves. When you put your mind to it, the work will be done, it will come. There are more things to be done and many people are able to accomplish many things if they prevent themselves from becoming sidetracked with meaningless endeavors. Possible is everything. Stop at nothing. Must convey message. Health is second to none. Evelyn Adams go forth and do it! There is nothing she can't do!

For Evelyn:

There is a hand that always leads the child, a person less experienced, the apprentice as they begin to learn to cross the street. They protect, they guide, and they assist, but there must come a time, in order to reach full potential, full development, and to experience all that there is in the world, when the young child, apprentice, the person studying, must let go of that hand and experience the crossing of the road on their own and to seek all that there is on the other side. An experience through the interpretation of others is not always best as it limits your view and your lesson and your ability. Much greater growth is had by taking on these experiences for yourself without the middle interference or relaying of information. You are capable of this now. Have no fear, this is not new to you. You've been here before.

For Evelyn:

Do I need to call my guide to bring forth energy before each healing session?

There is no reason for that to be spoken before each session. We are with you always. You have a direct connection to us. When there is a need for healing you may simply conduct it and we will bring what you are unable to pull from your environment. There is much that can be done on your own and many humans depend on something outside themselves or believe that something outside themselves needs to take place before a change can happen. All is done in the mind and with energy that is present in all living and natural things. This is where healing also comes from, not just the spirit side where many things like these are normal occurrences.

Should I let you know what I am about to do when I am beginning a healing session on another person?

This is helpful for us. Communication is simple for us, not difficult as you first perceived. Your thoughts about your actions will draw helpful entities nearer to you and will proceed with any advisement or help during the healing process.

Do I need to call my guides before each automatic writing session?

This is something you should do until the process becomes more natural and concrete for you. There is much that can be done by using a system or a routine until you become more confident and comfortable. There is a need for you to take the place of another at this table and you are doing it rightly. There will be a time when this is not the preferred method of communication for you. Though it is building your ability and strength and confidence at this time. These are all important. For there will be a time when your technology may not be as accessible as it is now.

Do I need to call my guide to place a shield around me before each healing or automatic writing session?

This is helpful but not necessary as each person is protected on their own from within. Because you are doing work for a higher good and greater good than selfish reasons, there will always be protection for you from within your own body and mind. This does not always come from an outside force. We do not always intervene since the majority of energy and action takes part from within you, whether you realize it or not. Calling it something that happens outside of you by another force is possibly easier to understand then the realization that all protection comes from your actions, commands, thoughts, and beliefs. Nothing good will come to you if you don't believe it first. Negativity will not join you unless you call it or introduce this with your actions.

Am I conducting my automatic writing sessions correctly?

There are things you can do to improve them, but this is not a concern at this time. This is the process by which we communicate at this time. There is not a need to rush things as all information will come as you are ready. You are looking for a confidence or confirmation of your ability to communicate with us. You may seek this if you wish but it is not necessary when you know by your own account, and that of others, that this information is coming from a place much higher than your current position on your human existence.

Is running or walking related to spiritual or psychic development and grounding?

This is necessary for you. There is a grounding that comes from it. There is energy gained and lost by this process and many will experience the joy from running or walking even if they do not perceive the entire change taking place on more subtle levels which they do not yet acknowledge. If those who were developing were to run or walk everyday there would be no reason to use other activities to ground themselves or seek out ways to

distract their mind through drugs or alcohol.
There is no reason to worry about exercise if a
regular fitness routine included only walking or
running. Much is done for physical and energy
body in these actions and there is much that is done
only with these actions. Energy is shaken from the
body and a calm is perceived as well as physical
blood and energy circulation. It enlivens the body
and awakens areas that may be dark or missing
energy. These are positive things that are achieved
by physical activity. There is no benefit lost by
their action, this should be undertaken as a spiritual
foundation for those who also wish to meditate or
develop spirit communication. It will help them
deal with higher vibrations as we contact them and
connect with them. There is much benefit in this
action by those who wish to work with energy.

How can I heal nature in the courtyard of my
apartment?

There is a nature here that is out of balance and
was only worsened when the trees were removed.
There is energy here that is scattered about and
comes from the various forms of life occupying
these dwellings. There is no reason to fear any
negative impact. In the long term plan this area will
once again be overgrown and run wild with
creatures, plants, forms of life. You can foster this
by meditation and sending energy do it. Brining
life into it with habitation areas will speed up this
process. Also, care for what is currently left and

still thriving. The lakes will run over if they are not watched but this too can be a helpful process.

Information Transfer: from Spirit Guide to a Medium:

What is the basic process that occurs when a spirit guide in one-dimension transfers information to a Medium in our dimension? How many spirits must be involved to form the energy required for this process?

The energy required varies depending on the manner of the manifestation. There are many present but not all contribute in the same manner. Much is done to prepare an entity for transference of information prior to the transfer taking place. There are energy adjustments and chemical alignments necessary for most communication. Many can return to your plane without much assistance and complete these tasks, others need to have this work done at a later time or a retuning because of the detriment caused to the body by living this physical existence. No matter if it is done on the earth or it is done prior to birth, the same work is done, again, in addition, this process may be restarted or recalibrated due to the spirit's ability to manipulate the body negatively through physical means. There are separate entities which will work with each being in order to deliver information. Often times there is not one singular person or entity conveying this formation. Many of those on your plane who are capable of giving information may assign a name to the messenger, or they may assume it is their highest or closest companion from this world as you live in yours. They may use this name, but this is not the sole entity that brings information for them to share. During communication there may be the use of the guide to relay the information, or the information may be direct from the chosen entity. Often a guide or spirit advisor from the questioner will provide information. The process in this regard depends highly on the vibrational level of the channel as well as the congruence between the spirit guides in question. Some may be harmful or otherwise incompatible with the channel, these will not be allowed within proximity of the channel, though they may converse with the spirit guides or observers of the channel. The energy may come from our plane, or it may come from yours, in most events there is a combining of energy. More energy is needed depending on the method of communication manifestation that is being used. Each requires different energy and different types. There may be a greater need for energy drawing from your world, or from ours. On your side this can come from other willing physical living participants, or the ambient energy that is existent in air, earth, water, the natural life-giving elements. There is much that you do not know about this, and we will do our best to share and enlighten you. Though you must understand that there are many terms and processes which may compound your confusion or illicit such a reaction from your curiosity that there will be only further questioning to a point where no discernable information can be gathered by you because of the subtle processes used and their explanations. Know there is much to transfer energy, all actions and thoughts are energy. They are transferred quite similarly as you would transfer a telephone call to another part of the world. A connection is created, a vibration must be raised in the channeler and the ability to focus on the task being conducted is important. It is important to maintain the human body of the channel. Much information is shared when the difference in energy is similar or reaching a closer point. There are those on this side, our side who can make this difference less and less with little effort, and for some it takes many entities working together to bring about this lowering and raising of energy to facilitate a closeness in mind and harmony and resonance so that the thought transfer can be conducted and maintained. Various means of communication all take part in the same way, through it is the physical body that may interpret it as hearing, feeling, or seeing, simply because these are the areas which have been focused and energy directed. There are other specific types that may be accomplished but all work on the same basic principles. A channel is created, then a thought, the energy travels that communication pathway to the human body, containing a spirit in the human existence, and the information is shared. In the same manner, trance will take place but rather than share your thoughts with that person expressing the skill to channel information and messages, the thought is not transferred, the physical energy of the entity is traversing the pathway and inhabiting the physical body, or they are able to use the pathway to send their energy through, as a telephone may be picked up and listened to and spoken to, this is true for manipulation of the pathway to deliver information. There is no need to worry about your communication Evelyn Adams. It is clearer, there will be an impact on your energy field to allow trance communication to take place. It may be possible to complete this skill at a later date, while in the absence of any other human, and verified using a recording device. This can build your skill and efficiency. Later you will have this ability to share with others. You are close to this now. There is much being done in your physical body and energy field to align your energy and physical makeup to allow this to take place. Questions could be asked now during your development, but it is imperative that the mind not overshadow the physical or energy bodies and that the mind not jolt the physical body and make it completely aware of what is taking place. Intend for your communication to take place, allow, and give permission for those you wish to energize to enter and those who are permitted to communicate with you should be given your permission to do so. There will only be a select few who can communicate through you, though they have information from many sources, they are not limited. These entities will begin to attune themselves to you and have begun to work on this process in subtle ways within your energy system. It is important to maintain the diet to allow proper nutrition for this to take place without the distraction of the energy contained within these foods. Many guides and companions, working towards the same mission, will accomplish the same task, all is energy, this is the manner in which it is transferred. It may be many times before the energy is transferred successfully but this process is the same for delivery of any manifestation. Physical manifestation is, again, the transfer of energy, though a different type. They are being used, the energy of the channel, to bring forth the entity so that they may manipulate the physical energy of the human body and extract from it what is necessary to create a physical apparition. Each time a communication or manifestation takes place this communication channel is created. You can see it as a tunnel or a tube between two separate destinations, depending on the work that has been done to maintain this channel or tube, the information coming through will vary, this too is depending on the mind of the individual channel and what they hope to achieve, what they have worked to achieve, and what they will allow to be achieved. All is, as always, dependent on the mind.

Evelyn's (heart) Episode:

Please share information about Evelyn's episode, and what caused it, which occurred today around 3:30 PM by our measurement of time.

This was an experience for Evelyn Adams which she will be more comfortable with in the future. There is nothing a doctor can remedy as well as what an individual can choose to put into their own body. There is a salt that negatively affects the heart, and it can cause physical reactions within the body preventing the natural flow of energy. There is an unnatural amount of this in Evelyn's diet, this should be lessened so to allow a greater natural and harmonious flow of energy within the body for an increase to occur. At present, the lack of water and increase of salt or salt-like products deters some activity of energy for her and an increase in desired weight loss would be achieved should salt be lessened. Understand that some salt is necessary, salt should be in foods you eat, though salt only as a preservative is unhealthy for the body. There is energy at work which will need a body with salt to a lesser degree than what is present, water can achieve a balance in the body, but salt should also be lessened slightly to prevent buildup of energy in this area and any problems which are associated with it. Evelyn has strong energy, and she will shortly become more aware of this, but the human diet can, in many ways, directly affect the ability and flow of energy. You should experience these things as a road sign on your path as allowing you to take in direct feedback regarding your trip. You shall choose to see a doctor at some point, but as in the past, there is not much they will do to ally your fears. More is done by you, on your own. Energy and healing to this area will balance it. Allow others to heal this area which will improve it greatly though you can benefit greatly from short daily meditation on each chakra to allow each to be fully operational and balanced and in line with the others. This would allow this area, your focus on it, the greatest amount of work to be done and allowing it to fully awaken and balance. What you experienced today was a culmination of energy as it works to undo what has been done in the past and in some part your diet plays a role. There is a working out of ideas and memories, and this is simply your body working through them in order to make room for new experiences. The new cannot fully be appreciated when always compared to the past, or what the past is so deeply and emotionally attached to the energy and physical body. You are allowed to forget things, events, and occurrences. The ideas you learned from experiences will be carried with you always and into future events and situations. You will remember all once you leave this plane. You will not have forgotten times, dates, and places. A releasing of energy, a natural expression of what was taking place but also a sign to you of work being done and work yet to be done or areas of focus. Reduce the sodium, increase clear fluids, but do not introduce salt and sugar into these fluids. When desiring taste, introduce those things that are naturally sweetened, not artificially so or purely for enjoyment. Squeeze fruit into your drink, though pure water is the better for regulating. Some tolerance of this on your part is necessary though we can appreciate the tendency for variety and using such things to sweeten or add taste will not harm the process. Remove fear and uncertainty from those corners of your mind where you know it still exists. You have shared much and taught many; you will continue to do this. Personal privacy and the status of a 'loaner' at work is a positive thing because there is much conflicting energy. Though understanding it and how it flows and why it flows is important to understand for future experiences. Love to all, but it is not necessary to let their energy overburden you. You can touch their lives without being fully altered by the experience to which it may cause you detriment. Help others without demoting yourself of energy. Do not take on the burdens of others, they are for themselves to experience. Guidance and wisdom are for them to consider, your job is to express it. Love is an amazing emotion and expressing it to them is helpful though many may not reciprocate by their exterior because of present attitudes in place. They are still appreciative and understanding though it will take time for them to express gratitude. Do not expect immediate results. It takes much to tear down mountains, but a single pebble can begin that change for many. Expressing anger in a positive manner should be understood. It is not necessary to contribute to the anger of others, allow yours to be released but in a positive act or turn of energy. Physically taxing work or movement will express this energy without further building and evolving this energy into something greater or without allowing it to become part of some greater collective of energy which might also be similar and a collective negative thought by the group towards one group, several people, or an idea.

Evelyn Adams does not have a physical problem with her physical body (heart) in this area. Any pain, discomfort, or uneasy feeling is the result of an energy imbalance in this area that she still experiences from a previous lifetime. It is necessary to repair this and move farther from it. There is no reason to leave love or move away from

it because of previous hurt or lost experience.
There is only the experience itself. It does not
detract from or prove the non-existence of certain
human and even universal emotions. She is to
bring her body into alignment by showing love but
also receiving it. Allow it to come from the most
unexpected places and places from which we do not
consider love and our intentions or those that we
believe to be with our intentions, to emanate. There
is a time for Evelyn Adams to transfer energy from
other areas of her body and seeming control and
focus them onto this area. Great wisdom shall be
your forte though you may not see the depth with
which it reaches humanity, but with knowledge and
wisdom there must be a balance of heart and love.
Great leaders do not lead alone, there are always
emotions and a separate being which may guide
them or be their companion in a physical form.
Steer with your mind and your heart and balance
will come to this area. Do not cause more problems
than what truly exists within your body. There is
no time to worry about this more than what is
necessary for worry for it will only bring you to the
same stagnate point, it will not bring change to this
area, and you will have only created a stressor for
yourself on its behalf. Action only. If action
cannot be taken do not concern yourself with what
may or may not happen. There is a time for action
and that is the motivator, not time for worry and
inconsistency within your physical body. You must
go and experience the world in addition to your
own experience and personal endeavors. There is a
life beyond an apartment, an interaction will be
brought within your path to allow you to experience

this love we speak to a greater sense than you have felt in this lifetime and also in lives previously on this plane of earth. Much is to be done to prepare you for this and you have done much, though a worry is only a worry. See it for its existence, not that which you add or detract from it. A being is a being, not a beautiful, bright, intelligent being, only a being. Added emotions and descriptors often cause further harm by asking that the being continues to live up to our expectations, our own thoughts create these expectations and do not always serve the good of those involved. Conflict can be experienced by it and then our thoughts are less pleasing because we feel they did not occur within or because or of our thoughts. Happiness comes from the life experienced externally. There is a diet for you, and you are slowly following it, exercise and sunlight are important. There is much to be discussed by this but none all at once. You must make changes gradually and slowly so that they become part of your regular life and routine so not to cause problems within the being that may cause the new activity to be ceased after a time or boredom befalls you. Create a peace within yourself and share this with others. A time is coming when you will need to experience strength in the heart area. While many actions in your past may be readily dismissed it is important to understand that they have caused an underlying problem in your energy because it was not dealt with or expressed at the time the event took place. Release all that is not for you, understand that which takes place. Replace hurt with the knowing that an experience is what was had, and an understanding shall come from this that shall carry over into other aspects of your life. There is nothing more that can be said on this for you now.

Who is calling Evelyn's name in her apartment and for what purpose?

This is a method of reminding her that she is forever present and connected with the spirit world. In its basic forms she should call aloud to the beings calling her. As much of this is a test and a call and answer session to further her communication abilities. There is much to be done, and while it is not always necessary to interrupt her down time or create more work for herself, it is always possible to do more. Balance. Do not run yourself ragged in any particular direction each day in any particular realm of activity. Balance yourself in all areas. Your attention is being called by her spirit guides and watchers. This is not a particular entity at all times as there is often a unified and neutral voice for testing. She may understand that there is a need for the physical mind to wander but wander and wonder in balance with critical thinking and deductive reasoning in her days. Acquire knowledge that is on the physical plane, not simply to better understand your world, but the act of knowledge acquisition is helping her grow in other positive ways. She is doing a great deal of work, do not feel as though you are just inching along.

Is it possible for me to see you (my guides) now, regularly, as we communicate?

It is possible for you, but you must elevate your mind. The communication by visually seeing anyone communicating with you is not important at this time. It is not important to see us; it is important to bring a message to you and for you to receive it without interference of your mind. Increasing your own confidence is not served by showing your mind's eye our physical appearance, nor is it readily available to you yet, later on, yes. You must achieve a deeper state in order for this to occur. There is not time for comparison between the ability of you and another. Your ability in other areas is stronger than that of other physical beings, this is same for many. There is no time for judgment or comparison, it is entirely dependent on your own ability and your own path, what you see, hear, and observe. In due time you shall have conversations with us physically and as readily as you communicate with those who are also in the human experience. It is not necessary to doubt any communication or message that you believe you are receiving, believing is not necessarily required in the sense of the world that many experience, you are doubtful of your receiving, you understand the message when you receive it, but you are not always convinced that it is us, that it is anyone other than yourself, giving it to you. Overcoming doubt and worry will aid in your ability to grow in your ability to communicate between realms. Meditation is the key to success. Sitting with no purpose is not helpful, but sitting in quiet mediation, in or out of a development sense, will aid in your ability to grow. Occasionally, in the human form we allow clutter to block the areas of the body and mind and true self which control and manage these abilities, often it takes the work of many to free these areas, to open them, to adjust them, to allow them to be receptive. Once again, the mind must be trained, the physical reminded of what it can do, and relearn what it once knew as true. Many times, young children have behavioral issues because they are receiving such information and receiving through greater number of senses than many adults who have come to ignore it. It is important to go forward knowing this. Know that all are capable through the will of their true self. Much change may be required to advance them forward if not initially prepared to achieve a high degree of realm crossover.

For Evelyn:

What type of work should Evelyn check into that would bring more harmony and tranquility for her in Florida?

There is a need to find employment that will meet your basic needs. There will not be a need for extra expenses like you have been entertaining. There will be empowerment for you to express yourself through your writing and the natural surroundings. This is not indicating to you that you should live in poverty but look to that which will give you the greatest joy and flexibility in terms of employment. It is acceptable to sacrifice the dollar for something that you can enjoy doing while you are required to do so to sustain your living arrangements. It is not that you will be in poverty, you can have greater advancing positions in working, but you do not need all that is available around you, you will have many opportunities for natural enjoyment and entertainment by your surroundings, they will not require finances. It is possible to look for employment that is near your home base so that you can rely less on your car or public transportation, thus eliminating the cost of fuel and maintenance by a sharp degree. There will be the same type of interaction for you with the public but not in the same capacity. There will be new lines of work for you, but they may not at first appeal to you. Consider the possibility of working with the public and interacting with it as a cashier or similar position. These are not stressful positions and can be found in places and locations that are similar to your beliefs and interests or in your surroundings. It is not necessary to worry about the complexity of the position or electronics; the position will be automated so that it is easily grasped and difficult to run afoul of its standard operation. There are several positions available now in natural settings. You will become a figure head at these locations because of your mindset, your attitude, your beliefs, and your presence. Some will offer better opportunities to share your beliefs, while others offer the ability of a low-impact position without stress while providing beautiful surroundings. It is not important to fret on these things as they will become evident to you.

You can pursue the same type of work if necessary and comfortable to you but understand that there will be a repeating of events that you have already experienced. It is important that if you obtain this employment that is similar to your last (Certified Nurse Assistant) that you should understand that it is only to provide temporary security until you are able to seek the freedoms of these new positions. Financial freedom is important and obtaining this previous employment will create further time if you see it as necessary but do not remain in it. The schedule for you will be inhospitable. As we see it, there are much more tolerable schedules in daytime hours that are greater in flexibility and offer greater flexibility so that they coincide with the natural cycles of the human body. Shift work is not for you and your body at this time. It is important to find what does not disturb the natural cycle but affords you these opportunities.

Floaters in the Eyes:

What causes floaters in my eyes?

Often times this is not something in the eye but something on the exterior, the fluid which lubricates the eye and reduces friction between the lid and the eyeball. This fluid can become thick and can become muddled with debris. This area can be cleansed with pure saline wash, no extra or outside chemicals. True tears or the natural wetness you experience is the only acceptable solution.

This area can be flushed and cleansed naturally by consuming more pure water. This will become more flushed and cleanse the area when greater amounts of fluids are consumed as it regulates the entire body. Fluid here will reduce tiredness; it will reduce small swirls or fragments that may seem to float in this fluid. The floaters in this area are caused by small sections of nerve and eye matter separating from the eye or nerves. This is caused by acidic or corrosive diets. Sugar can affect this area. Sweetness through unnatural means should be seen as a toxicity and harmful, though some small amounts in extreme moderation produce necessary chemicals within the digestive system. It is necessary to reduce that which causes the corrosion in the body and ferments. That which rots the gut also rots the nervous and sensory systems. Be prepared to make changes in this area Evelyn or your own eyesight will worsen. Water is the great equalizer, the great balancer of the scales. Much harm can be done to a body or much done to imbalance its system, but the addition of water prevents much or reduces the harmful impact. There is a fluid in the eye and when this becomes overly acidic or corrosive it begins to eat away at the flesh it encounters. Healing to this area in the form of reassigning the 'floating' matter to its rightful place or dissolving it to a state of pure energy is possible. Your consideration of anything similar to prayer or affirmations on the true context of the problem and how you would like it resolved create much energy and healing in this area. Direct healing can dissolve these, but it is hampered if the diet is remaining the same.

What can be done to eliminate floaters in the eyes?

Change the diet. Healing of any kind using energy of mind, word spoken, and direct energy by others on one's behalf. You are learning that all is energy. Energy is emanated by all that you do. Direct your energy to the positive result you wish to see and make the changes to prevent such measures from needing to be taken once more in the future.

What can be done to prevent floaters in the eyes?

There are often times no diet orders which need to be followed and the floating debris is caused by contamination of the blood. Though this is diet related it can be accused of carrying something negative for the body when it is working on its behalf to sanitize and clean and purify the body. Problems can also arise from any injury which may cause damage indirectly or directly to this area. Many changes come in the way of appreciation of sight and that which you refuse to see, because of the energy, can hamper your vision. There is not one simple remedy for most problems, though they are all simple, most will never undertake them because they require a change in thinking. It is your energy or the energy in which you involved yourself that creates much in your body, mind, and environment.

Book Writing:

What type of books and/or knowledge should Evelyn Adams seek to bring forth in the future?

There will be a time when people are needing to know more in-depth how to bring about peace into their daily lives. This will catapult them into creating a peace and understanding, though the world may not change, on a greater scale. This will allow them to fully understand the plight of their brother. This will allow them to understand that each is a human experience, there is a soul, a spirit, an energy being that will one day leave this place. There are many who are at a progressed portion of their path, referring to the knowledge they have gained, but they do not know how to break out of the knowledge shelter that has been created for them by society and their parents. Others have broken free but there is not material suitable to them. Much that is on the shelves and available today has much extra material. This is as we have said, how many will believe in the same sort of entity or process but call it by many terms, there is no need for extra wording or extra routine when simply the intention will do. There is no need to dress up the process or the knowledge when simply doing is all it takes. Many new ideas will come to you at a time when you are ready. Many ideas are presently available but not in an approachable format to those who are just getting off the bus and arriving at the destination which will take them into a greater sense of peace and understanding of themselves and those around them. The purpose of this lifetime is important for each who is completing it, knowing that there is more than what many popular beliefs hold is important. As you begin to speak on these things you will find more and more people with similar interest who will benefit. There should be a manual, a guidebook of information that will provide people with the general and basic understanding of concepts that many will not openly speak yet because of worry. There is other information that can be gleaned from books and rewritten for better understanding by those who do not need the extra decorations in ceremony and other pomp and circumstance. Using a church setting as an example, it is important to know that the idea is the reason why you attend, not the grand story, not the robes the preacher wears, not the decorations and ornateness of the massive cathedral. In this sense you will find a large audience will be reached by your work because you are explaining this material as though you were having a conversation in your living room. There is a certain gentleness and humbleness that you possess that will allow many to understand what you have said with much greater clarity than what others may have attempted to convey. It is important to know that there is no reason for one man to place himself on a higher pedestal than another. We are all the same. We can help each other grow. At some point the man on the soapbox will come down and the man on the pedestal will realize that there is greater similarity and teaching and education needed by him just as there are the many he was attempting to reach with his seemingly great and powerful knowledge. Many should know that even without this knowledge there is still no reason to fear. There is no reason to live a negative life. There is greater joy shared in giving joy to others than in destruction and negative actions. Greater numbers of people benefit through small positive actions compared to the negative impact of a small negative action. It is important to know peace, there are many things that will always exist. There will always be violence on an earth plane to some degree, not to the degree in which we are experiencing it now, but it will be possible to move far from wars, far from mass killings, and far from what has been experienced. There is still a change to come to the earth and learn these things once a greater change takes place, however many who are needing further development will not attend this place of learning if they are inclined towards these behaviors. Much energy is wasted, though it should be noted that the needs of many people are not being addressed properly because many who have material possessions see the needy as also wanting those things. The basic principles of human life are to have shelter, food, water, and community or companionship. There is no need by every living being to live in a mansion or own several expensive cars. While some may want those things, it is not necessary for all. Many who have power, control, vast riches, this is how they view those who appear to be of less value or less fortunate than they. If they are to understand anything it should be that there is no one that is going to steal their riches and knowing that this is a permanent life where others only wish to have the basic needs met so that they may teach and learn from and to others, this is important. Each working for their own, but also working to help those, this is the best use and the best area to direct energy. What the proper goals of humankind should be, simple texts, you know this. Many will read your texts.

Diabetes:

Does Evelyn Adams currently have diabetes, or could it be a misdiagnosis? Is there a spiritual message concerning diabetes?

Evelyn Adams does not have diabetes. There is a constant flux of sugar regulation in her body, and this is normal and will become more normalized and without peaks and valleys once she becomes accustomed to a new and healthier diet minus a surplus of sodium. There is a time, where another opinion of diabetes may be claimed but know that this is not something you should accept in your physical body. Mediumship is dependent on regulation and balancing of all energy and chemicals within the body. If anyone is not maintained it can be repaired but it must take time and consistency to allow us to establish what your actions will do to your body so that we can make adjustments on the level of energy and chemicals, we bring to it. This is why it is necessary to eat in a routine as there is less fluctuation. This is important to read about the things that you eat so that you know what you are truly putting into your body. There are many things that will cause the problems associated with blood sugar and related issues, but it is only a temporary problem and not the long-term problem associated with diabetes. Water will regulate the problems that are slowly being eliminated by the addition of new foods to your food routine. But it will take a period of time for proper adjustment. Never fear this word when doctors speak it to you. If your glucose were to stop because they seem to believe that you have consumed too many unhealthy foods and your glucose is failing, if it is true, it is possible for you to restart its production on your own and we can also aid you in this. As with any problem it should be not readily expected that you will meet a change immediately. There will be change after a period of time because of the unseen changes and balances to your body in addition to what you are doing. It must be seen at times that you are going to maintain a certain level within the body so that others aiding your energy and physical body will know how to measure and assist. There is no need to worry about this for you. Walking is important, look for fewer excuses not to take part in this activity no matter if you are at home or at your workplace. Look for more reasons for water. You will also get this from fruits you will be eating. Protein is important. Balance and regulate, all that you will be doing is based on your diet and the health of your physical body. There is much that you can still do to improve it. Focus on what you have been told so far. There is no emphasis on a medical doctor at this time or for what they may have given you in the past. Past information can soon be disregarded because of the energy and focus you

are now placing on diet and physical activity.
Know that your focus and actions are not unseen.
We too are working to balance and assist you.
Your development sessions, your meditations, and
many other times are times that we can aid your
physical body as well as your being on higher levels
and the unseen. There is no need to repeat what we
have said or done; you must simply maintain. Look
for new ways to express yourself when the old ones
have become mundane, outdated, or they are no
longer available to you. There is a fluctuation in
your levels regarding diabetes because of the
manner in which your diet is maintained and the
method which is presently used in a rudimentary
form to provide you with information and guidance.
This will change soon. Focus on the things you
have achieved but when small glimmers of new
skills appear it is time to take notice and make your
mind fully aware of them. It may be important for
you to write these into a book and review them later
as it will serve your ego when confirmation is
needed but also to focus the mind on these things
by reviewing your experiences. Focus on your diet.
The energy and will to complete and maintain will
become easier as the seasons change and once you
arrive to Florida, but work should be done now,
rather than expecting a switch to be flipped and a
sudden wave of interest or focus to come flowing
towards or out of you once your residence is in a
new state border.

What should I know about my working nights
and not seeing the sun?

There are many aspects of the sun that your body needs. You are getting little of them right now. It has adverse impact on the body. We are working on a position for you where you can be in the sun and outdoors. You will enjoy it greatly. There are many benefits to being in the sun and outside, many healing qualities. Many aspects regulate the body's normal function and systems.

What can I do to reverse the absence of the sun while I am working nights?

Vitamins, vitamins, vitamins. You are right to take vitamin D and C. There are many things you must do to combat no sun. Keep a regular routine, sleep at a normal time every day. Keep track of what you eat. Exercise.

Is there a light that I can use in my apartment or at work that will give the same benefit as the sun?

There aren't many things that you can do to replace it directly. Many lights just make claims. Having many lights on will help regulate cycles. Bright areas are better than dark ones when you must sleep opposite of the majority in humanity.

What about the lights at the office, fluorescent lights are not good?

They are not helpful and deteriorate your mood and energy. They often are dim, and this can impact your mood or psyche.

What can I do to prepare for the job on days and outside?

Become fit, work on this, you are. Show yourself what you can do. We will help but only so much. You will be happy. It is not unnecessary to want these things for yourself. Fitness for function is necessary, but not too much, don't overdo it. Be active, make peace with this now. Your dreams are coming true.

Is my ability to heal affected by missing the sun?

Not directly. We are helping you and when you heal yourself you are rebuilding your energy. This will be repaired soon. Patience, in time.

For Evelyn:

In this lifetime you have a justice theme. You are an empath, you absorb energy like a sponge from others, therefore you need to shield (protect) yourself from their negative energies.
You need to learn to deal with other people's personalities in order to grow your soul. No judgements, everyone here is doing their best or they 'think' they are doing their best. Need to be more patient with younger souls.

What causes Evelyn's legs to go numb (nerves in lower back)?

Lower pain, lower pain in legs. Belt. Pressure. Needs to be eased. Healing, stretching, walking. Relaxed clothes. Need stretching. Need healing, you can do this.

Does Evelyn need surgery?

No, not at this time. There is much to be done outside for that. Evelyn will have to go through surgery at some point but most likely not for leg or back related. All will be well. Pain is only temporary as you say.

Evelyn's Out-of-Body Experience:

Just after going to bed, I felt as if something grabbed me and started pushing me toward the wall. I was laying on my right side facing the wall my bed was pushed up against, which is an outside wall. At first, I resisted the push and pushed back. Then the force grabbed me again and pushed me toward the wall. That second time I stopped resisting and went with it. As I reached the wall I went right through the wall. It was like breaking a hole through concrete, yet with little effort. As I moved through the wall, I felt free of my body. It was dark outside, yet I could see clearly. I could now see houses and vehicles as I easily glided over them. I flew over water (creek) and even splashed my hand in it to convince myself it was real. I could fly fast or slow. I felt so free and alive and happy. The next thing I knew was that I was back in my bed, incredibly happy and excited. An absolutely wonderful experience. The next morning, I awoke and looking back on the incident, I convinced myself it didn't really happen, that it must have only been a dream. My guide Alexander popped in later and said I shouldn't dismiss what I had experienced as a dream. He said it did happen, and that many people have these experiences and simply ignore them as I did.

For Evelyn

There is a tremendous opportunity waiting there for you Evelyn. After you have attained this height, after you have achieved these goals, you still are going to feel as though you're falling short. Fear not. Let that feeling of not being the highest master of whatever it is you're mastering, let that feeling not turn you aside or depress you. You have no way of judging the amount of success spiritually that you have achieved. So, the physical you then many times is going to feel disappointed, disheartened. You'll have the feeling perhaps of failure. Simply because you lack the ability at that time to see the great achievements you've made. Even as you go through life and reach the age of an elderly woman, and you'll say, I wasted this life. That's simply because you do not have the vision to see the success you've made. It also works as a counterbalance, to keep you from getting the 'big head.' So, we don't want a prima-donna on our hands. We want you to stay levelheaded, keep both feet on the ground. Because you're going to soar anyway. We want you to be modest about it and proud of it, but not boisterous. Because you are just simply who you are, and that's something to be proud of, but you needn't brag it all over the world. Let other people brag on you, for you don't need too.

It's a good emotional outlet at times to get down and feel in a lower vibration. But don't stay there too long, because it's not justified, and it won't be justified. Yet, through your desire for perfection, you're going to have trouble seeing the perfection in yourself.

END****

Annoying Dead People
Book #1

Chapter One

Applying for a job online I was called in for an interview. I will not name this corporation, just know it is large and is involved in the hospitality industry in Florida.

I am a Medium or what many today simply call a Psychic, who sometimes feels compelled to use my gift's when those from the unseen world wish to communicate with those among the living, as it were. Being clairvoyant and clairaudient; which simply means I can see and hear the dead as some folks refer to them; I prefer to call them spirits. Because of my abilities the dead can and quite often do show up at the most inopportune of times, which can be annoying to say the very least. So, I just try and go with the flow and see what happens.

The Human Resource person, a genuinely nice, well-spoken lady who seemed to be in her early to middle thirties came into the waiting area and called my name. We exchanged pleasantries as she led me back to her office.

Sitting down inside her small office which contained only two chairs and a small desk she first looked over my resume and then began the interview process.

"I'm Maria Hernandez, and I see here that you have applied for the front desk customer service position, is that correct?"

"Yes, I'm very comfortable when dealing with all types of people, no matter what their culture or nationality might be."

"Tell me what did you least like about your last job?" she continued.

As she finished that question, I could now psychically see an older woman who was now standing to her left side. My first thoughts were please, go away, I really need this interview to go well, I need the income, and I mentally relayed that information to the elderly woman.

The older lady smiled and said she truly needed to make contact with my interviewer. She stood there, her form radiating peace and compassion, yet her eyes showed the desperation in her need to make contact. Knowing full well from past experience what might happen if I make her presence known, I still felt compelled to try.

"Did you not understand my question?" Maria asked politely. She had taken notice that I was staring at what appeared to her as the blank wall on her left side. She at one point momentarily glanced to her left to see what I might be looking at.

I broke off looking at the older woman and then answered her. "I'm so sorry, but this may seem very strange, but there is an elderly woman standing by your left side...she is telling me her name is Camila and that she is your mother. She is wearing

a blue dress with a red rose pinned on it. She also
has a white hat with a short white veil."

Maria looked to her left again, then back to me.
"I beg your pardon. How do you know my mothers'
name?"

"Camila is saying how sorry she is for not
coming to your wedding…that she honestly thought
Alfredo was not the man for you to marry. She felt
in her heart he was no good and would cause you
great harm. But now from the other side she can
see into his heart, and she sees the love he has for
you. She now knows he would never harm you or
the children. She is asking for your forgiveness…"

Maria had an incredibly surprised look upon her
face, to say the very least. "Is this a joke?" Maria
asked in a serious tone. "How dare you bring up
the memory of my mother…you have no
right…this interview is over. You need to leave,
and I mean right now!"

Maria had tears welling up in her eyes; I could
tell there was a lot of emotional baggage she was
still carrying around from her relationship with her
mother. "Your mother wants you to know…"

"Get out right now…I will call security if you
don't leave right now!" she threatened as she picked
up the phone.

As I went out the door I looked back and Maria
was now sitting, her face buried in her hands as
tears rolled down her cheeks between the soft sobs.

Getting into my car I couldn't help but think;
there goes another good job...I hope Camila is
happy now, because no one else is.

Early the next morning there came a knock at
my front door. I opened it to find a man in his late

thirties who had a profoundly serious expression on his face.

"Are you the one who came to see my Maria yesterday?" he said speaking very rapidly. "Don't lie; I know you're the one who upset my Maria!" he burst out yelling.

"I'm sorry, who are you?" I asked softly through my shaky voice.

"I'm Alfredo, her husband." His voice was gruff and angered.

"I was only trying to…" he cut me off in mid-sentence.

"You're a goddamn witch! That's what you are…stay away from my Maria!" He screamed as I closed and locked my door.

His rage was strong, before returning to his car he yelled through the door, "You will burn in hell!"

My hands were trembling, and I had trouble catching my breath. I wasn't sure what Maria had said to her husband about our conversation the day before, but I have had similar reactions like this before. But this is the first time anyone came to my home. I guess Maria let her husband see my resume which contained my address and other personal information.

Three days later I received a phone call; to my surprise it was Maria Hernandez. She wanted to apologize for her husband's visit to my home. Apparently after she informed him of what took place several arguments ensued between them and some other family members as well.

I told her it was not my intention to cause her, or her family any stress or grief concerning her deceased mother. I wasn't really that surprised when she asked if I were a psychic and could she come to my home for a private reading to discuss Camila. I said it would be fine and we set a date and time.

Two days later in the evening I heard her pull into my driveway. I invited Maria in, and I put out a bowl of potato chips and we each had a glass of cold Pepsi poured over ice.

"I wish to apologize for my husbands' behavior; his beliefs come straight from the Catholic faith as do many of my other family member's beliefs.

My two younger sisters however do not follow the old religion; they call themselves 'spiritual, but not religious' as many of the young do in today's world. I too do not follow the old religion.

After much discussion they have convinced me to listen to what you have to say; to not let my fear keep me from the truth."

I thought to myself that when Maria said 'after much discussion' she really meant to say after much yelling and arguing between the family members she decided to call me.

"Your husband did frighten me I must admit, but you don't owe me an apology. I knew when I started to tell you about your mother things might get ruff. So, let's just start with a clean slate." I said smiling.

"Do you want money from me?" Maria asked in a low voice.

"Oh, heavens no, I only told you about your mother because she wouldn't stop pestering me during the interview." I was surprised as we both laughed.

"Yes, that was my mother alright; she never knew when to stop talking." We again laughed together.

"I hope you are prepared…" I said looking over her right shoulder.

Maria looked at me then turned to look behind her. "Is she here now?"

"Yes, she is."

Maria started to cry softly as she turned to face me, "Please tell her I forgive her."

"She can hear you, so you may say whatever you wish." I said in a reassuring tone. "Camila is saying how sorry and how wrong she was about Alfredo and that she only wanted what was best for you. She loves you very much."

Maria was wiping tears from her eyes, "I love you too very much Mama."

I now could see standing next to Camila a little boy, he looked to be about four years old it seemed to me. He was holding Camila's hand and was smiling. Mentally I asked Camila who the little boy was. She said it was Maria's little boy. I asked what his…

"What is my mother saying?" Maria interrupted my thought.

"Well, there is a small boy who is about four year's old standing by your mother. She says he is your son."

"What…my son…how can that be? I have two daughters, and both are alive! I have no son. I don't understand?" Maria seemed completely caught off guard by her mothers' statement.

"Your mother says you became pregnant four years ago and you did not want another child; that your two sisters took you to a clinic where you underwent an abortion. You did not want Alfredo to know so you all swore yourselves to secrecy. You felt your husband would not understand due to his strong belief in the church ways. Your mother says you do not believe in the Catholic faith because she raised you in another faith. She says you only became Catholic to please your husband and his family."

Hearing this sent Maria off the couch as she fell onto her knees sobbing uncontrollably. I rushed to her side trying to console her. After several minutes she regained her composure and got up from the floor and sat back down.

Maria explained she felt she did not have the time or strength to take care of another child. She was afraid to tell her husband, so she told her sisters who said they would support her decision and help her make arrangements to go to the clinic in another city. Alfredo had left to go work at a construction site in another state during this time.

She did not know the tiny fetus was even a male she said in between bouts of crying. Maria asked if her mother and the boy were still present in the room, and I told her yes, they were still here.

"Please ask my mother what she calls my son?" Maria asked in a calm voice.

"The boy, she said, named himself; he is called 'Alfredo Benito Hernandez, Jr.', he took his father's name. They simply call him 'Junior', and your mother says he loves you very much. She said he comes at times and sits next to you and holds onto your arm to express his love for you. She says you have felt this before, have you not?"

"Oh my God…yes, yes I have, I never knew what it was, but I would feel so calm when I felt that odd sensation as if something was completely embracing my arm." She was smiling and looking off into the distance as it were; seeing and experiencing the love and gentle comfort the little boy had brought to her.

"Junior says on his birthday he would be so joyous if you would buy him a birthday balloon and release it in the small park down the street from your house." I said as Maria's gaze fell back upon me.

"Oh yes, tell Junior I will from now on…each and every birthday, I swear it!" An odd look came over her face as she asked this question, "Please ask Junior…when is his birthday?"

He answered before I could send the thought; I wasn't sure how Maria was going to react to his answer, "His birthday is the day you aborted him on, he says you know that day very well." Maria looked stunned, and then burst into tears again. I gave her more tissues and waited while she processed that statement from her son.

Camila now spoke to me, and I relayed everything she said to Maria verbatim, "Abortion is not a sin as many religions upon the earth may claim. It is simply a lesson for many to learn to understand this great choice. Abortion will never completely be understood in this physical world you inhabit. There are no unfavorable circumstances when deciding to have an abortion or to not have an abortion. There should be acceptance of this practice; though the goal should be to overcome the fear associated with it by those who are wishing to carry it out. Overcome the worry, fear, and selfishness you place upon yourselves because of this act. Your son chose you as his mother knowing full well that you would abort him, this was his choice too. He came to experience this short life in your womb for his personal spiritual growth. You may never fully understand his decision during this lifetime, but you will come to an understanding once you cross over and reunite with us. All will be made clear then. If you understand nothing else, just know, abortion is not a sin and God does not judge those who choose to bring this experience into their life path."

Maria stopped crying and said she needed to do some deep soul searching over what her mother had just expressed to her. She said she felt much better overall, but that she couldn't bring herself to tell her husband about Junior or the abortion. She was afraid of what he might do, so for now she would remain silent.

"Maria, your mother says she has one more thing to tell you and then they must go." I spoke very softly and reassuringly.

She gasped a little as I said that "Oh my God, there's more?!" Her eyes were large and wide open with a look of mock disbelief. "I'm not sure I'm ready for this, I'm all cried out." She forced a little grin followed by a short chuckle as she slumped back into the chair.

"Don't worry dear, Camila said this is about your husband." I said smiling at her.

"Please don't tell me he's cheating on me?" A serious look befell her thin face.

"Oh no, this is nothing like that." I shot back which changed her negative facial demeanor immediately. "Your mother simply wants you to know that Alfredo is a very good-hearted man, even though he is quick to anger, he shall always be there for you and the children. Things you will discuss later in life; just remember to give him time to think about things. He is slow to make changes so just be patient with him."

"Yes, I understand." Maria said.

"There is one last thing she wants to say before she goes. Your mother says after she passed, her home was sold, and the money was divided among her living children."

"Yes, between me and my sisters, we all split it equally. It was not very much; we each got three thousand dollars." Maria said.

"Your mother says that you took her personal items, furniture and the like and placed it all in a large storage unit. She said you girls talked about one day getting together to go through her stuff to decide what to do with it, but no one wants to go there because of the sad memories of her passing."

"Yes, that is true, we are having trouble letting go I guess." Maria spoke from the heart.

"Your mother said she wants you and your sisters to go to the storage unit. There in the far back you will find an old chest full of family photos from when she was a young girl. It is especially important that you go through this small chest; she keeps repeating this to me, it is very important she keeps saying. She wants you to promise her you will do this for her." My voice was strong as

Camila's thoughts came with such force into my mind.

Maria looked at me first with surprise and then with conviction as she answered her mother's request, "Yes, I swear we will go and check out the family photos, just as soon as I talk with my sisters, and we can work it out so that we can all go together."

"Your mother and son are now going to leave; they both expressed their great love for you and the rest of the family." I said as they vanished as quickly as they had appeared.

"I love you both so much!" Maria said, almost shouting as she placed her hands over her heart.

We chatted for a short time before she said she had to get home before her husband did, as she didn't want to explain where she had been. I completely understood as we parted company.

Three weeks had passed, and I was no closer to finding employment. I was making some money doing private readings here and there but that only paid for food and gas money. I was farther behind on my rent then I had realized; opening the mail I found an eviction notice from the management company. I had thirty days to leave, or I'd be put out by the Sheriff's Department it read.

Talk about stress! It would be an understatement to say I was very worried and fearful. No relatives to fall back on as I was raised in an orphanage until I was eighteen and on my own from then on. I called my spirit guides and literally begged for their assistance, and then prayed to God to help me through this unnerving time in my life.

No longer a young girl, I didn't want to end up homeless, living and begging on the streets. I had some pretty rough times when I was younger; sleeping in my car, washing up in gas station restrooms until I could get a waitress job or one cleaning homes. Working as a childcare worker at a group home, working with the mentally and physically handicapped and other low paid jobs was mainly all I could get with a high school diploma.

Finally, in my late twenties I saved up enough to go to one of those 'Certified Nursing Aids' classes. Pay was better than most of the other jobs I had. After thirteen years working many different nursing homes and hospitals as a 'CNA' I just couldn't handle the physical work anymore; my body was simply wearing out and exhausted.

I'm just a hair over five feet tall and only weigh one hundred and twenty pounds on average; my thin build has been a disadvantage most of my life working as a CNA.

My last job was working as a waitress at a small corner restaurant. It paid the bills as long as I kept to my budget. But when the last stock and housing markets and all that other stuff went south, I was laid off and the restaurant closed. I lived off the unemployment benefits until they ran out; now it's sink or swim time I'm afraid.

There came a knock at my door in the late afternoon; as I opened the door not sure what to expect, Maria and two other women were standing there with great big grins on their beautiful faces.

She introduced her sisters to me and said she had told them everything that had happened and what their mother said when she came to see me. They had finally all gotten up the courage to go to the storage unit and face their fears and emotions.

I never expected so much excitement from them as Maria told me the details of their visit. They could hardly sit still as the story unfolded in my living room. Opening the unit brought back much grief and sorrow Maria said as they entered.

After a few minutes of tears and hugs she said they decided to find the little chest with the photos and take it to Maria's home so they could go through it there. They felt there was just too much sadness among all of their mothers' things to check out the photos in the storage unit.

Maria said to their great surprise not only were there family pictures inside the box, but there were also U.S. Savings Bonds. Their mother and father had been buying one fifty-dollar savings bond every week for over thirty-five years; the total came to over one thousand eight hundred bonds.

They did some quick calculations online and said the bonds were worth over $200,000.00 dollars. You can imagine how ecstatically happy they were. It was as if they hit the lottery; hugs and kisses and joyous crying all around! I felt so overwhelmingly happy for them as they spoke of paying off their car and home loans and having money for their children's education and the like.

Maria also said they told their husbands who were dumbfound at first; then fully embraced their good fortune after the shock wore off. She went on to explain that her husband, Alfredo, asked why she all of a sudden decided to start going through the storage unit and she hesitantly confessed that she had come to my home and told him what had transpired concerning her dead mother. She did not mention Junior or the abortion.

She said he sat quietly and seemed to be pondering over what she told him all the while she braced herself for his short temper to show itself; but it was not forthcoming to her surprise. Another surprise came her way when several hours later he asked her to find out if he would be welcome to visit me and ask about his younger brother who died at age eleven due to a drowning incident.

I was genuinely surprised by this, but immediately told her he was more than welcome, and I would be glad to see if we could make contact with his brother.

The very next morning Maria called, and I agreed to see them that very same afternoon. Answering their soft knocking and before entering Alfredo came forth with such a heartfelt apology I was moved to tears. I could genuinely feel this man has such love and passion for his family that I accepted his apology without hesitation.

After entering Alfredo said he couldn't help but notice the eviction notice on the front door of my rented house. After making themselves comfortable we talked a little about my circumstances and then I noticed a young boy had appeared standing close to Alfredo and he told me he was his little brother, Julio, who had drowned.

Maria had noticed my attention was now focused as I gazed upon Julio. "Is he here?" she asked almost in a whisper.

Alfredo turned to Maria, "Is who here?"

She pointed at me and as Alfredo looked to my face I began to speak. "Julio is here and he wants you to forgive yourself Alfredo. He says the day he fell out of the fishing boat and drowned was a planned event in his short life. He knows you are going to have trouble understanding this, but he wants you to forgive yourself for not being able to save him."

Alfredo had tears welling up in his eyes as he spoke, "No, had I only moved faster I could have saved my little brother."

"Julio wants you to know that before he was born, he chose to live only a short time in this life and that he also chose the manner of his death. This was done for his spiritual growth, the growth of the true spirit being that he is. He did not need or require a longer life to experience the lessons he had chosen."

Alfredo suddenly had a strange look overtake his face, "You are saying Julio died on purpose…that he committed suicide? No, no, he was a good Catholic and suicide is a sin! This is a lie; it cannot be so! My little brother would never do such a thing!" Maria had wrapped her arms around her husband and was softly trying to calm him.

"Alfredo, Julio wants you to know he did not commit suicide, it was simply a planned event. He wants you to know that God gave his blessing to Julio for this short life he asked to experience." I said in a soft, reassuring voice.

"No! No, no, no…this is all a lie!" Alfredo took his wife by the wrist as he stood up and headed out the door. In the blink-of-an-eye they were gone.

My eviction date was only six days away so I was boxing up what I could fit into my car when there was a loud knock at my door. A wave of fear and panic flashed through me as I thought maybe I had misread the eviction notice and today was the day I was to be put out. I slowly peeked out the front window and to my surprise Maria was standing there with her two sisters.

After inviting them in Maria told me Alfredo had announced in the car on their way home the other day that they were to never speak of Julio or what had transpired in my home ever again. She said he is a good man, but he is a devout Catholic and he cannot go against the beliefs he was taught as a child and those beliefs of his family and friends.

I told her it was fine for him to believe whatever he wished; that we all have free-will and that we are all on a spiritual journey of self-discovery, which leads us to follow many paths in many lifetimes as we seek to know ourselves and to know God.

Maria and her sisters were all wearing big grins as one sister nudged Maria and said, "Go ahead, give it to her." Maria pulled an envelope from her purse and held it out toward me.

"Oh, no, you don't owe me anything. I told you from the start I wouldn't charge you for the readings. It was my wish to simply help, but now it looks like I may have caused you more problems and I am terribly sorry if I made things worse."

Maria was no longer grinning, "You don't apologize to me or anyone else, you have helped me and my family in ways you will never know.

We are so grateful to you for everything. Please take this gift, it comes from our hearts. We will not take no for an answer," she said as she placed the envelope in my hand.

"Well, thank you so much, I do wish you all well…"

Maria and her sisters were grinning again. You could almost feel their excitement as Maria spoke, "So, open it already!" They were like a bunch of giddy schoolgirls who just saw a celebrity at the mall.

As I opened the envelope and pulled out the check, I was overcome by what I saw and burst into joyous tears. The check was for $5,000.00 dollars. We all hugged, and I cried for several minutes before regaining my composure. These selfless women went on to help me find a new place to live and also helped me with new employment as a cashier at a large supermarket.

Words truly could not express how happy and genuinely loved these beautiful women had made me feel!

* Note to Readers: I do psychic readings to help off-set my meager income. My spirit guides have always helped me with any financial problems that have popped up from time to time. You never know how they do it but when dire money problems have come to me, they always seem to work things out to where I end up okay.

Our spirit friends and guides are not here to make us rich or wealthy, but they do provide opportunities in order to assist us with completing our chosen lessons and life experiences.

Chapter Two

Earlier in the week I had received a phone call from one of my steady clients as I prefer to call them. A steady client is simply one that comes for a reading every few months or so. She said she had a friend who wished to make an appointment to get a reading from me. I agreed and made arrangements to see her friend that afternoon.

It was a rainy day; mostly scattered showers here and there which helped lessen the humidity and heat. She arrived a little early which was fine with me. We settled in; I usually just have my client sit next to me on my soft little couch. That seems to work best for me, I can pick up on their vibration as I tune into my guides.

When I'm not giving readings, I meditate three days a week for one hour and tune into my spirit guides as I seek to raise my vibration level and form an even better connection to the unseen world.

I do not use tarot cards now or other things of that nature to give a reading. When I first started out tarot cards were a great help to me, they gave me focus and reassurance that what I was receiving from my guides was accurate. But as time passed the strong bond which has developed with my spirit guides, I found I no longer needed the cards assistance in giving a reading.

She told me her name was Donna and she looked to be in her late fifties or possibly in her early sixties if I had to guess. Short, no more than five foot or so and very heavy for her height. She had some difficulty breathing at times but seemed very pleasant, yet she was perspiring a lot, so I asked if she wanted me to adjust the air conditioning to make it cooler, but she declined.

Donna said this was the first time she had ever gotten up the courage to go to a psychic. She said her family in general viewed psychics as fakes and people who prey upon the elderly and superstitious people in order to cheat them out of their money. I took no offense at her statement.

Then she brought up the question of what I charged for a reading, and I explained for legal and tax reasons I do not charge, but simply ask for a 'love donation.' She asked how much the average person donates and I told her $30 dollars for thirty minutes was the average. I explained some give more; some give less depending on their financial circumstances and on the quality of the information they receive from my guide. She handed me $30 dollars and said she was ready to begin.

"So, Donna, I work in one of two ways. I can have my main guide I work with give you information that your spirit companions, those who watch over you in this life, wish you to have at this time and then you can ask questions or if you wish you can simply start asking the questions you are seeking guidance on. Your choice," I said pleasantly hoping to calm any fears she might harbor about talking to those on the other side.

"Oh, I have no questions for myself; I'm seeking some answers about the young man who saved Stephanie, my granddaughter three weeks ago." She spoke.

"Well then, let's see what my guide has to say about your granddaughter then."

"Yes, anything would be very helpful." Donna added.

After a few moments, the information started pouring into my mind. "Was your granddaughter playing between your house and your neighbor's house with another little girl?"

"Yes, she was. She was playing with Ashley, my friend Geneva's little granddaughter. They are both five years old. We live on a dead-end street so the only people who come on the street are the ones who live there. No one else usually comes down our lane." She explained hurriedly.

"They are showing me a man of average height and weight who looks to be in his late forties. He is wearing jeans and a dirty T-shirt and has a slight beard and light-colored hair. He approached the girls and said he found a lost kitten and wanted the girls to come to his car to see if they knew who owned it." I said as the information kept coming from my guide.

"Yes, my next-door neighbor Geneva was coming outside to check on the girls when she saw the strange man talking to them and her description of him was the same as you just said. She yelled for the girls to come to her, and Ashley ran to her grandma, but Stephanie was afraid and froze. Geneva yelled at the stranger that she was calling the police. The man then grabbed Stephanie and started carrying her to his car parked out front. Stephanie was now screaming and struggling my neighbor said but the man was too big and strong for her to break free of his hold. Geneva then said a younger man came out of nowhere and started fighting with the bad man, so she ran inside to call the police." Donna was now crying softly as she said this.

"They are showing me the stranger was trying to force her into the trunk of his car when a tall, dark haired man who looked to be in his early twenties ran up and grabbed the older man. The stranger let go of Stephanie while the two men fought with each other. The young man yelled for your granddaughter to run home which she did."

"Yes, she ran into the house and grabbed me around the waist crying, I asked her what was wrong, and she told me about the bad man, and I immediately called 911 who said they already had units responding. I ran to the front door and locked it and peaked out the window. I saw the bad man driving off in a dark colored four door older model Buick.

The police arrived a short time later and asked me and my neighbor for descriptions of the car and the bad man. The police said he was most likely a pedophile and that the young man my neighbor described saved my granddaughter from a terrible fate. But no one knew or had ever seen that young man on our lane before. He was nowhere to be found. He saved my Stephanie and I wanted to thank him for what he did." She said through her soft sobbing.

I handed her a box of tissue, "Are Stephanie's parents doing okay after this upsetting ordeal?" I asked very sympathetically thinking how scary it must be to think someone almost took your child from you.

Donna regained control of her emotions, "My daughter Danielle had Stephanie when she was twenty and the father, who was an asshole, left before she was even born so he was never in the picture. So, I was babysitting one afternoon when the police came and said a drunk driver had ran a red light at a high rate of speed and slammed into Danielle's car killing her. Of course, the drunk lived, so I've been taking care of her ever sense. My husband passed two years ago of a sudden heart attack, so it's just me and Stephanie now. So, I would like to know who the young man was so I can give him my heartfelt thanks for saving my little Stephanie." She let out a deep sigh as tears welled up in her tired sad eyes again. One could tell she had experienced much sorrow in her life, yet she seemed to be holding up very well indeed. I sensed she had a lot of inner strength.

"Alright then, let me see if my guide can give me anything on the young man." After a few moments, a flood of information came through to me. It was even a surprise to me what came through as I started to explain what had occurred.

First my guide explained for Donna that everyone, each spirit before they are born work up a blueprint, for a lack of a better word of what will take place in the life they are about to enter into. This blueprint contains lessons that the soul wishes to experience for its personal growth and enlightenment.

The nature of these lessons can come in many different forms. A spirit being may wish to experience, for example, the lesson of a disease such as cancer, diabetes, or heart disease. They may choose to experience rape, murder, or some type of sexual and/or verbal abuse and so on. These things are not to be viewed as negative things; just view them as experiences that cannot be experienced in the spirit world or that which many call heaven. Only here in the physical world do you have the opportunity to experience these events first had. I asked Donna if she understood so far and she said yes, so I continued on with the information my guide was sending me.

To simplify it for her, I explained that each person who is alive on earth have a spirit companion, some have several who watch over them and assist them with their chosen lessons. These spirit companions are called by many names. Some people say they have an Angel or Guardian Angel who watches over them, others seeking help call for Jesus, or for certain Saints, or for certain Archangels and the like.

The main focus of your spirit companion is to assist you in having the opportunity to experience the lessons you specifically chose for your personal spiritual development. Now understand that all spirits living in a human body have free-will. So even if you change the path you came to earth to experience, your spirit companion will still work behind the scenes, as it were, so that the lessons you chose still come to you.

Now, free-will also allow others to come into your life that you were not programmed to encounter. I explained to Donna that this was one of those moments in time. It was not a part of Stephanie's blueprint to experience being sexually molested and possibly murdered by a pedophile in this lifetime. My guide went on to say that when Stephanie's spirit companion was alerted by her vibrational change, due to her screams of distress immediate action was then taken by her spirit companion to stop this event.

The majority of the time your personal spirit companion will not interfere with your life because you have free-will. Only if it concerns death or certain other events will they intervene if the event is going to stop you from having the ability to learn your chosen lessons. The exception is, should you call out or mentally ask or pray for some kind of help or assistance then your spirit companion comes forth to assist you. For example, I explained to her that if you ask for guidance or for healing for yourself or for others your spirit companion then seeks to aid you with your request, because you asked for assistance.

Donna had a look on her face that told me she didn't understand all of this fully. "Is this making sense so far?"

"I'm not really sure what that all means. I just want to know about the young man." She said softly.

"Alright, let me see what he can tell me about him." I said as I sent the thought to my guide.

It wasn't long and the information came through. I began to tell her what my guide relayed to me. That the young man who came to the rescue as some might call it was not of this earth. Stephanie's spirit companion once alerted to the situation called upon higher beings to intervene in order to stop what was not programmed to occur in her chosen blueprint. A spirit being then was empowered by higher beings to penetrate into this world in order to stop the abduction of Stephanie by the so-called bad man. Once the spirit being stopped the event he simply returned to the unseen world. Sometimes these beings are referred to as 'walk-ins.' That is why no one had seen him before the event, and no one could find him after the event I explained.

"Oh, my goodness, so…in a way, it was God who sent one of his Angels to stop the bad man, is that right?" Donna asked trying to make sense of what I had just explained to her.

"Ah, yes, I guess you could say it that way." I agreed.

"Thank you so much for your time, I better get home now. I can't wait to tell my neighbor Geneva about God sending an Angel to save my granddaughter," she said hurrying for the door.

* Note to Readers: A 'Walk-In' in the above-mentioned instance is a being that can be here temporarily, and they do not experience birth or death. There have been many instances when a walk-in intervened in an incident and later was never found or seen again. It is not some great mystery; life by physical means is simply a matter of bringing together the correct particles, atoms, and ions. It is not a matter of the stork bringing into existence the necessary arrival. Now there are walk-in's (Soul's) that do trade places with Soul's who were born and are living a human life. For whatever reason, a soul may decide it can no longer continue its chosen lessons and with its permission and the permission of a higher group of spirit beings it can be removed from a physical body and

replaced with another soul who is willing to finish up that lifetime.

Chapter Three

One evening I was relaxing and watching television when the phone rang. As I answered a soft female voice spoke.

"Hello, is this Evelyn the psychic?"

"Yes, it is how may I help you?"

"My name is Jody and my mother said I should call you about my youngest daughter Lisa." She went on to explain about her mother being one of my clients and that her mother felt the spirits could help with her daughters' problem.

"When would you like to come over for a reading?" I asked looking at my wall calendar. I make notations on my calendar, so I don't schedule too many clients on the same day. If I do more than six readings in a day, I get very tired, so I try not to overdo it.

There was a short pause before Jody spoke, "Is there any way you could read for me over the phone? My mom said you charge thirty dollars and I swear I'll send you the money but I'm so worried about my little girl, she's only five years old."

"Ah, sure, I can do that, can you hold on while I get myself situated?"

"Please, take your time," she said waiting patiently on the other end of the phone.

Sitting the phone down I then turned off the television. Closing my eyes, I took in a deep breath and held it for the count of seven then exhaled and held that for a count of seven. I do this a total of seven times to relax my mind and body.

Then I mentally call for my spirit guide. Picking up the phone, "Alright Jody, I'm ready. What is the problem or question you wish to ask about?"

"Lisa has these awful 'night terrors' where she wakes up screaming and crying and it's extremely hard to calm her down. I just don't know what to do. This happens a couple times a week now. I've taken her to two different pediatric doctors, and they say there's nothing medically wrong with her and one suggested taking her to a child psychiatrist. So, my question is should I take her to see a psychiatrist?" I could hear the fear in her voice.

"Well, let me see what my guide has to say on this matter." Before I could mentally ask for the information, it was already flowing into my mind from my guide.

The main guide that works with and through me I call 'Alexander' simply because I cannot pronounce his true name, he goes by in the spirit world. Names in the spirit world are different from those in the physical world we live in. He told me true spirit names are a combination of sounds and colors and can even convey emotions or smells which those in the human form cannot begin to understand.

So, as I said I simply asked him for a name I could pronounce and he said Alexander was a name he was called by during a lifetime he lived in the physical form many, many centuries ago before our current history timeline even began. He said we know so little of our true origins and of those who dwell on other worlds.

I started to relay the information as it came to me, "Alexander said concerning the night tremors, as he calls them, that Lisa does not need to see a psychiatrist, and she does not need to be medicated. He said a pill will not address, nor cure the underlying cause of the night tremors. He stated she experiences these tremors in her sleep because of concern for her family. There is much worry and grieving by her over the actions taking place within the family and the negative energy being expressed. Do you understand what he is saying so far?" I asked trying not to sound judgmental.

Jody paused for a few seconds then responded, "Yes…your guide is right. Me and my husband have been arguing and fighting over the bills and I think he may have even cheated on me with another woman."

"He says there is a great need to create a harmonious, peaceful and loving environment within your home. He says though you may not feel Lisa is fully capable of understanding the complex intricacies of the world around her; there is much taking place that she sees, hears and is aware of, even subconsciously. She experiences these things because she is living in it with the rest of the family. She has no other way of expressing this conflict she observes and experiences; thus, it manifests itself as night tremors. Are you still following what he is saying?"

"Yes," her reply was simple, but I felt she wanted to ask a question but felt uncomfortable in doing so.

"Jody if you have anything you wish to ask, please do so. There is no judgment from those on the other side, none what-so-ever." I tried to be positive and reassuring.

"So, what needs to be done then?"

"Alexander says the elimination of certain aspects that are not a part of anyone's highest good should be acted upon. Know what is important for the harmony of the family unit. For Lisa he said to share time and love with her directly. No passive enjoyment from her; assist and guide her now. He says do not worry that she has been neglected in any way up to this point. Start anew with her right now or she will continue to experience these sleeping night tremors. If improvements are not made with the energy pattern of your current family situation, he says there will be a wearing down of her mind and therefore she will become accustomed to this negative energy which can have dire consequences for her later in life. The harmful effects of this prolonged negative energy will manifest in her future relationships and interactions with others she encounters. He says create peace and balance now within your family or this pattern will continue as it has through the previous generations."

"What does he mean through the previous generations?" Jody asked.

"He says you are the product of such a family unit that Lisa is now experiencing. Your parents were at great odds with each other and you as a child experienced night tremors yourself. That negative energy pattern that became a part of you is now affecting your compatibility with your spouse. If you do not break this pattern now, your daughter will grow up to…"

(Click) Jody hung up the phone. She never called again, but I did receive a $30 dollar check several days later in the mail. It contained only the check. I was hoping for some kind of explanation for the abrupt hang-up, but nothing was ever forthcoming.

I can only speculate on what had upset her so much that she felt inclined to stop the reading, but denial can be one way many try to deal with negative situations in our lives. It is not for me or anyone else to make a judgment against another. You the reader can draw your own conclusions concerning what happened.

Chapter Four

Andre Washington's wife, Eleanor called me to set up an appointment to receive a reading next Sunday afternoon concerning a dream her husband had experienced.

At the appointed time Mrs. Washington, absent her husband knocked on my apartment door, a very soft knock. She looked to be in her early seventies and was dressed modestly.

Answering the door, "I'm pleased to meet you, I'm Evelyn, please come in and make yourself comfortable."

After exchanging the usual pleasantries, I felt we were ready to proceed with the reading. She did not seem hurried or restless as some of those who come to me are inclined to be.

"You said on the phone your husband had a dream you wish to ask about, is that correct?"

"Yes, he had it last month. My husband is older than me and has always been afraid of dying. He won't visit anyone in the hospital; he won't go to funerals even if it is a family member or close friend. He will be coming up on his eighty-third birthday next month. You know how men are, he says it's nothing to dwell on, but I know better. Back in my forties I started reading about spiritualism and things of that nature. I know a lot of my friends think its hocus-pocus and con artists just out to take your money, but I know in my heart there's more to it than that. They believe what they want, I believe what I want, Amen." She was straight forward and spoke softly.

"Can you tell me about the dream your husband had experienced?"

"Yes ma'am, he says he wakes up and he is in a hospital room. Everything is white; the walls, the ceiling, the bed sheets, and he's lying there in the hospital bed, but he is not feeling any pain or sickness and doesn't understand why he is there. He says a nurse comes in wearing a white uniform and comes over to his bedside with a big smile on her cheery face. Andre asks her if he is alright. The nurse takes his left hand in her left hand and begins to pat the top of his hand with her other hand which he says makes him feel very loved and comforted. She then answers his question by saying everything is all right Mr. Washington, you're dead, and she stands there smiling. After she tells him he is dead my husband says he is not afraid but feels great joy and love in his heart and then he wakes up. I know in my heart he has had this dream more than once, but he won't talk about it and told me not to bring it up again. So, I come here to see what meaning this dream is bringing to him."

"Alright then, let me see what my guide, Alexander has to say about this dream." I relaxed and took a deep breath. Alexander was already sending the answer to me before I exhaled. "Those spirit companions who watch over Andre know of his fear of death and dying and they have been implanting, so to speak these dreams into his subconscious mind for several months now. So that when he does cross over to the unseen world, he will not be traumatized by his death experience. They are bringing these dreams now because his time of crossing over is drawing near and they wish for him to be more prepared when it comes time for his soul to leave his physical body. If he is in a more understanding frame of mind and not so fearful it will make the transition from the physical world to the spirit world go much easier for his soul, his true self. Alexander is asking if you have another question."

There was a short pause before Eleanor spoke, "Will his death be quick or long and drawn out by sickness?"

"He says it will be a short and easy departure for him. The hardest part for him will be his misunderstanding that he is leaving you behind and will never see you again, which is not true. Once he becomes acclimated back into his true home world, he will then realize how much closer he is too you at that time; rather than to how separated you two are in the physical world of earth. That will be a great relief to him when he comes to that realization." I explained.

"How long before this happens?" She asked in a low fearful voice.

"According to Alexander, Andre has only weeks before its time for him to return." I said straight forward. "He says he will not give an exact date and time so as not to put that stress and worry into your mind."

"So how long before I can cross over and be with him in the spirit world? My children and grandchildren are all moved away to other states, and we rarely get to see them. Am I destined to be alone for the rest of my days? (She began to cry) I truly don't think I could stand living without my beloved Andre."

Handing her some tissues, "May I ask how old you are Eleanor?" I made the request to see if Alexander could give me a time frame for the question she just asked.

"I'll be seventy-two on my next birthday." She had stopped crying for now.

Alexander was sending me his answer as she answered, "He says you still have a mission so-to-speak to complete on the earth plane and that you will be here until it is completed."

She began to plead, "What mission? Why can't Andre stay with me until this mission is done? He's always been the one to make the important decisions in our life together; I don't know what to do. I'm already afraid; I don't understand this new world we live in; all these fancy gadgets and machines. I can't work a computer or one of those new-fangled phones. Andre takes care of all that stuff. What am I to do? Please don't take my husband. We need more time together..." She burst out into tears!

Eleanor leaned over toward me, and I wrapped my arms around her. I held her tightly as we both now cried together. I truly felt so sorry for this elderly woman, and I didn't know what to do for her. My emotional feelings changed my vibrational level, and I lost my connection to Alexander. It took several minutes for us both to regain some of our composure.

Finally, after much nose blowing and almost a half box of tissue, we each, one after the other, retired to the bathroom to wash our faces, fix our make-up and whatnot. Sitting quietly on the sofa again I told her I was going to see if I could reconnect with my guide and see if we couldn't get more information on her future situation.

Relaxing, I did my deep breathing exercise which helps me mentally, physically, and emotionally to tune back into the other side. Now I felt I was ready to make the connection again to the unseen world where Alexander patiently awaited. In an instant his thought came to me asking if I was ready to resume, and I most definitely was ready to seek some guidance to help this beautiful woman sitting nervously by my side.

Taking her hand in mine to reassure us both the communication came forth, "Alexander says that Andre cannot stay because it is his chosen time to depart. He has experienced and learned or not learned all that he came for, so now he is finished with this lifetime. He says that you have allowed Andre to make all the important decisions concerning your lives together and now as he departs it is time for you to come to the forefront and make decisions for yourself. You are stronger than you realize and are very capable of directing your life from this point forward. Do not fear for your spirit companion will always be with you when you need help or assistance now and in the future. So, you are not alone, and you may call upon Andre and he will send you comforting thoughts to help you through your remaining years on this planet..."

Eleanor interjected, "Years? How many years will I be here for?"

"He says your mission will keep you in a physical body for a little over…twenty more years." I was hesitant to answer at first not knowing how she would take this news, but if Alexander gives it to me then I figure the person it is for can handle it. I never censor what information comes through even if it seems negative; for there may be more to it then I myself realize since I cannot see what they can in the unseen world.

As her jaw dropped open, she sat staring in disbelief. A few moments later she uttered loudly, "Oh my God!"

Alexander continued, "He says he knows this is a lot for you to take in and he wants to stop for now so that you can have time to digest all that has been spoken here. He wants you to make arrangements to return in sixty days after you have had time to think and dwell upon all that has been presented to you. Then at the next reading he will explain the mission you are to undertake which will take almost twenty years to complete. This is a particularly important mission, and you were specifically chosen for it. You agreed to it before you were born into this life; for up to now he says you have only been 'existing' in this lifetime, but now you are going to truly become alive and give this lifetime true meaning."

Alexander withdrew at this point and the communication stopped. Eleanor and I made plans to meet up again in sixty days' time to further explore her 'mission' that was brought up by Alexander.

My desire was that it would give her a glimmer of hope for the future to know she was chosen for a special mission, but she seemed overwhelmed by all that was said concerning Andre and her limited time remaining with her husband. If I were in her shoes, I guess I too would be fearful of facing the unknown future by myself, without my loving companion by my side.

(Two months later)

Much had taken place since I last met with Eleanor Washington. She had telephoned to confirm her reading day and time earlier in the week. I could feel the loneliness in her soft voice. We spoke briefly on the phone, and she said her husband Andre had passed quietly in his sleep two and a half weeks after our first reading. Most of her children, two sons and three daughters and their families flew in early to help with the funeral arrangements and the like; only her youngest daughter Abigail couldn't be located.

Eleanor said it was wonderful to reunite with her children and grandchildren even during this time of sorrow in her life. All had to leave after the funeral to return to their hectic lives in other states, which she said she understood, but that brought on a slight depression and feelings of isolation she said.

Yet, overall, she was coming to terms with her new life; she had a neighbor who was helping her with all the new financial responsibilities and things of that nature. Mastering new things also brings with it a certain comfort or feeling of improved self-worth which she had not experienced before. She said it was like a freedom she never knew existed and that it was an absolutely wonderful feeling of empowerment.

Eleanor arrived early and I invited her in. We got settled in; both of us sitting in the same spots on the sofa as we had done on our last visit together. I had already prepared myself and was quietly awaiting her arrival, so I was ready to begin. She said she too was ready, so no chit-chat was necessary at this point.

Mentally I asked about her mission that had been spoken of at our last encounter. Alexander jumped right in with sending me the requested information, so I began to relay it to Eleanor.

"Alexander says there is an incredibly special child that will be coming into your life very soon. Your mission is to raise this child and provide it with love and compassion."

"What? I...I can't raise no more children. I'm an old woman now. I don't have the strength for something like that." She gasped and sighed heavily.

"He says you do have the strength for this important mission and your spirit companion, that which you call your Guardian Angel will be assisting you. Your so-called Angel will infuse you with healing energy daily so you will have the needed physical and mental strength for this task. When you are unsure of what to do simply close your eyes and mentally ask your Angel for guidance. He will send you the thought that will answer your question. Go with the first thought that comes into your mind for that will be from your Angel. Take action on that first thought, do not sit and second guess or keep repeating your question; for if you do, then your own mind will interfere and cause doubt and try to sway you to another course of action, which will be wrong action. Many times, a person's mind well choose fear over love, so do not be swayed. Have confidence, over time you will know when your Angel is guiding your thoughts and simply follow them. He says when doubt enters your mind simply release it and think of something beautiful, something pleasant. Do you understand so far?"

"Ah…yes, I'm following what you're saying, but where will this child come from? How old will it be…is it a baby? Is it a boy or a girl?" She now had many questions on her mind that needed answered and Alexander was ready for them.

"He says not to worry; all your important questions will be answered within a few days' time."

This wasn't what Eleanor wanted to hear; you could almost feel the desperation coming from within her, "So there's nothing your guide can tell me about this child right now?"

"He says you will know what to do when it comes, your soul has been eagerly awaiting the arrival of this special child all these many years. Your mission is to raise this child with unconditional love. With compassion and joy, you are to fill this special child with the understanding that all creatures in nature are a part of God and are to be treated with kindness and love just as all humans are to be treated the same. You will give this child no religious instruction of any kind; religion is not to be pushed or forced upon this child. It will follow its own path in this lifetime, and it will choose what it will believe or not believe while on its chosen journey. This child will not attend what you would call normal or regular school. You are to home school this child. Those of the unseen world as some term it does not wish this child to be exposed to the traditional schooling of this country due to its misguided representations of the factual truth of the world at large. This child will have an ability to communicate with its spirit companion as it grows to adulthood. When this child tells you of its 'so-called' imaginary friend just know it is not someone the child has invented in its mind to play with. This will be a spirit guide that will come in a form that will be in harmony with this child so as not to frighten; it will be seen as another child. As this child grows so will the appearance of the spirit guide change to mirror the age of this special soul. This spirit companion will be teaching universal spiritual truths and the laws of nature to this special being as it grows and will remain with it from birth until it returns to its true home."

Eleanor broke in, "What am I supposed to teach this child? What subjects; I haven't been to school for over fifty years or so. I…"

Alexander told me to interrupt her thought pattern and convey this to her, "He says you may go to the nearest school system, and they will register the child as a home school individual, and they will provide what the state requires to be taught. Do not fear; when these types of troubling thoughts arise simply sit quietly, close your eyes, and mentally ask your Angel for help and in a short time you will receive the needed assistance. He also says to tell you that as the child grows his spirit companion will tell the child to tell you what is needed. The

child may not understand the information he
gives you, but you will understand and then will act
upon it accordingly. Do not concern yourself with
the child's education; its spirit companion will teach
it of the true world and assist it with its homework
assignments required by the school system. He
says to take the child to the playground at the park
and let it interact with other children. Let it see
nature and God's beauty for it will grow up
normally. It will have many questions which it will
discuss with its 'imaginary' friend, but it will seek
its love and affection from you. Hugs and kisses
and laughter you two will experience together. You
will find a new love of life in your heart as you two
explore new adventures together. As the child
explores its new world you will rediscover the joy
and serenity you felt were lost to you many years
ago. Never fear again, for you have your Angel
standing right behind you and behind your Angel
stands God, who would dare stand against you! So
be not afraid for you are watched over and
protected always." This seemed to calm Eleanor
down quite a bit. She seemed more relaxed and
more at ease, at least for now.

"Why is this child so special?" She asked
hesitantly not truly expecting an answer.

No answer was forth coming from Alexander,
but then I felt a vibrational change from within.
Alexander was no longer in tune with me. Another
spirit being had come forward and over shadowed
Alexander. I felt as if this other being was much
more enlightened, more spiritually advanced then
my guide. I could not see him in my mind as I do
Alexander. This spirit came to me almost as an

intense glowing white light; yet expressing and radiating pure love. I felt humbled to be in its presence. The decision seemed to have been made by that great being that Eleanor's last question could and should be answered. As this divine being now communicated to me its thoughts, I felt so at peace within myself; words cannot describe how I felt on all levels; physically, mentally, and emotionally.

As I was about to open myself to its message it simply placed me in a trance state and used my form to convey its message directly to Eleanor, which I completely allowed as it asked my permission to do so. I heard these words come forth, "This soul has returned to earth to help usher in a new type of peace that was lost to this world centuries ago. This great soul shall draw thousands of lost souls to it who will be desperately seeking to find their way out of the darkness of this misguided world. Much darkness shall befall this world in the future and souls of this kind are now incarnating to be of great service to humankind in those times of great sorrow. Mankind has brought this destruction upon itself and now must learn a most severe lesson." I felt this great presence move slowly away as I was released from the trance state, I had been placed in. I was now aware of Alexander's presence.

"Oh, my goodness." Was all Eleanor could say.

Alexander then withdrew and the reading was now closed. Eleanor and I shared some tea and discussed her message for a short time before she had to leave. She said she would keep in touch as she departed. I now sat quietly and contemplated on the 'destruction' that the advanced spirit had mentioned was coming in the future.

(Seven months later)

Drying myself off after a most refreshing bath I heard the faint ringing of my telephone. Dressing quickly into my bathrobe I scurried into the living room, but the caller had already hung up. Checking the Caller-ID display I dialed the number; to my delight it was Eleanor who answered in her sweet voice.

She gave me an update on what had happened since our last reading. A young man carrying a small red gym bag came knocking on her door late one evening. He looked to be in his early to middle twenties she stated. Peeking out the window she was afraid to open the door to this stranger. As this man kept knocking, he noticed her looking out the window. Placing the red gym bag down in front of her door she said he seemed to be writing something on a piece of paper. Then he pointed to the bag with his right hand and then turned and drove off in an old black Honda Civic.

She watched for a few minutes before opening her front door. There was a folded-up note lying on top of the gym bag. Opening her door, she reached down to retrieve the note when she heard the baby inside the gym bag crying. She said she knew immediately that this was the special child she was to care for and raise.

After bringing the bag and note inside she removed the infant and discovered it was a boy and began to mother it, soothing it and caring for it. Eleanor said she had already bought diapers, formula and all that would be needed in preparation of the arrival of the special child.

After it fed and finally fell asleep, she sat down to read the note. To her shock it said the baby was from her youngest daughter Abigail and that she had died just two days ago at the county hospital and that her unclaimed body is there now in the mortuary. The note further said the man could not care for the baby and explained that he was just a friend and not the baby's father. The note was unsigned.

Calls to the hospital said Abigail had been shot once in the left side of her face while sitting in a parked car. She never regained consciousness and died a short time later from the complications. Police have no suspects in the shooting at this time. Police think it may have been drug related Eleanor said.

She called the family, and all came and helped her with the funeral arrangements. Some family members were surprised she said after telling them she was going to raise the infant; but all said for her to call if they were ever needed.

No birth certificate could be located so she got an attorney and established through the court system she was now his legal guardian and said she was inspired in a dream to name him 'Martin Luther Washington.'

After that call we would have no further contact. There were times later in my life that I had wished I had stayed in touch with this wonderful woman. But, like so many others I was caught up in the rat race of my personal life and missed the opportunity of what could have been an endearing friendship.

* Note to Reader: Concerning Andre's returning home; spiritually speaking death is like opening a door and walking through it. There you find yourself back at your true home; with true friends, companions and family who rejoice at your return. You completed that lifetime, learning and experiencing as much as you could or couldn't. Later, you will be waiting to greet those loved ones you left behind on earth when they have finished their lifetime and they cross over. You will rejoice with them at their special reunion.

Yes, many people fear death because of their religious faith and/or upbringing. They fear the 'Hell' that was programmed into them by their misguided religious beliefs. Religion told them they 'Sinned against God' and therefore they must be damned to a burning 'Hell' with Satan torturing them throughout eternity. But once their soul crosses over and they are met by their friends and loved ones they soon realize no one is there to judge them or to send them to hell. They then realize that Hell and Satan and all the other negative things; were just made-up devices to control them while living in a human form on the earth plane. Religions and governments on the earth use various means to control the people they hold influence over. Most times it is of a negative type of control.

Humankind created religions, not God. The 'Source of all Life' as God is called in the spirit world loves all of his creations unconditionally. When you return home to the spirit world, he does not judge you for what you did or did not do on the earth. You will review that lifetime and decide whether you did or did not accomplish certain lessons and then with higher guidance you will plan your next journey of discovery. No punishment of any kind will be placed upon you.

The negative events you experienced, or you created while upon the earth were simply for learning and spiritual growth; that of yourself and that of humankind.

Chapter Five

My friend, Winston Thomas who is a trance medium invited me and several other close friends over for a séance. This was held in his basement. We were given the option of receiving a 'Past Life' reading or a 'Future Life' reading. Winston's spirit guide who will be speaking through him is known as Dr. George Wilson.

Dr. Wilson: Yes, this is Dr. George Wilson. I'm the spirit companion or what some my term guardian angel for this instrument. Greetings, my understanding is that some may be interested in past or future lifetimes. I have looked into this for those who are present here tonight.

We will be working under a time restraint this evening due to the physical limitations of the instrument. Therefore, in order to accommodate everyone gathered some may feel as though their reading may be a little short, and I do apologize for this in advance.

Now at this time I wish to give you each a choice, and I want you to simply see before you two doors. The door on the left will be the door to a past life. The door on your right will be the door that opens to your next physical existence in the earth plane. I will give you your choice of choosing whether you wish to have discussed a past life or the life that you will live the next time you incarnate into the physical body of a human. This will be your choice you see. Now did everyone understand what I said.

Group: Yes.

Dr. Wilson: Alright then, Keith, do you wish to go first?

Keith: Yes.

Dr. Wilson: Which door do you choose Keith?

Keith: The right door.

Dr. Wilson: Now, I want you all to understand that there is a spiritual law that I will be working under, and I'll explain it to you. The law is that I will not always give you a date, and I want to explain that. If I were to say, for example, in the year 2037 you were going to be born and do this and that. Then when you reach a certain age in this life, you may say, 'Hey, I've got to die in order to get over there in time to get everything ready for my next life.'

You see, so I don't want that. So, I will not give you certain dates. I wish it not to be in your subconscious mind. Everyone understands if you pick the door to your right, I will withhold the date because your subconscious mind will cause you concern and worry and a lot of wasted effort in thought.

However, I will tell you that being in your subconscious, any information that is given to you while in the physical state will be most difficult to erase after you have been reincarnated. Do you understand?

You will have more recall then at the actual time of birth. The spirit itself is being instructed into its earth life before birth. Do you understand?

Keith: No.

Mayme: If you're born-again Keith, you will remember what he's telling you now.

Dr. Wilson: Yes, because you are being given the information now, while you are in a human form; you will recall it in the next life. You will have more recall; you will remember what takes place here tonight. Understand?

Keith: I think so.

Dr. Wilson: When you are living that future life, if I say on a particular day a certain thing will happen, you will have total recall and say, "Well I was looking forward to it happening."

Keith: Okay, I understand now.

Dr. Wilson: Good, very well. Of course, for those who choose the door on the left, the recall will not have a plus or minus for you.

Jane: I have a question, if you choose the left door, are you going to give dates?

Dr. Wilson: Yes, dates are always given in past life readings with only a few exceptions.

Jane: Oh…okay, I didn't know.

Dr. Wilson: This knowledge will be coming from the Akashic Records. It might be called the Higher Hall of Records. It has many names, or it means many different things to many different people. It is the Higher Hall of Akashic Records when the future life is there.

Now I will begin with you Keith. If you have questions, feel free at any time to ask. This is Dr. George Wilson; I will be working tonight.

Keith: Okay.

Dr. Wilson: In your future life, the life that is already planned, the life that has been laid out, the life that you are working towards now; that you are obtaining knowledge and information and being guided towards. I will now begin. I will turn the page of the book and I will start with the very beginning of the time of birth.

This may seem insignificant to you tonight but in the next life it will mean a great deal. It will mean a great deal to people who study the stars and the planets. So, the time will be important to them and to you.

You will be born the Earth time of 6:03 am. It will be a Thursday. Your mother will end her physical existence at 6:08 am, Thursday.

You will be raised in a home that is not unlike the homes of today of an orphanage, but it will be called more of a training institution.

Your father will not reject you, if you're wondering why the institution, your father will not reject you, but it will be the way of the time that you have been born in.

Your father will be a man in the service of the government in the way of, not a politician, but as a keeper of peace. You may in your lifetime, this lifetime that you are living in now call the gentleman a career soldier. But he will be a gentleman of peace instead of this other term.

I will reveal to you at this time the names of those people. Your name will be...now this is no pun. Your name will be exactly the same as your first now, but it will be spelled backwards; Htiek. Do you understand so far?

Keith: Yes.

Dr. Wilson: Very good. Your mother, whom you will never know, will be named 'Navarone.' Your father's name will be 'Harmzes.' The last name, the family name of your family will be 'Eiruman.'

Now then, through the institutional care and through the studies and the schooling, you will go into the scientific study of planetary study. This will be normal study for that time.

You will spend your career not upon this planet. Your life basically will be a dweller of space. You will be traveling from one area to another. Much similar to the airlines of today, which go from one city to another city or from one continent to another continent. But this will be of a more colorful, advanced type of flight which will take place out in space. More like going from one planet to another planet.

You will never marry. You will perish and return to the spiritual dimension after a period of earth years numbering forty-seven. I will not disclose the nature of the death, for it will have no bearing upon this life when you do recall. You will be in another dimension. You will be in another galaxy, and you will perish. But know that you shall be as close to spirit then as you are now. There will be no reason to fear being lost there in a vast nothingness because it is not a vast nothingness.

Keith: Will I have the same feelings and emotions as I have now?

Dr. Wilson: No. You're going to be developed as a scientist. You will have no emotion. You will have feeling. You will not have emotions; you have primitive emotions now. You will not have emotions in the future life. This is Dr. George Wilson.

Keith: Ah, thank you.

Dr. Wilson: All right Renesha, which door would you like to choose?

Renesha: I'll take the left one.

Dr. Wilson: In your past life, I'm going to skip with you and at a later date I'll go into your last existence.

I want to go back into time when you were what many people of today would call a monk. You were of the male sex. You spent a great deal of time in monastery work, which was primarily praying, gardening, and teaching.

Renesha: Wait a second…you're saying I was a man?

Dr. Wilson: I shall explain for those who wish this knowledge. Your Soul or Spirit, whatever word you desire to use is simply made up of intelligent energy; the essence of this energy is a part of that which many call God or Great Spirit or Creator which is also intelligent energy.

As an energy being, you are part of God, you are not male or female but may then choose to be either when you incarnate into this physical plane where you must take on the mantle of male or female. Your race, your nationality, your parents, to be rich or poor and much more are chosen by you before your birth into this world. Are you following the pattern I am speaking of?

Renesha: Yes, I understand.

Dr. Wilson: Very well, now then, as a monk in that life you had reached a certain knowledge and degree of your own. You did not die due to old age. When the hordes of Genghis Khan came through your area, you were cut down, decapitated.

You lost your head, your arms, your legs and were disemboweled.

Renesha: I was told by a psychic friend of mine that Genghis Khan was punished for what he did in that lifetime. Is that true?

Dr. Wilson: He was not punished for that lifetime, just as Adolf Hitler was not punished for the life he lived in Nazi Germany. But to balance the karmic debt incurred for the life he lived as Genghis Khan, he later reincarnated and lived that lifetime of the one known to many as Joseph Merrick the 'Elephant Man.'

Now then, to continue with your past life Renesha, upon entering the monastery he did not take the vow of silence because he was a teacher and instructor.

The name of the monk of this existence was Xavier but was of a different pronunciation. He went only by Xavier.

Now the date of passing, due to a new experience of another life that is to come, I wish not to divulge the date of death because of the horror of the death. The second of that death will carry over and into another life with a similar earth experience. I wish not to place the date of death because the date will correspond with the coming date of death.

That being the one that is important in mathematics in that lifetime, in that mathematical equation of death; she will find the answer, and it will cause much disturbance to her, so I will not divulge that date for her.

Renesha: So, I'm going to die the same way in this life as that one?

Dr. Wilson: No, not this life, but your future planned life you will be…I will be cruel with this, yes, in your future programmed life you will be murdered on the same month and day you were murdered during your past life we are discussing now. It will simply be a different date for the year, which will be far into the future as you count time. So, there is nothing to fear, simply new experiences of your own choosing. This is Dr. George Wilson.

Renesha: I get it, thanks.

* Note to Readers: Concerning Adolf Hitler, my guide Alexander said he was not judged or forced to punish himself but was to undergo a form of counseling. Many of the actions, developments, and forms of review he underwent upon his return to the spirit world were self-imposed. Alexander said it is possible, for any being, to accomplish such acts as were carried out in his lifetime and be unaware of the severity of their actions. Hitler was able to return, if he chose, and not fully become aware of the direct involvement and severity of his acts while in the human form. This being (Hitler) has made progress through counseling, through reviews, through reflection of the actions that were taken during that specific lifetime. It is in this process now that he currently finds himself and there is much progress being made. There were many things that were not reported through historical records or through media, or through the controlled outlets. There were many things that were taking place within this lifetime that led to this series of events for many souls to undergo. It was not necessarily an evil act but an attempt to display

the atrocities of the relating actions and ideals
that brought forth this mentality into the physical
world and led to the violent death and actions taken
in the name of the government who sanctioned and
made right, true, or correct the actions of the people
for the sake of power. It should be evidenced by
historical document that there were no lasting
positive outcomes that could have been brought
about by acting in this manner; developing hatred,
annihilation, these are not useful. Yet the men and
women of this planet regularly engage in them on
some scale. This was the lifetime of Hitler to
involve himself in these actions in this manner,
though there was a great deal of external motivation
and influence by those with whom he surrounded
himself. For, it was not entirely his motivation
alone that lead to the final outcome.

Dr. Wilson: Now Mayme, are you ready? Which
door do you wish to open?
Mayme: The left.
Dr. Wilson: You wish to seek a past life
experience. Very well, I'd like to place you at this
time in the nation or country of Canada. I'm
placing you there and giving you the name in which
you will not enjoy. You have never in any life had
a name you enjoyed. I wish to give you the name
of your last, next to last incarnation. This is not the
last one. This is the one before. The name that I
give you is Malinda.
Mayme: It's better than the one I got now.
Dr. Wilson: Yes, but you didn't think so then.
Mayme: Probably not, it's not the prettiest.

Dr. Wilson: Now Mayme, like the 'M' is particularly important in your life to you. You feel closeness to the 'M', and I think it's because of the spirit god sound of 'OM.'

Now then, let us go along with this and you can see some of the character peculiarities coming out, because of the Canadian life and to this one. I skipped a life. It didn't show up in your last life that's the reason I picked the one before to speak on this evening.

This is why you are always hot. You like cool weather. You're cool natured. You like cool places. Many of your lives which have been few have been spent in cool areas on the earth.

Now, the family name of this one of which I'm speaking of was Sheller. You were not French. You were a Duke's mixture. You were English. Your parents came from England.

Now, Malinda Sheller was born in the year 1637. You were married and raised three children. You gave birth to seven children, four did not live. They had short life spans. Three that survived lived to adulthood.

You were alone a lot in your life, for your husband was an explorer type. He was working for the government in bringing about mapping of the land. He was exploring the land areas for the leaders and officials of that time period.

You live to be the age of eighty-seven. So, you may add your birth date to see the date you died. You passed away in October of that year, the 21st. The month of birth wasn't as important as it would have been to Keith. It was May 12th.

You had a great deal in common through that experience with the Indians in that area. You were not an Indian lover, but you tolerated the Indian people. You were no missionary by any means.

Mayme: What was my married name?

Dr. Wilson: Malinda Bonyea. He was French.

Mayme: Well, between this last life and the one in 1600 must have been a long time in between there.

Dr. Wilson: Yes, you needed a long period of development in the spiritual dimension. Now then, do you have another question about that period?

Mayme: Is that the reason I want to go to Canada now, because of that prior life?

Dr. Wilson: Yes.

Mayme: Where did I live?

Dr. Wilson: You were close to a large Indian village or encampment they called it. This is Dr. George Wilson.

Mayme: Oh…thank you.

Dr. Wilson: Now then, moving on, let's see…David are you ready?

David: The right one please.

Dr. Wilson: I would like to explain how it is arrived at a future existence, and it is the future life as programmed, so to speak, from your past experience. In many past lives you're being guided in a direction to be of future service in a coming life or experience. It is basically the same life; you are the same being, same soul. You are being placed in a different experience.

Now David, are you ready to open the door on your right?

David: Yes.

Dr. Wilson: Very well, again I will not be giving you dates or ages or years so as not to concern you dearly or deeply now.

In your next earth experience you will be female. You will be from a large family. The time and day of your birth I will give although it will again not carry the importance to you that Keith's will to him. Your birth will be 8:12 pm on a Sunday. It will be raining. You will be in the country known as France.

As I spoke earlier, you will be of the female sex. You will have tremendous abilities as a child in the Arts.

You will not marry young, but you will marry; however, you will not produce children.

You will develop in your thirties a writing ability. You will write many volumes of knowledge on the Arts. You will develop a philosophy through your writings.

You will, for a time, live in seclusion during your periods of deep thought in your career.

In your twilight years of your life, you will expand and broaden out in the field of appearing before audiences in speaking and lecturing.

Your passing will be normal. Everything goes according to the records as I see them, you should live to be eighty-one years old in your next earth existence, not this one.

Now then, the birth name of this child will be a strange name too. It will be Feon Monet Break. When she does marry, the married name of the gentleman she marries will be Marchant.

Do you have any questions?

David: No. Thank you.

Dr. Wilson: Now Evelyn, I have for you two doors, one on the left and one on the right. Which will be your pleasure?

Evelyn: Left.

Dr. Wilson: We open the door and enter into a room of a past life. In the past life that you have completed, you are seeking some verification. I will give you something here for you to puzzle over. You were not a doctor; you were one who worked as a doctor.

I am placing you right in the middle of the Revolutionary War in this country. You were not Martha Washington, yet you knew of her and some others. But your name, a common name, was JoAnne Wilcox.

Now there were three marriages. JoAnne Wilcox Circee was the first, JoAnne Wilcox Circee LaMarz was the second and the third was JoAnne Wilcox Circee LaMarz Blankenheimer and it was a Jewish name. Two of the gentlemen were killed in the war and the other one outlived you. Yes, you lost two close together.

You were close to much of the fighting at that time, which spread all over a great area. Most of your life though was spent in the Virginia region.

Now then, May 30th was the date of your birth. The year was 1741. In earth years you were going into your ninety-third birthday when you passed.

You were born in what the Indians called a wigwam...

Evelyn: I wasn't American?

Dr. Wilson: Yes, you were an American citizen.

Evelyn: You said I wasn't a doctor?

Dr. Wilson: You had a limited nurse training, but you were called upon to do the acts that a doctor would do in a type of emergency. You did many midwife acts, and you doctored many people. There were no doctors available many of the times in the areas where you were at, and you assumed the duties. You had a lot of courage. You liked to use or were adept at using a knife in the way of surgery.

Evelyn: Was this from a prior life?

Dr. Wilson: Yes, I feel as though you got your fill.

Evelyn: I used up all my courage (laughing).

Dr. Wilson: I will say this, in a prior life even before this one we're speaking of; you were a man. You were a brute. You did commit chaos and murder. You bludgeoned people to death with instruments of war.

So, in that life I am speaking of, the last one, the sight of blood and gore didn't annoy you.

Now you have come a long way because you have outgrown that. See the improvements and progressions you have made?

Evelyn: Yes.

Dr. Wilson: This is Dr. George Wilson.

Evelyn: Thank you very much.

Dr. Wilson: Now then, which door would you like to choose Michael?

Michael: The left one for a past life.

Dr. Wilson: I'm placing you in the nation or country of Italy. Now I wish not to divulge the name because he was born to a family of prestige in that era. You were very much at the forefront of a major religion; that is where you found your structure, your belief system, and in the end your demise. You were well known in your circles because of your dedication and pushing for release of information, and for release from oppression.

You were fighting for equality, for fairness and understanding for the people. Your past life was one of exile and persecution, dying at the hands of those with differing world views from your own.

You had been assigned a personal quest in that lifetime and because of this you did not give up your beliefs or change for the sake of a better life outside of imprisonment.

Michael: So, I died in prison?

Dr. Wilson: You were being held by the religious organization. Through torture and imprisonment, they were trying to force you to stop speaking out against the oppression and control they were exerting upon the people who followed this major religion.

When they saw that you would not be swayed, they decided to end your existence through the avenue of murder.

Michael: How old was I when they murdered me?

Dr. Wilson: You were forty-three. All of your previous lifetimes, with the exception of two have been short lifetimes.

This is Dr. George Wilson. God's blessings upon this gathering.

End

Chapter Six

It had been almost two years since I last did a reading for my old friend from high school. Bonnie Sue Anderson is a forty-two-year-old mother of a beautiful little eight-year-old named Jenny; her only child. Her husband is named Jason and they all live in southern California in a large ranch style home.

Bonnie Sue and family had flown to Florida due to the death of her husbands' uncle. After the funeral she called the next day and asked if we could get together and also if she could get a reading. I was delighted and looked forward to her arrival the next morning.

She came alone, leaving her husband and daughter to get acquainted with some of the relatives that never had the opportunity to meet Jenny before.

We reminisced a little about the old days and talked about what had been going on for the last two years since we last saw each other. It wasn't long before she broached the subject of a reading, and I was most happy to accommodate her.

"So, would you like just a simple reading, or do you have something specific you wish to ask about?" I began.

"I have been having dreams that all seem to have the same basic theme to them. I just want some clarity." Bonnie Sue stated in a straightforward manner.

"Okay, tell me about the last dream." I closed my eyes and started my deep breathing exercise relaxing myself for Alexander's arrival.

"My dreams all revolve around my older brother Karl. In my dreams it is made known to me that he has a brain tumor and is going to die. I saw him not long ago and he is in perfect health. So, I wanted some kind of confirmation before I tell him of the dreams I'm having. I don't want to alarm him, but if he has a brain tumor, he needs to see a specialist as soon as possible." You could hear the love and emotion in her voice.

"Alright, my guide Alexander is saying the dreams you are having have nothing to do with your brother Karl. He, nor you have a brain tumor. These dreams are for you. There will be much loss around you, and you will view this as devastation and traumatic. Your spirit companion has been sending these dreams to your subconscious in order to prepare you for the coming tragedy that will unfold in your near future. Your spirit companion is using your dreams to prepare you because he has no other way to instill this message to you. He says you have a strong psychic ability, yet you have relinquished all interest and use for it. You are very much involved in the material side of life; the buying and gathering of things which have no true worth. Material things do not bring true happiness, they only offer misguided hope to those seeking to foster love in their empty lives. A change in your thinking about this future event now will prepare you to deal with the fallout that will occur afterward. He is saying you need to prepare now, prepare your mind and thoughts so you are mentally and emotionally ready to make the necessary decisions at the time of the impending tragedy."

"What tragedy?" She asked hesitantly.

"Alexander says you already know the answer to that question. That you have already discussed this with your husband." I must admit I was curious to know what the tragedy was, but if Alexander didn't tell me then it wasn't for me to know.

After a short pause, "Yes, your guide is correct. I do know what he is referring to. Can he tell me when this may come about?"

"Within the next three-year period as he sees it in our understanding of time."

"Will there be financial help available to me after that event?"

"He says there will be almost no financial help available to you at that point in time. Your world as you now know it will crumble and disappear. You will have two paths placed in front of you: one leading to a new way of life and one leading into darkness as he sees it. You will have the free will to choose which path you will walk for your remaining days upon this planet." As I brought forth that information Bonnie Sue began to cry.

Through her tears she asked, "Is there nothing I can do to stop it before it happens?"

Alexander seemed to pause before he sent me the answer, "No." That was all he gave me and that was all I conveyed to Bonnie Sue as I felt Alexander withdraw from my vibration.

She excused herself to my bathroom and after emerging she said she needed to get back to her family. They would be flying back to California in the early morning. We hugged and I wished her

well and gave my condolences on her husbands'
family loss. I would never hear from her again in
this lifetime.

(Seven years later)

It had been a long day for me. I was mentally
and physically tired. Preparing to enter a hot bath I
had just made the phone started ringing. I decided
to ignore it and would call whoever it was back
tomorrow.

As I was disrobing Alexander popped in and
said, "Evelyn, please answer the phone. It is
important." I was a little caught off guard for
Alexander had never done this before; I always
made first contact so to speak.

Putting my robe back on I headed into the living
room. To my amazement the phone was still
ringing. Answering, it was Karl Anderson, Bonnie
Sue's brother. I had only new him from our old
high school days and had not seen or heard from
him since that time. We were never close as they
say, he was two years ahead of us in school, so he
wasn't in our 'click' of friends so to speak.

Karl said he wasn't sure why he felt the need to
call me; for some unknown reason, my name just
popped into his head, and he's been thinking about
me for over a week. He said he felt compelled to
look me up and he finally gave in and called.

We had a truly short phone conversation before I
asked how his sister Bonnie Sue was doing. There
was surprise in his voice for he had thought his
sister had surely called and told me of the events
that had taken place. He then told me of the

tragedy that had befallen the family four years ago, three years after the reading I had given her.

Jason Anderson her husband had just received a plaque in recognition of his outstanding work achievement at his place of employment; manager of the year it read. After the presentation Karl said there was a staff party. During the celebration it was noticed Jason was missing and several employees went in search of their boss and friend.

Jason was found dead in his car in the parking lot. He had shot himself in the head with a revolver. Beside him on a notepad he had simply written; 'It's time for me to return home my love. I look forward to seeing you in the next world. Please explain to Jenny and give her my love.'

All employees questioned by police said he seemed very much in good spirits after the ceremony and said the same concerning the party afterward.

Karl said his sister's life deteriorated rapidly over the following year. Bonnie Sue told him and the other family members how they were hiding from everyone the fact that they were very much in financial debt. They had two mortgages on their home; their credit cards were almost maxed out. They were having trouble paying their monthly car payments and the list went on and on. They didn't want anyone to know how they were robbing 'Peter-to-pay-Paul' he said.

Bonnie Sue had confided in Karl after Jason's death that he had been very depressed and was seeing a psychiatrist who had him on medication. But the medication only seemed to dull his mind and added to his mental and emotional problems she told Karl. Toward the end they could no longer afford the doctor visits so that was stopped.

It had gotten so bad that Bonnie Sue had told Jason if he was thinking of suicide, he had better not kill himself in the house. She did not want their daughter finding his body. Jason said if it came to that, he would comply with her wishes Karl said.

There was a small company insurance policy used for funeral expenses, but it did not cover all the costs. They had already used Jason's 401k money and cashed in their life insurance policies trying to stave off the mounting debt. They were trying to live the lifestyle of the American dream Karl said, but Bonnie Sue told him that dream could no longer be maintained.

The house went into foreclosure, and they were forced out; her and her daughter. Jason's parents were already living on their meager social security so they could offer no assistance. Bonnie Sue's parents had already passed on. Karl said they stayed with him for a short while.

He said her so-called friends all gave good lip-service at the funeral, but none could spare a dime or any personal time to help her or her daughter when they truly needed it. Maybe they too were all striving for the great American dream but were secretly struggling just as Bonnie Sue and Jason were. I try not to judge for who truly knows what lessons other people are facing in their personal lives.

Karl said Bonnie Sue was very depressed for almost a year over losing her husband, losing her lifestyle, losing her so-called friends, and losing her self-identity. All her material things; house, furnishings and even some treasured personal items had to be sold to help pay debts. Both cars were repossessed. She had to declare bankruptcy. A small one-bedroom apartment was all she could afford for herself and her daughter Jenny.

He went on to say that his sister spiraled down the dark path of alcoholism, which he felt was brought on by the severe depression she had succumbed to. She was fired from her job because of the complications arising from her drinking problem.

Bonnie Sue was shortly thereafter committed to a State Facility after she tried to commit suicide by mixing old prescriptions with vodka. Jenny found her unconscious and called Uncle Karl because she didn't know what to do. He called 911. Family services became involved.

Karl said he stepped in at that point and moved Jenny in with him to keep her out of foster care. Jenny was an emotional mess and was assigned to see a school counselor twice a week.

Bonnie Sue had been placed on a suicide watch at the facility. She refused to eat and only kept stating she wanted to go back home. When her psychiatrist asked her where home was; she repeatedly said she was from another dimension. She kept asking that her body be destroyed so she could free her spirit from this world. That brought on strong medication and forced intravenous feeding from her doctor's he said. I felt so sad for her, and Jenny I was softly crying as Karl continued on with their saga.

Then something miraculous happened on the seventeenth day of her confinement; she sat up in her bed and said she wanted to see the man-in-charge of her care. The head psychiatrist was summoned, and she told him she no longer wished to die, but now wanted to live. She began to eat on her own, to exercise, showing interest in everything and everyone she came in contact with. Months later she was released from the facility with a new lease on life as it were.

During her confinement Karl felt it would be better if he and Jenny had no contact with her, which had come at the behest of her attending Doctor. At first, Bonnie Sue who was now only going by the name 'Sue' made no attempts to contact her daughter or her brother. She found employment in the healthcare system and established a residence in a lower-middle class area of southern California.

To his great surprise a close friend of his said she had attended a psychic fair held by a local spiritualist group and that Sue was there giving psychic readings.

After not hearing from Sue for almost a year Karl decided it was time to see what Sue's intentions were toward Jenny. Karl's friend alerted him to the next upcoming psychic fair which was four months later. The fair was being held at a Holiday Inn on a Saturday and Sunday only. Arriving mid-morning he entered the large room and saw that Sue was sitting at a small fold-out card table, as were five other psychic's giving readings at separate card tables.

Paying for a reading he awaited his time slot and approached the small table and sat down across from her. She greeted him as if she had never laid eyes on him before. Stunned, he sat quietly as she started to give him a reading. Abruptly she stopped and asked Karl if they had been acquainted in some fashion.

Not knowing what to believe he began to explain who he was; about her husbands' suicide and the events that had led her down the road to attempting suicide herself, and that she had a daughter who loved and missed her very much. She told him she had vague memories of the things and events he now spoke of but did not feel any connection; mental or emotional to him or Jenny.

He asked her about this new psychic ability she now alleged to have. Sue said not long after leaving the facility she woke up one morning and just knew she had the ability, and she started using it. It was just so natural she said.

No further contact was forthcoming on his part he said. He provided her with his phone number and home address if she changed her mind and wished to have contact with him or her daughter. After all this time Sue has made no attempts to contact either of them, he said sadly.

Karl then asked if I could give him a reading over the phone. As I was about to explain how tired and exhausted, I was, hoping we could schedule it for another time I suddenly felt energy surging into my body. No longer did I feel mentally, emotionally, or physically tired. It was as if I had gotten eight hours of refreshing sleep. Knowing Alexander was behind this I told Karl to give me a few minutes to prepare myself and I would be glad to read for him.

"Okay Karl, what would you like to ask first?"

"Was it the depression and drinking or was it the strong medications they were giving her at the state hospital that caused her overall memory loss?" His tone not only conveyed confusion but a hint of anger.

"Alright..."

"How could she not remember us...especially her own daughter?!" I could hear the negative emotion attached to his words; the anger and frustration of what had played out over the last several years.

"Karl?"

There was a short pause, "Yes, I'm here. Sorry, I'm just so bewildered by all this."

"Take a deep breath and let me see what my guide has to say about all this. Can you do that for me?" My tone was soft and reassuring.

"Sure, I can do that." His voice was no longer angry but came across as simply tired and stressed.

"My guide Alexander is saying this may be hard to understand at first, but later once you think on it, you will come to a better understanding of what he is going to explain to you now. Your sister Bonnie Sue had reached a point where she felt she could not continue in this lifetime. During her attempted suicide while she was unconscious her spirit companion, along with a highly advanced spiritual being, allowed her soul to leave her physical body so that it could be counseled. At that time, it was determined that her soul could not continue on at which point it asked to be allowed to return to the world of spirit. The higher advanced spirit after communicating with her spirit companion gave approval. Her soul was released from the body and another soul (walk-in) agreed to take over her body in order to fulfill its own personal set of lessons it was working on. My guide says that is why the one now known as Sue has only a vague remembrance of you and Jenny. Do you understand so far?"

There was a long pause before Karl spoke, "Are you kidding me? What are you trying to feed me? One soul taking over another soul's body…what a bunch of bullshit! You know, I never liked you and I told Bonnie Sue to stay away from crazy people like you. Go sell your voodoo somewhere else." After his abrupt hang-up, I never heard from him again.

* Note to Readers: From a Spiritual standpoint suicide is no different an exit from earth than any other manner of death. This, as others, is a physical action manifested from the thoughts and stress that persist on a person's mind. These can be overcome in the physical, and if not, there are many counseling sessions and advisements when that soul returns to the spirit world so that they can understand what torment they felt they were experiencing. Often times, those who commit suicide are young souls; those who have not yet had many life experiences in a physical form, and this is something they must overcome in order to continue learning in the lifetimes through the human form. Young souls who no longer remember their true home world become confused by being trapped in a human body and desperately seek to escape from their perceived confinement on a subconscious level. Committing suicide is no more or less

negative or positive than any other action taken
on the earth plane. Self-inflected death only returns
a soul back to the spirit world; just as dying from
old age, a disease or even murder or war
accomplish the same. There is no judgment from
God for a Soul to exercise its free will. Once a soul
has been counseled and it decides it is ready, it will
incarnate again into human form facing those same
conditions with the desire to overcome them and
grow spiritually. There are times when suicide is
not only for the individual committing it but may
simply be a lesson for those family and/or friends
who are associated with the person committing this
act. In that instance it becomes a matter of
restoring love; you have seen family's that seem to
be scattered yet when such a perceived tragedy
occurs, they come together again; re-establishing
their love and commitment for each other. Suicide
can be a lesson in its own right, not just the act of a
seemingly desperate individual.

Chapter Seven

Mark and Linda Goldman live in the apartment down the hall from mine. We have exchanged pleasantries passing in the hallway but nothing more. They seem like a nice young Jewish couple who have a beautiful one-year old baby boy named Davin.

Several days ago, the Goldman's discovered their son had died in his sleep and the authorities had ruled it a 'Crib Death.' Needless to say, they were very distraught and devastated at this event. Both husband and wife fell into deep depressions, the mother more so than the father.

As they struggled in the following months to reclaim their lives; one could say 'time' does heal all deep emotional wounds, but it does so slowly.

I was in the community laundry room washing two loads of clothes when Linda Goldman came in carrying a basket full of dirty clothes. She gave a short, half-hearted attempt at smiling as she passed by me and headed to the end washing machine. Returning her smile with a nod of acknowledgement I went back to a romance novel I had been reading while waiting for the spinning cycle to finish.

Looking up from my paper back novel I then noticed the elegant older woman, who was holding a small infant standing just several feet from where Linda was now sitting. My psychic ability told me immediately this regal woman was her grandmother, and the infant were her son who had died from 'Sudden Infant Death Syndrome.'

From past experience I knew her grandmother wanted to make contact with her bereaved granddaughter, yet once again I wasn't sure how to initiate the communication between the two. Summoning my courage, I got up and sat down in the chair next to Linda Goldman. She was just staring at the floor.

"I'm sorry to bother you, I'm Evelyn Adams and I live down the hall from you in apartment forty-nine."

Linda broke off her intense stare and turned toward me. "Are you speaking to me?"

"Yes, I'm Evelyn…"

"What do you want?" Linda was very direct and plainly didn't want to be disturbed.

"I'm sorry for my intrusion but I just wanted to offer my condolences on the passing of your son."

After a long blank stare, she finally spoke, "You have never said more than two words to me or my husband since we moved in. Now after all this time you now dare to offer your condolences on the tragic death of our son. You think I don't know who you are? People in the building talk about you…you're nothing more than a fortune teller who preys on the weak minded. You need to get away from me before I call the police and report you. There are laws against con artists like you. Go sell your lies and superstitions somewhere else." She then fixed her gaze back to the floor.

"I'm sorry to have bothered you." I said softly heading back to the other end of the laundry room.

When the washing machine stopped, she placed her wet clothes in the basket and left the laundry. She did not stay to dry them, nor did she look in my direction as she walked past me. It was at that moment I realized her grandmother and infant son had already vanished.

For me, it would be a true statement to say the dead can be very annoying, with their constant intrusions into my life seeking help. I would be visited by her grandmother and son on four more occasions; all occurring in my bedroom. Each time they would just appear at the foot of my bed with the grandmother communicating the same message to me; 'She needs to know her son is loved and cared for.'

Finally, a week later I wrote a short letter and placed it in an envelope and then late one evening I attached it to the Goldman's apartment door since I truly felt uncomfortable in approaching Mark or Linda Goldman in person. It read:

Mr. and Mrs. Goldman,

My name is Evelyn Adams. I know because of your religious beliefs you do not put any faith in what I do as a psychic. Nevertheless, I am going to tell you of a vision I have had from a lady who identifies herself as Margaret, grandmother to Linda Goldman.

She has asked me to convey to both you and your husband the following message from the great beyond. Your son Davin is happy and well and is loved very much. She wants you to know that once a mother gives birth here on earth, from that point up until the approximate age of two years old the new soul that has incarnated into this world through the baby's body has a decision to make. It can choose with its free will to stay and work on the lessons it has chosen for this lifetime or it can back out of that planned life and simply leave and return to the world of spirit.

If it chooses to vacate the body sometime during the first two years of life, for whatever reason, the baby's body simply dies when the soul leaves it. The physical body cannot sustain life without a soul inside and it shuts down. Doctors who cannot find a medical cause for the death of an infant then call it a Crib Death.

The soul leaves the physical body not to punish the parents, but for its own personal reasons seeking the best life possible to help it advance spiritually.

Margaret wants you two to know the death of your infant son had nothing to do with either of you personally. It was simply its choice to leave for its own personal reasons. So do not blame yourselves for this outcome. There is no fault to be assigned here, none whatsoever.

She and your son love you both very much, but it is time for you both to move on with your lives. God Bless.

It was my great hope the short letter would bring them some comfort in their loss and grief, and maybe bring some understanding to this unfortunate situation.

Their response to my letter came two days later. As I opened the door to very loud knocking, I was stunned to see two Sheriff Deputies standing there. They informed me an official complaint had been made saying I was attempting to use my position as a fortune teller to illicit money fraudulently from the death of the Goldman's son.

They said this was my one and only warning to 'cease and desist' making intrusions into the lives of the Goldman's or face criminal charges. I informed the deputies I would have no further contact of any kind with the Goldman's.

Three days after that incident I received a certified letter from the apartment management stating I had thirty days to vacate my apartment. It listed several reasons for the eviction; namely that I was harassing other tenants with my religious beliefs, that I was operating an unlicensed business from my apartment, that the police had to be summoned to my apartment and that others in the apartment community didn't want me practicing or directing 'black magic' toward them or their children.

After reading the eviction letter I must admit I sat down and cried for nearly an hour. I was so disheartened at how my small gesture had caused such a severe backlash against my open and honest intentions.

Pulling myself together over the next week I began looking for a new residence. Not one to wallow in depression I quickly found my positive footing again and moved on with my life with the assistance of Alexander.

*Note to Readers: Some people say the loss of a child is the most severe loss one can experience, but this is not true. Anyone who loses a mother or father, a wife or husband, a brother or sister, a son or daughter, a true friend or companion, or even a beloved pet; that loss to 'them' may be the most devastating. Each person experiences the loss of a loved one in their own way. No one can measure how much grief we will go through or for how long it will take us to come to terms with our loss.

Chapter Eight

My friend Madelyn and I crossed paths in the supermarket. We were chit-chatting about her grandkids and the like when she brought up her ailing mother. She would be undergoing testing for liver cancer at the end of the week and as expected she was very afraid indeed. Many still view cancer as a death sentence.

Madelyn asked if they could come for a reading the next day, but I had already made plans to work at a psychic fair in another city and would be staying there for two days. I was leaving early the next morning and told her I would be glad to do it after that, but she had already planned to be with her mother for the testing which was also taking place in another city. They were flying out the day after tomorrow. Therefore, we decided to hook-up the day after their return flight back.

Truly I felt bad not being able to help her mother before seeing her oncology specialist, but I needed the money and many of my regular clients were counting on me being there at the psychic fair.

A week later they were back and after a brief phone call they were on their way to my apartment. They arrived within the hour and after making them comfortable we got down to business.

Madelyn's mother, Bertha was noticeably quiet and seemed to be in the early stages of depression. Just from her demeanor I could tell the cancer testing didn't show any positive results.

Madelyn did most of the talking as her mother seemed very tired and was doing her best at this point to just exist. She confirmed my observations about the test results; that she was basically given a death sentence. Her doctor wants to do a massive round of radiation followed by a heavy dose of chemotherapy but was not overly optimistic they would have any effect.

Bertha knew about psychics and the like through her daughter but never put much stock in it. She was raised in the Baptist faith and never understood why her daughter left it to seek a new path into Spiritualism. She was not a fan of the so-called 'New Age' reality her daughter was always babbling about, as she put it.

"Well Evelyn, I'm not sure we still need a reading now that the test results are in." Madelyn was patting her mother's knee gently. Her mother just stared off into space with watery eyes.

"Since you're here let me just tune in to my guide Alexander and see if he has anything else to offer on this situation. It can't hurt to ask." She started to retrieve some money from her purse, "Oh no dear, put that away. Let's just see if my guide has anything to say."

Madelyn closed her purse and snuggled a bit closer to her mother and held her hand as she spoke, "Okay then."

Alexander started sending me information, "He is saying that cancer is a scary word to most humans and that there are many reasons for cancer to appear in someone's life. From a spiritual point of view cancer can make a person take note of a life they are wasting through frivolous life pursuits;

cancer in that case pulls them from their complacent lifestyle and refocuses them to what is truly important for their spiritual growth. Cancer allows many to tune in to who they truly are and allows them to forgive themselves as they then seek to live the life they had chosen before being born. Some go on to die because they feel worthless, and some because of self-hate feel they do not deserve to live. Other cancers come into a person's life because of poor diet and lack of exercise; your body is your home so-to-speak and 'you' and only 'you' are responsible for maintaining it. Cancer in and of itself can be a most profound lesson and can be a chosen path for those wishing to use it as a way to leave your world. He says there are many other reasons for cancer, but these will suffice for now. He says most cancers, like many other major diseases are simply here to teach specific life lessons to those who have chosen a certain disease for that very purpose. Don't see cancer or any other disease as a death sentence, but as a learning opportunity. Yes, he says it may lead to death, but that, at times, is what was desired by the soul who is experiencing this disease through the human form; for its spiritual enlightenment."

Madelyn had a look of uncertainty on her sad, tired face as she asked, "So…what type of cancer is my mother experiencing then?"

Alexander answered quickly, "Oh!" I wasn't expecting his response.

"What?" Madelyn chimed in.

"I'm sorry, his answer through me off a bit. He says your mother doesn't have liver cancer; she has been misdiagnosed."

"What?!" Madelyn was also a bit surprised by the answer as I was.

"He is saying she needs to go to another doctor for a second opinion. They will confirm the misdiagnosis. He also said if she had undergone the chemotherapy treatment, that the chemo, which is simply a poison, would have caused her organs to start failing. He says she would have succumbed to the treatment, not from any cancer. He says the problem now facing your mother is the shock she is experiencing from the cancer diagnosis. She has lost her will to live. She is so physically, mentally, and emotionally drained she has been quietly praying for death to take her to end the misery. Prayers are thoughts and thoughts which are sent out with strong emotion attached to them do bring results; whether positive or negative. She is trying to bring an end to her physical existence through her own free will. This is her right to seek such an ending, and should her spirit companion receive validation from a higher spiritual being; her prayer to die may be allowed to come to fruition depending on whether most of her life lessons have been experienced, and whether she would have the future ability to still accomplish any remaining lessons or not have the ability to do so because of the state she is now in. At this point it could go either way concerning whether she lives on or dies and returns home."

"So, what now?" Madelyn asked with great uncertainty displayed over her weary face.

"Alexander says it's all up to her and her spirit companion now. You will know their answer within a few months' time he says, one way or the other."

Madelyn helped her mother out as we exchanged 'goodbyes.'

I received a phone call just short of three months later and Madelyn said her mother did confirm the misdiagnosis, but it didn't seem to have any effect on her. Enzyme testing found she just needed to be put on a gluten-free diet. She still did not want to live and nothing her daughter did could pull her out of her deep depression. She had her mother put on anti-depressants, but they seemed to make things worse overall.

As she began to cry, she told me her mother had passed quietly in her sleep just four days ago and asked if I would come to her funeral. I told her I would be there.

* Note to Readers: Do not fear death, for it is simply your Soul returning to your true home. Those you have known throughout eternity; true friends and companions who have been with you through many lifetimes will rejoice when you return to the unseen world. They will be waiting with open arms to receive you and surround you with feelings of pure love and peace at your return. It matters not what your beliefs are, for we were all created by the same God.

Chapter Nine

I was happy to hear the news that two friends of mine were becoming engaged and were planning a small marriage. Shortly after hearing this wonderful news, I received a phone call from Joni Jones, who simply went by 'JJ.' Young and impetuous, she was the impending bride-to-be and was seeking a reading from me, and I was happy to oblige.

Alan Crane, a very dashing young man was the impending groom and was not coming with her she said because he had to work. So, after her early morning arrival and some girlie chit-chat about the upcoming nuptials we got down to business so-to-speak.

After preparing myself for Alexander's arrival I began, "So JJ what is on your mind?"

"Well, this is a very important step in my life, and I would like to know if Alan is my one and only true soul mate?"

"Alright then, let me see what my guide Alexander has to say. First, he wants to give you a better understanding concerning the term soul mate. He says certain souls incarnate for the purpose of interacting specifically with another soul in a specific lifetime. This does not have to be a long-term interaction or a significant interaction; only that the interaction occurs, by both souls agreeing and by positive consideration by those above you. There are some who are soul mates who are engaged in long term relationships and others who only have short involvements with your life. The purpose of these relationships ranges the full spectrum of needs, emotions, and for development, or receiving an experience. He says it is important to know that simply because you are soul mates does not make you 'lovers.' You can have friends and colleagues who are soul mates. Soul mates can refer more to your similarity in progress that has been made through your development as an energy being, your true self. Though, it is possible that there is a link between beings that do not reside in these areas of existence within your true home. He says there are soul mates who work together on spiritual progress; often these can be groups, not limited to just a singular pair of souls. These groups work to promote and motivate or help to understand the experiences had by the group for the sake of evolving and, as you might understand it, educating each other for the purpose of ascending to a higher frame of knowledge. Can you follow what he is saying so far JJ?"

"Yes, I guess so, but does that mean me, and Alan are true soul mates or not?"

I could tell by her response she wasn't truly understanding Alexander's message, but more often than not people hear only what they want to hear, "Alright JJ, let me see if Alexander can clarify it for you. He says it is possible that significant or insignificant relationships also be of your own free will or those that were destined to happen or created to happen for your experience, or even by chance, and that those individuals share nothing in common with you on any plane. Though in many cases, in order for a successful long-term relationship of any kind to take place and be maintained there is often a meaningful accord between the two beyond the physical realm in which you currently reside."

"Evelyn, can your guide simply tell me yes or no, please?"

"Well…he says yes, but…"

"Awesome!" She yelled as she stood up, leaned over, and kissed me on the forehead, grabbed her purse and raced out the door. I was stunned for a moment at her response.

Too bad she didn't let me finish what Alexander had to say. He was trying to convey that although Alan is one of her soul mates, he was not here to have a long-term relationship with her. He came into her life to bring her a lesson she requested before they both incarnated. Therefore, their time together would not be long term, not in the way of marriage or as life partners in this lifetime.

Alexander could have told her Alan came into her life to bring a specific lesson; yet he could not tell her what the lesson itself was so as not to influence the outcome of the experience she chose to receive.

I mentally asked Alexander if I should try and convey the rest of his message to her and he said no. Her free will was in play he said so she has the right to move forward with her life, with or without seeking all the information available. Sometimes, actions do speak louder than words.

Chapter Ten

Henry and Loraine Robinson arrived at my apartment knocking softly on my door. They were referred to me by Henry's brother Scott who was a regular client of mine.

They were a pleasant couple in their late thirties and wanted to see if I could shed some light on an incident that happened several months ago concerning their fifteen-year-old son Drew.

Henry had hardly spoken a word while Loraine was doing all the talking. I sensed he wasn't very comfortable, and my impression was his wife made him come with her. I told them I would be glad to see what my guide had to say on the matter.

Loraine told me she was very much into the 'New Age' philosophies and loved reading about psychics, karma, reincarnation, and the like. But she said Henry basically thought it was all 'hog wash' as she put it. She laughed as she told me he believed it was all the Devil's work. As she was telling me this Henry made no facial expression; but seemed to be surveying his surroundings as if he truly expected to see a Demon appear from a dark corner.

"So, Loraine, I'm ready to begin if you are?"

"Oh yes, please do."

"So, what was the incident with your son Drew?"

"Well, it was late November and Drew wanted to take Henry's twelve-gauge shotgun and his thirty-eight revolver out by himself and do some target shootin' and maybe a little huntin' to boot.

We live way out in the country where it's mainly woods and corn fields. So, we don't see too many folks out there. So, after Drew pestered his daddy and me for a few days we finally gave in.

He was fifteen and Henry taught him how to handle guns. They had been on many huntin' excursions and whatnot since Drew was twelve. But this was the first time allowin' him to go out by himself, but we felt he was ready. You know how it is; you have to let them fly on their own at some point, so we turned him loose.

It was a cold day, the corn fields had already been ploughed over, so they were muddy and partly frozen in spots, the trees in the wooded areas had no leaves; you get the picture."

"Ah, yes I can visualize what you're saying." I said softly. Henry was now fixated on my face. Just starring with only short eye blinks every now and again; I got the impression he was waiting for me to turn into a witch and fly around the room on a broom. I stayed focused on Loraine and listened as she continued her story.

"Well, Henry and I were in the family room which is on the backside of the house. We have sliding glass doors that look out into the fenced-in back yard. There's a small gate in the far-left corner which leads to the muddy field behind our house. Farther out its all trees and a small creek that snakes through the wooded area.

It was a gray overcast day with the hint of snow in the air. Drew had been out huntin' for about an hour, I guess. We were watchin' TV when Henry saw Drew just standin' outside the little gate. He was just standin' there, in the cold.

Henry brought it to my attention and we both watched Drew just standin' there, not movin'. Then Henry jumped up and started puttin' his boots on and I asked what was goin' on. Henry yelled back as he went out the glass doors that Drew wasn't holdin' the shotgun and that somethin' was wrong. I ran to the doorway and heard Henry callin' Drew's name, but he just stood there like he was in a trance. As Henry opened the gate Drew just seemed to collapse into his arms. Henry carried him back into the house yellin' for me to call 911; Drew's right hand was bloody, and his thumb was missin'.

I told the 911 operator we'd meet the ambulance at the county road, so I wrapped a clean T-shirt around Drew's hand and we loaded up into our pick-up truck. Drew was in shock and basically unconscious. Once the ambulance got him to the hospital, they got everything under control and said he'd be fine, thank God."

"That must have been a tremendous relief for you and Henry?" I spoke. Henry was still watching me with no expression on his face as Loraine continued.

"Oh my God, I was so afraid, you just can't imagine. Henry was just beside himself with worry." She pulled a tissue from her purse and dabbed at the tears that had run down her cheeks.

"So, Loraine, what questions do you wish to ask about?"

"Well, Drew recovered physically pretty much, but he is a little uncomfortable with his missing thumb. So, I guess there will always be some emotional stuff for him to deal with. But Drew has no memory of what happened in the field.

The last thing he remembers is he was bored because there weren't any critters to hunt, so he had been shootin' the revolver at some old soda-pop cans and whatnot until he ran out of bullets. Then he saw a big, half frozen mud puddle and decided to blast it with the shotgun.

He said he remembers firing off a shot which sent mud and water flyin' all over the place. You know how men are; they just love blowin' stuff up. Drew then remembered slidin' the bolt lever back loading another shell into the chamber, but when he aimed at the mud puddle and pulled the trigger, this time he said it didn't go off. Then he said everything just went black. Next thing he knew he woke up in the hospital.

Because his accident involved a gun the Sheriff's department had a deputy come talk to us at the hospital, and then sent a deputy to our house to find the guns since neither were on Drew when we found him at the back gate.

The sheriff deputy went out our back gate and traced Drew's foot tracks back to where the guns were. Both were layin' on the ground near a single old tree in the middle of a ploughed-over muddy corn field. The deputy picked up the guns and took them to the station as part of their investigation.

A few weeks later after Drew was back home recuperatin', we got a visit from the deputy who retrieved the guns. He said it would be ruled an accidental shootin' and wanted to know if we wanted the guns back. He said the revolver was fine but that the shotgun was nearly blown in half.

Testing showed he said that the first shot went off okay but when Drew thought he had ejected the spent cartridge, it did not eject and stayed in the chamber. So, when he used the bolt lever to put another shell into the chamber it simply forced the other empty shell to be lodged into the gun barrel. So, when Drew took aim and pulled the trigger the second round had nowhere to go so it exploded, blowing the shotgun almost in half.

The deputy said there were two things their investigation could not account for. First, he said that since Drew was righthanded and had the shotgun up near his head when he pulled the trigger, the resulting explosion should have struck him on the right side of his head, not just his right thumb.

Then he said they also noted when they followed his muddy tracks back to the guns, the tracks ended there. There were no tracks leading back to our house. It looked as if he simply walked out into a muddy field and then vanished. No other footprints could be found anywhere leading back to our house.

Of course, we told him we didn't have any answers either, so he left it at that. We told him we wanted the revolver back, but that they could destroy what was left of the shotgun.

So, we'd like to know if your guide could give us some answers to the deputy's questions."

"Alright, Alexander is saying that many times a person's spirit companion or that which some call their Guardian Angel are connected to the one they watch over through their vibration. If it suddenly changes, they then tune-in so to speak to see what is going on with their charge. Sometimes they are actively observing the person they are charged to oversee.

My guide says he wants you to understand your spirit companion does not spy on those they are watching over, but they are ready if called upon to come forth. For example, it would be like saying your spirit companion is on the second floor of your house and you are in the basement. You can mentally ask for assistance and your spirit companion will get your message. He will receive your request, but he will not be with you in the same room. He will simply send you the answer mentally, as if you were both communicating over the telephone for example. He would not be with you in the same room but would still be connected to you.

Now if you called for help because of a dire situation, then your spirit companion can lower his vibration and leave the second floor of the house to come to you in the basement, so-to-speak if need be. Loraine, are you following what he has said so far?"

"Yes, it makes sense. Go on."

I glanced at Henry, he now had a distant look in his eyes as if he were bored and ready to leave all this 'hog wash.'

Alexander started sending information again, "Alright, he says concerning Drew; his spirit companion was aware he was going shooting and was in close contact with him.

Drew fired the first time, and then thought he had ejected the empty cartridge; the empty shell casing did not eject. It remained in the chamber. Drew then loaded another shell on top of that empty one, it was at that moment his spirit companion then realized what was about to occur.

Drew took aim at the half-frozen mud puddle and pulled the trigger. Now my guide says you must understand his spirit companion was in the spirit world so to speak and your son was in the physical world.

When the trigger of the shotgun was pulled it set into motion a physical chain reaction of sorts. As the gunpowder inside the shell ignited, this causes the steel pellets to travel at great velocity down and out the barrel of the gun heading toward its target. But because the barrel was blocked by the empty cartridge the gunpowder which was already in motion had to follow the path of least resistance; that being the weaker outer layer of the gun barrel itself; which is the area that holds the shell in place.

Drew's spirit companion then seeing what was now about to occur materialized a shield of energy and placed that around the ignited shell hoping to contain the blast. The problem was this was a physical event happening in a world of physical matter; Drew's spirit companion did not have enough power so-to-speak to stop the exploding shell, and now realized it could not contain it for very long. At that point he mentally sent out a distress call for Drew's Master Teacher as he is known.

Responding to the distress call, Drew's Master Teacher, who is greatly advanced in spiritual awareness and can call upon greater energy immediately penetrated itself into the physical world and seized the shotgun and forced it down away from Drew's face. As the shell exploded it missed his face but blew his right thumb off.

Alexander says had it been possible for the Master Teacher to have arrived sooner, he would have had the power to pull the gun from Drew's hands no matter how tightly he was gripping it, but that the explosion was already in motion and could not be contained at that point in time.

This was just an unforeseen event brought on by humankind's free-will he says. Do you understand Loraine?"

"Yes, it makes sense…so he is saying if Drew's Master Teacher had not come, the exploding shell could have blown part of his head off. But what about there being no footprints in the mud leading back to our house. How could he have gotten to the back gate without leaving any trail?"

"Alexander says the impact of the shockwave from the blast and the injury to Drew's right hand sent his body into shock. He was virtually rendered unconscious as his body reacted to the sudden incident. His body started to collapse to the ground but was stopped from doing so by his Master Teacher.

This was not a programmed event for Drew to experience in this lifetime, so the intervention was allowed to proceed. To stop the blood loss from his hand and to keep the effects of the shock from killing him his Master Teacher placed a shield of pure oxygen around Drew's body. My guide says he was then pulled up several feet off the ground and levitated to the back gate behind your house.

His Master Teacher then lowered him to a standing position and kept him suspended in that state until your husband then came to his aid. Once your husband opened the gate the shield was released, and your son collapsed into the arms of his father.

The Master Teacher then withdrew, and the spirit companion then resumed his vigilant watch over his charge. Throughout the three nights Drew spent in the hospital his spirit companion was periodically infusing his body with healing energy. Does that answer your questions, Loraine?"

"Oh my god, yes, it does. Thank your guide for his help and thank you Evelyn, you're the best." She leaned over and hugged and then kissed me on the cheek. Henry stood up and his body language made it truly clear he was ready to leave my apartment.

They left without saying another word; Loraine was softly crying, and Henry never looked back as they walked out. I was happy Loraine was pleased with the information from Alexander, but I was very relieved when Henry left; that guy creeped-me-out.

*Note to Readers: The Master Teacher is the most advanced energy being that oversees your human experience, and also oversees those who are assigned to assist you during your lifetime. Periodically he observes those who watch over you, and makes any necessary corrections concerning those who assist you. When you reach the point of returning home through the avenue called death, he has the final say as to whether your soul will be allowed to leave your human form, or whether it will remain to complete unfinished lessons. For example, if he determines you have progressed as far as possible, he will then instruct your main spirit companion to shut down the human body and assist your soul in removing itself from it. The death process, depending on the type of death you chose prior to birth can be instantaneous or a long-involved process. Now if you are near death and this was not your chosen time to die, then your Master Teacher will instruct your spirit companion and his helpers to bring forth healing energy to restore your health to a level where you can resume seeking to accomplish more of your chosen lessons. When a situation arises that cannot be handled by your spirit companion then he may call upon your Master Teacher to come forth and solve the problem or dilemma. Keep in mind; all decisions made by your Master Teacher concerning your human existence are for the benefit of your individual 'soul' growth.

END

More Annoying Dead People
Book #2

Chapter One

There came a knock at my door that was so soft, I almost didn't hear it. As I opened my apartment door, I recognized an old friend who I once worked with at a nursing home in another city. I hadn't seen her for nearly twenty years, yet I knew her right off.

She was only an inch taller than me and had put on quite a few extra pounds. Tears streaked down her cheeks and her reddish-brown hair was in disarray. As I peered into her gentle green eyes, I could tell without my psychic ability she was experiencing some dreadful circumstance.

"Molly, it's so good to see you. Please, come on in," I said as I opened the door wider.

Once inside she fell into my arms, and we held each other for almost a full minute before she spoke.

"Whatever it is, you can tell me," I said reassuringly as I led her to my sofa.

Molly finally spoke in a low voice, "I've missed you, Evelyn. I'm sorry I didn't stay in touch; but I fell in love with Tony, and everything revolved around him, and later we had a son and…"

I interrupted her, "Molly, you don't owe me an explanation, that's just how life works out sometimes. I knew you went off with Tony and I was happy for you both. So, how did you find me after all these years? I've lived in so many different places."

"I was at the salon getting my hair done about three weeks ago, when I overheard two ladies talking about a psychic one of them had gone to for a reading. I was so surprised when I heard one say your name. I dared to ask what you looked like, and I knew it had to be you. They gave me your address. I finally got up the nerve to come see you."

"Well, I'm so glad you did, but I feel you're here for another reason. Would you like a reading?" I said patting her arm softly.

Molly seemed to relax a little as she looked into my eyes and said, "I didn't come here for myself, but for my son Ross. Could you read for him?"

"Why, yes, of course. Where is your son?" I wasn't sure what to expect.

Molly pointed toward my apartment door, "He's outside in the car. I was afraid if we both came to your door you might get worried since you never met him before."

"Oh, well you can have him come on in. It's okay."

Molly left, and a short time passed when I heard her soft knock again. Opening the door there stood a young man who looked to be about sixteen or seventeen years old. His hair was blond, and his eyes were brown. The mirror image of his father. Ross was only about three inches taller than his mother and was very good-looking. She introduced me as I invited them in. Molly and Ross sat on the sofa, and I sat in a rocking chair nearby.

"Well Ross, your mother says you would like a reading."

"Ah, yes please." A bit apprehensive I felt as he made no eye contact; just looked down and every now and again he'd glance at his mother.

"Do you have a specific question for my guide Alexander, or do you just want him to bring what he feels is important for you at this time?"

Molly moved closer to her son and placed her reassuring hand on his thigh as she said, "It's okay, don't be afraid to ask her."

"I can't, please Mom, you ask her, please…" His voice was low and sounded like that of a fearful pleading child.

Molly turned to face me, "My son is gay, and he wants to know if there are any bad or harmful implications from being a homosexual."

Ross leaned closer to his mother and whispered something. Molly continued, "He would also like to know if he's going to burn in hell, like it says in th Bible."

"Very well Ross, let me see what Alexander has to say about your questions." The information came through very quickly.

"He says there are no adverse consequences to being gay. There are physical damages that can occur through long-term sex of a specific nature, such as 'excessive' anal sex, which could cause both homosexual and heterosexual individuals health problems later on in that area of their anatomy. Simple 'moderation' is the answer.

Alexander says, there is no definition of who may love who, and in what way, as far as God is concerned. As for the bible, he says that passage concerning man, laying with another man, being an act of abomination, punishable by death, was placed there, not by god, but by organized religious authority as a means of controlling the uneducated and superstitious masses of that time."

I wasn't sure if Ross was understanding all of this, so I asked, "If you have any questions, please feel free to ask. Okay?"

"Sure," Ross answered without looking up.

I continued, as more information was coming through. "Alexander says a balance of love in all forms is necessary. Physical desirability of any kind is acceptable as long as it is not to the disadvantage of others.

He says, there are some that choose this path prior to incarnating to earth; there are others who choose it once they are here, and it is an outward expression of their lacking love from specific parental or 'parent-like' figures in their life.

Though it is no less important, the lessons learned in that situation, no matter their motivations or the decisions to undertake them; many have not learned universal love, and perhaps the greatest lesson is not for the soul to undergo terrible persecution for sexual beliefs, or the love of the same gender, but for humankind to understand that there is still a soul in each physical form.

So, in a manner of speaking, no matter what is viewed on the exterior, and no matter the beliefs held inside that physical form, there is still a being of energy and light within that physical body that is learning, experiencing, and changing just as those who might be eager to judge, blame, and persecute are still evolving."

Molly chimed in, "Honey, do you have any questions so far?"

"No...I get what that Alex guy is saying." Ross blew his nose with a tissue his mother handed him.

Molly glanced over toward me, "Sorry Evelyn, I didn't mean to interrupt."

"Oh, no problem dear. Let me see if Alexander has anything else to say." I almost didn't get the last word in before more started to come through, "He says, often, there is previous debt that must be paid for prior actions, and there is persecution experienced in a current lifetime that was a direct result of the actions taken by that soul in a previous lifetime. Quite often there is a balance in what one experiences by choice; choosing to experience both sides of the coin, both sides of the situation, this can be by choice and can be called karma.

Yet, even if they do not choose, in order to understand, you must be both the murderer and the victim, this is karma. You cannot only experience the rosy side of each action, karma is not a punishment, but the polar opposite of actions had before, in order to better allow you to understand what has taken place, what is taking place, and what is being experienced by those when the other side of the action is experienced.

There is no gay individual that can be 'learned' or 'loved' or 'forced' into being a heterosexual. Gay is not a disease; it is not a mental illness. There are other problems, as with all humans, that can accompany any underlying desire, urge, or preference and these are what should be addressed.

Alexander says if they are uncomfortable with some aspect of their body or mind, this is for that soul to come to terms with, learn with, use as a tool, experience, and learn not to judge just as they wish to experience this lifetime without judgment and hatred towards them.

He says, all should love each other and through the physical form more is often associated with love through sexual acts; there is nothing negative or detrimental to the spirit or soul by any form of sexual experience that gay individuals may undertake. God does not judge; you are the judge concerning your chosen life."

Ross looked up at me and his expression no longer seemed so despondent. It was like that old-line people use, 'as if a great weight had been lifted from his shoulders.'

Molly asked him, "Anything else you want to ask?"

"Well, after what your friend just said…you still think it's your fault I'm gay?" He stared right into her eyes genuinely wanting to know her answer.

As tears rolled down her cheeks she said, "Not any more…it is, what it is, and that's nobodies' fault." They both hugged and cried together.

I couldn't contain myself, I too started to cry softly as this mother and son embraced each other with such love and forgiveness in their hearts.

As we all finally regained our composure, I asked if there was something else, they'd like to ask Alexander.

Molly and Ross made eye contact just before they both faced me. "No, you and your guide said all we needed to hear, I think. We want to thank you both, but we need to be getting home." Molly reached into her purse and produced thirty dollars which she leaned forward to hand me.

As I accepted the money, I don't know why, but I asked, "I don't mean to snoop, but how is Tony handling Ross being gay?"

Molly glanced toward her son and then back at me, "He doesn't know yet. We were going to wait for the right time to spring it on him."

Ross spoke up, "I don't think dads going to take the news his only son is gay very well. I've overheard how dad and grandpa talk about fags and how they should line them all up and shoot them."

"I'm a bit surprised, Tony seemed so open-minded back when we all worked together," I said.

"Tony's dad isn't going to win the father-of-the-year award any time soon." She stated.

"That's for sure. I think dad loves grandpa more then he loves us," Ross popped off.

Molly spoke quickly, "Please don't say that you know he loves us very much."

"Really? Well tell me how much he'll love me when he finds out I'm gay. Tell me then what he thinks of me." The fear and stress were clearly evident in his strained voice.

"Oh honey..." Molly tried to hug her son, but he pulled away.

Ross now turned on me, "You know what my dear old loving father had to say about psychics...he said they are scam artists who take advantage of the elderly and the weak minded.

Well lady, we sure the hell aren't elderly, so I guess that makes us the weak minded!"

"Ross, you apologize right now!" Molly screeched.

He shook his head from side to side as he spoke, "I don't know why I said that. I'm terribly sorry, and I do thank you for the reading. It really has helped me. I'm simply scared to death what my dad's going to do when he finds out."

"You don't need to apologize, trust me, I've heard much worse," I said in a most reassuring manner.

"It's time to go, your father will be home soon," Molly said as they headed for the door.

To this day, I've not had any more surprise visits from Molly or Ross. After a few months, my curiosity got the better of me, and I did ask Alexander what had happened with my friend Molly and her son.

He wouldn't tell me what occurred between Tony, Molly and Ross. Yet, he did say this; divorce does not always destroy a family; many times, it brings understanding, learning and the true meaning of unconditional love for those involved.

*Note to Reader: The bible is a collection of stories that may be considered fables or moral stories. Some were based on actual events, while others were simply handed down word of mouth as lessons for those who needed the symbolism. There are many sections that were originally written by those with spirit communication, and even sections that were given to this planet by other beings from other planets, and other beings of light. There has been much work to control this book and use it for selfish purposes and realizing this will remove the controlling hold it has over an individual or a group of people who are following this book as though it were an inflexible document and all binding. There was much done to it to change it from its original format, which was intended to be a symbolic guidebook and positive reference for the people of that time period. There are many who included Jesus because they knew of his power; though the threat was added of his return to further ensure that a proper behavior was had from subordinates. There are many true stories in the bible of healing, prophecy, positive affirmations, levitation, and other phenomena. This book allows those who need greater instruction to know that there is a peace far greater than what they presently know. Though this book is used as such, it was not intended to divide and should be used to unite. Reading it as you would any other book is the way for those who are seeking guidance; it is unimportant to develop a new ritual for reading and following it. There is much that is unimportant in the bible, but the basic tenants of life and kindness to, from, and between humankind are wrapped onto the pages. Each shall have their own view of the world, but the bible may be a basic building block just as many other stories serve the purposes of learning basic concepts such as kindness, love, and forgiveness. There is no wrathful god to cower down before, as this was also added by those who sought control of the masses.

The so-called 'Ten Commandments' did not come from God, but from those who needed a weapon, of sorts, to rule over the people. As many have heard before, 'words' are mightier than the 'sword.' Such commandments would have negated your soul's use of free will and limited your ability to create while in the human form.

Many sovereigns and religious leaders of the past, when re-writing various stories that later became this collection, also created more elaborate stories to provide them with power, from their point of view, while others were simply attempting to show the gravity of the situation. This book was to give purpose and direction to those who were wandering aimlessly. It is still useful if those sections which are glaringly untrue to you are ignored. Many on certain levels will feel a specific phrase vibrate or resonate with them, these sections are true for them. Inclusion and love are what should be taken from the bible; not many reasons for exclusion and persecution, this was never the original purpose or intention.

Chapter Two

Early one beautiful summers morning, I received a phone call from a female caller who said her name was Susan Jones. She had gotten my phone number from a business card I had pinned on a bulletin board in a local laundromat advertising psychic readings. We agreed to meet later in the afternoon.

Susan arrived promptly. She looked to be in her late thirties, and had short black hair, of which I could tell, it was not her natural hair color, yet it looked becoming. She had a light complexion which showed off her pinkish freckles and made her blue eyes sparkle.

We no sooner sat down, and Susan asked, "You charge $30 dollars, is that correct?" She produced the money from her pocketbook.

"I don't really…" Before I could finish, she thrust the money toward me. She seemed very anxious, so, I took the money gracefully and placed it next to me on an inn-table.

"So, how does this work? Do I ask questions or what?" Susan was very impatient.

"Well, you can ask about anything you wish, and I will tune in to my guide, who goes by the name Alexander, and see what he has to say, or if you prefer, Alexander will just provide you with information that your spirit companion would like you to know at this time. So, it's really your…"

"I got it, so, like whatever…just give me your usual spiel lady."

Susan seemed very impatient, and even a little condescending in her tone. I never had anyone act this way before who was seeking a reading.

As I opened myself up to Alexander, he simply said, 'be strong little one, and just know I am there for you, always.' He then withdrew.

This too had never happened before. I wasn't sure how I was going to explain when Susan suddenly stood up. I looked up at her face and I admit I was startled, to say the least.

"Evelyn Adams, I need you to stand and turn around; place your hands behind your back." She said this as she pulled a pair of handcuffs from behind her.

"What?" Was all I could think to say as I flushed bright red.

Susan leaned down and pulled me to a standing position; whereupon she spun me around and proceeded to cuff me.

I couldn't think, or even speak. I was freaking out, to say the least. I think I was in shock. She explained that she was an undercover officer and that her and her male partner, who was standing outside my door, were taking me to the police station to be booked into jail.

She read me my rights while I sat stunned in the backseat of their police cruiser crying hysterically. I don't remember much of that ordeal; yet, when I awoke the next morning, I was in a cell and dressed in jail attire.

A jail matron came a short time later, and said my court appointed attorney was here to interview me for my appearance before a magistrate.

She let a young man into my cell as I sat up on the small bunk. I felt dizzy, and that I might actually faint.

"Ms. Adams, I'm Larry Baker, I am your attorney. I was assigned to represent you after it was determined you could not afford one."

All I could think to say was, "Okay."

"I see by your record; you have never been arrested before. Not even a parking ticket. That fact will help us a lot." Larry said as he shuffled through some papers in a folder.

Energy started to surg throughout my body. I could feel Alexander's vibration now; he was fortifying me with healing energy. My mind now seemed clearer and alert as I asked, "Sir, what am I charged with?"

"Please…call me Larry. Well, you violated article-17 of the city's criminal code pertaining to Psychics and Fortune Tellers.

You did not obtain a city permit to work as a psychic. The permit cost's $347.00 dollars and requires a criminal background check and that you be fingerprinted. It also states you must clearly display where you perform this service, the rate you charge and provide a receipt to your clients; this is for tax reasons.

Did you not obtain a permit and comply with the city's code?"

"Oh my gosh, I didn't even know you had to have a permit in this state." I was feeling bewildered.

"Sorry, but the judge won't want to hear that old 'ignorance-of-the-law' line, everyone uses it. All he is going to ask is one question when we appear before him; how you plead, guilty or not guilty."

"So, what am I to say? If I plead not guilty, would I go to trial with a jury?" I inquired.

"No, what's happened in the past is that the judge can order, if he so chooses, to have you committed for 72 hours of psychiatric evaluation at the state mental facility.

Let me be very clear on this Ms. Adams; you don't want some underpaid state counselor asking if you hear voices in your head, or if you see or talk to dead people. I know it's hard to believe, but some institutions still use electric shock treatments and heavy medications on those they think are having hallucinations and stuff like that."

"Oh, my goodness…if I plead guilty, what will happen?" I now noticed my left eye was starting to twitch from the stress and strain of this overwhelming ordeal.

"Well, this particular crime, in this city is a 'Class B Misdemeanor,' which means the judge can sentence you up to 180 days in jail and fine you up to a maximum of $2000.00 dollars.

Now, I do need to warn you, we are scheduled to appear before Judge Rex Niemeyer, and he isn't known for his leniency. He likes giving out maximum fines and jail time." Larry said with no hesitation in his voice.

I leaned back against the wall and cupped my hands over my face as I started weeping uncontrollably. I just wanted so desperately to go home.

Poor Larry, he did not know what to do, so he sat quietly as I had my little breakdown. It lasted only a few minutes and I pulled myself together.

The matron came and announced it was time to go before the judge. I was led into the small courtroom followed by Larry and the matron. I stood behind a small podium with a microphone on it. Larry stood next to me as we awaited the judge's arrival.

Judge Louise Parker came in and sat down. She was an African American woman who looked to be in her late fifties. Picking up the gavel, she struck it twice and the court stenographer stood and read the charges against me. I looked at Larry about the same time he looked at me; neither of us knew what had happened to Judge Rex Niemeyer.

"Alright Evelyn Adams, how do you plead?" She was straight to the point; a no-nonsense kind of woman I guessed.

I cleared my throat and said sheepishly, "Guilty."

"Very well then; I fine you $60.00 dollars to cover court costs. Pay the clerk and you're free to go." Striking her gavel twice, "Ms. Adams, please approach the bench," she said as she gave a little wave gesturing me toward her.

Leaning over, she whispered, "Sweetie, my mother has been a psychic for over forty years; do us both a big favor…get your damn permit," She then smiled and gave me a quick wink.

"Yes, I promise. Thank you so much." I was so overjoyed…words cannot describe how I felt.

Larry was so dumbfounded and yet, he too was elated at the sentence I received. As a goodwill gesture he paid the $60.00 dollar fine for me.

A week later, back home and feeling safe and free, I asked Alexander if what I had just gone through was a lesson or experience, that I had asked for before I incarnated into this lifetime.

He said it was not; that it was the free will of the undercover female officer that set this into motion. Her mother had been seeing a fortune teller; and this unscrupulous person swindled her out of over six thousand dollars claiming she was channeling her dead husband, which she was not.

Now, after discovering what had happened to her mother, the female officer is targeting any fortune teller or psychic that is practicing outside the legal guidelines.

After seeing your business card at the laundromat, she looked up your name and saw it was not registered for a city permit. You became her next target.

Alexander also wanted me to know, by using her free will in a detrimental manner toward others, she was opening herself up to incurring undesirable karma.

*Note to Readers: Karma is simply the balancing of energy. Energy only changes form, it is never lost. There is always a reaction, in the same amount of energy, to that which is done by you. It may not be in the same form, but it is still experienced, sometimes scattered, sometimes in one action, but it is always in the same measurement of energy. This ensures direct learning by what one's own actions are creating. This is direct information on what one is doing but also by what one is thinking. Like attracts like, a law of attraction is not merely a passing fad. For what you do, there is always a vibration with that of similar consequence. There is a change coming where people will come to understand that energy must be balanced. In this lifetime and with other lifetimes, though many are attempting to work out karma in current lifetimes, there is much that is done from one lifetime to the next to balance the energy that is doled out and experienced to ensure that there is a balance. This does not always mean seemingly good is always balanced with what is called evil or negative, but that there is a set purpose for energy and a set level of energy. With that being said, it is always possible to create a new direction. There are those who have created atrocities against life and may move from that quite quickly and do much good to balance the world in which so much negative energy was directed. However, there are some who will be seemingly trapped by it because they do not experience that act and then learn to move away from it. Some repeat acts because they enjoy it but are counseled upon return to attempt to allow them to gain the knowledge that was contained within that action. There is much good in all, that is to say, there is the potential for the good in all to shine forth, but there is not always an influence of good. It is possible to create what you wish to experience but know that certain trials will be experienced if you planned them before your experience on earth. Emanating good will give you the impression of release from this karmic operation. Though know that you attract what you do, you attract by actions and thought. Know that you may commit a terrible act and you may seem that in order to balance it you must be on the receiving end. This is the case in some form but know that you may have already done so in another life, or that you will in the next. There is balance to everything. A label of karma only explains the nature of balance in the universes and those dimensions the 'Source of all Life' has created.

Chapter Three

One of my frequent clients, Cynthia, called to make an appointment for a reading. She said it wasn't for her, but for a friend of hers, Vicky, who had just gotten out of the hospital a few days ago.

I told her that would be fine, so we arranged a day and time for them to come over to my apartment.

Later that week, they arrived early, which was okay as my previous client had already departed. I try and leave at least thirty minutes between appointments just in case the reading runs over a bit.

Cynthia, who was in her late thirties had a slender build and short blond hair. She was what some would call 'spiritual, but not religious.' Her friend Vicky, who looked a little younger, had long dark hair that went down past her shoulders. She too was slender. Vicky seemed in good health overall for just getting out of the hospital not so long ago. She was a devout Christian. After exchanging pleasantries, and making ourselves comfortable in my living room, we came to the point of their visit.

Vicky said she had been in a car accident. As she proceeded through a green light at a four-lane intersection, a young man of nineteen who was texting on his cellphone ran the red light and struck her on the drivers' side of her small hatchback car.

The young man was driving a large extended cab pickup truck.

The force of the impact rendered her unconscious and she had to be cut out of her car by a fire rescue team. Her physical injuries were minor, yet she had suffered a major brain concussion. She was transported to an emergency room at the nearest hospital.

Vicky said she remembers becoming aware that her body was floating several feet off the ground, and she was in a corner of the room watching two nurses and a doctor who were examining her body.

There were many wires attached to her head and chest area that were attached to several machines. She listened as the doctor told the nurses that she was brain dead, and that they should check her driver's license to see if she was an organ donor, and to notify her next of kin.

As she floated above this scene, she said she was not afraid and felt a sense of being surrounded by love. Vicky became aware of another being hovering near her. She said it was Jesus.

They had a short conversation about moving in a more positive direction with her remaining lifetime, and about not being so afraid and not to entertain thoughts of suicide. Then Jesus said it was time and pointed toward her body.

The next thing she knew she was back in her physical body and awake. The nurses were calling it a miracle. Even the doctor was amazed at her full recovery. Vicky said she didn't tell anyone at the hospital about what had happened to her. When Cynthia came and picked her up from the hospital a few days later, she then told her trusted friend everything that she experienced.

"My goodness, you sure have been through a lot," I said amazed at her ordeal.

"Yes, it's been quite an eye opener indeed." Vicky noted.

"So, how can I help you today?" I asked as I felt Alexander's presence.

"I just wanted to know 'why me.' What was the reasoning behind this accident, I guess is what I'm asking? Cynthia thinks there's more to it than meets the eye. That new age stuff she's into." Vicky seemed genuinely baffled by all of this.

"Well, my guide says he wants to give you the basic outline of why some people go through a 'Near Death Experience' and you will see the correlation of what you encountered to what others have endured.

Alexander says there is an experience for many that involves their belief in the afterlife. It is important that some be broken from this or be righted on their path away from what they were currently pursuing. Some merely attempt to break from their physical existence prior to their scheduled departure, not that it is to be understood that there is often a specific date or time. There is a set of goals, a loose configuration of what should be accomplished, once it is so, or it is seen that it can be only accomplished so much and you are ready to make an exit, then you shall.

He says near death experiences are physical bodies that are being kept alive, usually through spirit intervention, so that the energy being can be counseled or consoled in the higher dimension.

It is important to know that there is not always physical trauma that needs to be experienced in order to bring this to a soul's existence. The trauma, usually interpreted by the mind, is often a catalyst for such behaviors to be understood.

There is a clear break. This is merely an intermission allowing a break so that counselling of the soul can take place. This often brings about development of skills or abilities that use other senses of the mind to produce psychic perceptions or a stronger spirit connection, so that communication in some or all forms is much more possible.

Alexander says it is necessary to understand that there are many who experience this but never return with the information they were given. Often, in subtle ways, their conversations while out of their body, will affect their life subconsciously. Others may not change. Others experience this information and retain the memory of such. To some extent, this is dependent on the person; partly this is dependent on the situation.

He says there are many who have observed their body while on the operating room table or after a severe trauma has taken place. There is much that you do not understand about the mind's perception and relation and connectedness to all things.

Yes, your mind can give you the perception that your energy body is leaving, though still connected, to your physical body. But there is an awareness of all things that are available to all who exist. This experience is often that awareness being freed from the confines and shackles of the mind; it is being freed from the cell and therefore can perceive all that is taking place.

Alexander says because the last moments before unconsciousness were focused on the impending injury, there is the ability to experience the areas associated with this energy, therefore, it is remaining in close conscious thought proximity to that which is taking place to your body.

The others that experience this will also remove their entire being from the physical body, though the physical body has not yet completely been used or expired. This is, again, experiencing that which is completely able to be experienced now. It is often trauma which unleashes the full mind's potential and ability to see what is always readily available to it.

He says it is not some trauma which makes it or awakens it for you. It was there all along. It is the ability to access this information which is realized after the incident. You can awaken or focus on these areas prior to having your awakening through a car accident, a motorcycle accident, a fall, something that incapacitates the physical leaving the mind to not be fully controlled or encompassed and governed by the physical senses.

Spirit workers can do many things to sustain your body while you are removed from it, though extended absence results in death.

He says there are specific incidents where other activity is taking place; where the entity never leaves the body but is counseled within; there are others where they meet with their guides and higher masters in order to alleviate some confusion which has possibly brought this being to a point of neglect and destruction.

Others may have come to this point through no direct fault of their own but again, the mind is freed from the control the senses may exercise over it. It is freer. Your mind does not, and its awareness, does not take up only that which fills the empty space within your skull or that knowledge which you choose to read and surround yourself with.

The expanse which your mind covers and can assimilate and acquire and is currently aware of covers all the known stars, planets, universes, and galaxies known to humankind on your plane of existence.

Alexander says it is becoming aware through subtle hints, or what you perceive as subtle indications, that will awaken this. Many need to be told of the greatness beyond this current life you are living in order to understand the scope of themselves and those they encounter.

It is not necessary to always consult spirit guides or light workers directly for assistance and guidance; it can be lived, a life without psychic ability, and live a productive life spiritually speaking, but to know of the vastness of all creation, in your knowing and beyond it, this is why and the purpose for some needing to see the greatness that is truly all of the eternal known existence.

Alexander says there is much that is needed to be shared in order to awaken focus into other areas. Realms are not limited to only those inhabitants that currently reside in them, and in order to fully grasp the complexity and yet simplicity and of the purpose of this lifetime it is important to understand this.

Many are seriously on the wrong tasks; many are on the right and true tasks but not in a determined effort. Many are urged. You may not have a connection to spirit which you consciously use or call for information for yourself or others, but this is still present, the ability to communicate, for there is always information sent, there is the ability for information to always to be sent to you to assist you.

He says it is your will that exercises the judgment and ability to carry it out, acknowledge it, or to completely ignore it. You may decide what to do.

Do you understand?" I asked Vicky.

"Yes, I get it for the most part. I see where the parts of my 'Near Death Experience' fit into what he said. Time for me to make some changes in my life and head in another, more positive direction with my life. I have been existing, not living. I see that now. Thanks sweetie, you're the best." Vicky said as she and Cynthia got ready to leave.

"Well, the credit goes to Alexander. He has all the answers. There're things he talks about that I don't understand at times, but when I sit and think deeper, I start to get the overall meaning of what he's explaining."

After our goodbyes, I closed the door and then I noticed two twenty-dollar bills on my coffee table.

*Note to Reader: There have been many who have had 'Near Death Experiences' and relate seeing the image of, or communicating with, the being known as Jesus. Just know, Jesus is not presently a being that you can readily relate to in any way. There are many who worship him and expect him to come to their aid, but this is simply not possible. This does not mean that there is no aid, no one listening, no help or guidance, it is simply not the being you believe it to be. In many cases there are similar looking presentations, for various beings for those who are in a physical form, and cling wholeheartedly to the image and idea of Jesus. We do not at all discount or discredit the work of Jesus; many of the stories shared in bibles are accurate in their entirety, partially, and many others were ignored or dismissed over the years. It is simply a manner of crossing over and seeing what is most comfortable to you. You question these things because there are children adding to the claims of seeing Jesus. There are images that are shared, and this is simply the universally accepted image because it is the true physical representation of Jesus, as he appeared on the earth plane in the human form, but it is not Jesus as the true being of energy and light. If you were to truly experience another being on the plane of your true existence, the spirit dimension, they would not necessarily, and in most cases, not at all, appear to be a being in the physical form that you are used to seeing because of living a life in a human form.

There are those who may not comprehend this; but as with death, as with all things, there are no universal truths that are true at all times for all people; a truth can be simultaneously true and untrue. While it is not possible to communicate directly with Jesus, it is possible to communicate, for many, with Jesus. These communications are currently based on the life and teachings of Jesus and are related by a being who takes the physical form of Jesus. It is not important that a specific being is aiding you. What is more important and what can offer more assistance to you in the future is the understanding that this being you are seeking aid from is more often yourself, your true self, this is the being that can help you the most. We do not mean this in an abstract way in which you are viewing yourself in some type of mirror, you are currently, if you are reading this, in a physical body. You will not see yourself unless you leave your physical body and even then, you are not viewing yourself, you are only able to view a physical body, which you have inhabited along with many other bodies before, in many other lifetimes. Many will see what is comfortable. Many should see that there is a group of beings willing to help and assist you at all times. No matter your current state, you are never alone. Many religions and many belief systems will have different names for these beings, many can call them angels or guides or spirit animals, but what you see is what is more comfortable to you, to allow the message to be the most receptive that it can be. We understand that for many it will be and has been a shock to learn about these things and to experience them. We would not send a form, and none would visit you that would cause you to mistrust the message. What is more important is the message, not the vessel that brings it, but often it is the image or the vessel that causes mistrust or doubt. You are not seeing Jesus.

Jesus is not able to assist you. That energy being known as Jesus, who walked the earth over two thousand years ago, has mastered and moved from this holographic illusion into a higher level of awareness, never to return. Yet, there are many who work from his teachings to assist those on this physical plane who still seek such guidance.

*Note to Readers: This added information concerning Jesus comes from a higher evolved source and deals with Easter. The time for Jesus was not that rising from the dead, there are many accounts of this. He was not dead. There were illnesses of the time, he was not susceptible to many of these but would infrequently succumb to one. Easter is rebirth. This should be shared with you and others as though it was the new year. Many seek out the new year as their purpose for starting fresh and beginning anew, Easter, and the energy associated with it through various religions, is more powerful for new beginnings than any other day. It is shared with many and shared on many dates. Typically, May 1st, and the week leading up to it, that is when the energy is the strongest. This is energy associated with past acts and the intentions of those who focus on this time. Even in the modern Easter there are many representations of various religious traditions. It is not a time to segregate. Start new and fresh. The savior Jesus was not an immortal man, he was a mortal man who was sent to deliver messages and show diverse populations the message of peace and love, and that all that we seek externally is available internally.

Humans, are very literally, a representation of the universe. You can create, you literally impact the universe and are creators of the world, the actions, and the physical and non-physical that takes place within it. Jesus was not in a mysterious tomb only to be risen from the dead. He was to be moved to another location for medical treatment. It is important to say that no one was impervious to this disease, he was able to heal himself. It is also to be known that the length of one's life, the age, this was a different measurement than used today. It is important to know that recordings in the bible, those that have not been altered, many are physical and accurate depictions of that which occurred, but there is much that has been destroyed and abolished for the sake of control. There was much added to include hate and segregation. This was not in the true spirit of the man Jesus. This was not in a unifying and loving tone. These are not the messages that he would have wanted shared. It was his world to spread unity through honesty and caring between people no matter their station in life, no matter their money or position or education or sickness or health. Those who attempted to show their importance were only using money and their greed, these are not true things, these are not necessary things. These are not the willing gifts of the righteous who pursue their highest works. This Easter, it is time to move beyond what is shared in a biblical text and honor the true feelings in your heart. Start yourself as a blank slate as you awaken, allow all that is near you to enter your mind and consider it a beneficial possibility before all else. Consider it carefully. Before passing judgment, determine how this idea, situation, determine how it directly impacts your life and your heart and your mission. There is much judgment on topics that do not impact but a few beings on your plane, but many will use this as a weapon for disaster among people. Include in your thinking one opposing thought per day. Examine this opposing thought to your current thinking. If you consider it to be valid at present, determine what bearing it has on your true being. Determine what must be done so that it cannot impact you. Determine why it does. If it does not alter your true path, release it from your being. It is not for you to pass judgment nor carry judgment in your heart that is unnecessary. This is carrying unnecessary hatred. Honor those ideas and beliefs which are sincerely yours, which you feel truly impact your life, that which can change it positively. Share them, live fully in them, but be forever open to change. If you change nothing, consider yourself open to change. Open to new ideas, you are not a book, you are an open journal that is open and willing to receive information on your blank pages. After reflection, if the page does not speak to you, tear out this page. If the page is for you, keep it with you, turn the page and experience more. At no time is it impossible to remove or add information. You are an open and growing being. You are living through various points, periods, and time frames of education throughout life. Do not maintain rigid thinking that you may have acquired at a younger age, open yourself to the vast possibilities.

The reasons for many of these to manifest later in life is that we are typically less frightful, less worried, and have less concern for the status quo. Often, these may be through a series of events which have torn down the walls of what we know, and it now makes the being more accepting of new ideas. This does not mean you shall willingly take on the ideas and impressions of anyone you are with as if you are a puppet to be controlled. You are merely experiencing new possibilities that were before closed. Allow no judgment in your heart. See beings and the world as an opportunity for learning. Learn not from the poor actions, do not judge an action as poor. View the life of another and learn. Learn their perspective. Learn their purpose. Learn and be open. Be inquisitive. The more you are open to other beings the more you will grow and confront and grow within your own being.

*Note to Reader: Concerning 'accidents,' there is much adjustment that takes place in your life depending on your free will, so that events that are planned may take place, that is, not the specific event in most cases, but the event that brings about the desired experience or goal that you planned to achieve and experience in this lifetime. There are many things that influence free will and influence events during your lifetime. There are many things that are planned, simply because they appeared accidental or inconsequential makes them no less important, though they might be. An accident can bring your attention to an area that you were neglecting, even in terms of thought, though the accident may have some physical impact. There may also be implications for your emotions. It is important to adjust your thinking to understand that there are no negative actions. There are many things that unfold so that the desired plan, that which you were counseled and chosen to experience with your own desire, that these be accomplished. You may learn love, for example, through any number of experiences, so it is not dependent at all times that you meet a specific individual or care for an individual so that a bond is formed, or any other part of love or caring be experienced. There are times when it is very dependent on the person because of their path and yours and how they interrelate, but many goals and experiences will be brought about by the circumstances no matter how your free will has intertwined with your plan. It is of the utmost importance to keep your mind open and clear, and not worry on how the event has been formed; but to understand the fundamental reasons, those important beyond the physical world, those that you will carry with you after your physical death. Examine these reasons, the motivations, and the areas being affected. These are what often determine growth or an area to review for some potential lesson or meaning after you have come through physical death. It is not necessary at all times to feel as though you experienced a specific incident and then reacted poorly to it, though you may not understand the process now, you will understand, or you still may not, upon your exit from this physical world. Your reflection upon this situation and understanding the correct, or universal response that may have been more positive is as

useful as if it were your initial response.
Typically, it is not known by you whether this also
was the required response for the growth of
yourself or others involved, though all actions
should be considered and reviewed on terms of how
you feel, much later, after the incident. Were you
better off because of your reaction to the accident or
were you feeling as though you reacted negatively
towards yourself, or others involved? These are
important if you are considering growth and
evolution in your lifetime, and beyond that life.
Please understand that it is important that all
humans know of lifetimes, there is much said to
deter any thought or thinking regarding this, and
many are expressing themselves, their emotions,
and reacting as if there is no life beyond that of
physical death, that there is no impact, as if this is
the only life. It is important to know that you have
many attempts, many incarnations, if you chose to
call them that, and many reviewing of an immediate
previous life to examine and understand. There are
also many things that may not be depending on this
knowledge for you but to understand this, it is to
remove oneself from the hold and control and ill
focus and motivations that many hold. Process
information when you receive it. When there is a
pressing situation at hand you can learn to
recognize the correct behavior. Many may call this,
listening to their inner voice or angel, but being
developed enough to understand your own intuition
or guidance is important. It should be noted that all
should attempt to withdraw from all outside
stimulation at least one solid hour per week, and
there are many benefits to this being completed

several times, in short increments, throughout one's waking hours. Pleasing the self is not as important as developing the self. Waking hours are spent too often on that which causes the mind to be idle.

Chapter Four

As I was taking an afternoon nap, the buzzing from my phone awakened me. On the other end was the nervous, yet calm voice of a man who identified himself as Dr. Benton Cline, a psychiatrist.

He wanted to know if I would be available to come to his downtown office sometime next week.

I explained that at the moment I had no transportation, as my car had been repossessed by a used car dealership for failing to make the payments on time, which was okay since I couldn't afford to make the car insurance payments either.

Dr. Cline said he would make the necessary arrangements and pay for a taxicab to bring me downtown and to return me to my apartment afterwards and pay me $150.00 dollars in cash for my time.

The offer sounded exceptionally good, but I felt it was way too much and told him so. Then he explained that because of his reputation as a psychiatrist, it would not bode well with his colleagues or clients should they find out he consulted a psychic.

He asked that if anyone in the office building should inquire as to who I was, he'd prefer that I simply say I was a client of his, and not mention my psychic talent, as he called it. Understanding his dilemma, I agreed to meet with him at his office the following day. As for the money, it had the appearance of a bribe, but I learned not to question how spirit helped out when I was in true need.

A taxi did arrive and had been paid for in advance and I was taken downtown to a nice office building. It was some twenty stories high. Dr. Cline's office was located on the top floor and was very stylish.

It was late in the afternoon as I entered the receptionist area. There was no receptionist, nor were there any patients or clients as he referred to them. I felt the doctor was already finished for the day and that would help to keep my visit a secret.

His office door opened, and I was invited to join him. I could tell he was someone renowned in his field of psychiatry from all the diplomas, certificates and honorary plaques that adorned his office walls.

Dr. Benton Cline was in his late-forties I guessed. Grayish-brown short hair and matching goatee, with gold framed glasses. Average build with a developing pot belly. Impressive pin-striped suit.

Sitting across from each other we settled down to business. He clarified why he had called me for a psychic reading. One of his clients that he had diagnosed as a schizophrenic, had to be institutionalized because of her inability to differentiate between reality and fantasy; culminating in hallucinations and delusional behavior causing her to become disabled and unable to function in normal society.

He was now using anti-psychosis drugs with little to no effect and was now considering using electroconvulsive therapy (shock treatment) which had been suggested by a few of his colleagues.

"I've asked you here because I'm unsure of the direction I need to pursue. I must admit seeking help from a psychic had never crossed my mind." Dr. Cline stated with concern in his voice.

"What changed your mind, if you don't mind my asking?" I was curious to know his answer.

"Frankly, it was my oldest daughter's idea. Rachel is into this 'new age' movement if that's the correct terminology. She told me to forget what I was taught and to open my mind to new frontiers. So, here we are."

"She's right, it's never too late to try something outside of mainstream thinking."

"I like to think I have an open mind." He seemed a bit more relaxed.

"Very well then, let me see what my guide, Alexander has to say about all this." I already felt his vibrations around me.

"Yes, please." He crossed his right leg over the other as he settled back into his chair. Producing a small tape recorder, he held it up for me to see. I nodded in the affirmative and he turned it on and placed it on the arm of the chair.

I've had many clients who record my readings with them. Some do it because they can't remember all that is said, and others have told me it was so they could play it for friends or family later on.

As I took in a deep breath, Alexander started sending information. "My guide wants to say first off; schizophrenia is not just a disease of the mind but a problem of the overall person. This is what your medicine does not yet understand.

There must be another approach, differently, to overall health, that focuses on what is not yet directly or scientifically measured by your experts. There is much in the way of science that needs to interweave with your beliefs, and this is starting to happen in your lifetime. There is much that can be done to improve the state of a person suffering and undergoing this trauma.

Alexander says lesser spirits and entities, from lower levels of the spirit dimension, are torturing theses poor souls who have deformities, so to speak, of their creation.

The problem they are experiencing is that they cannot stop or tune out those lower evolved beings because of this defect. So those lower entities bombard them with incessant communication that causes, over time, the breaking down of their mental and physical makeup. They must learn to stop these entities and take control.

He says ignoring a problem with medication does not lessen the impact the spirit world, of any spirit kind, is having on a person. They must associate body, mind, and spirit as one complete element.

Now, Alexander says there are some who go through this with the intention of learning and experiencing it in this lifetime.

There are many who may come to this life and have an error in their creation or development that allows these lesser entities to communicate with them. It is not easy to stop this. Drugs quiet receptors in the mind and body and simply dampen the messages. A drugged mind is less receptive and less open to messages and input, but this also includes input from any higher being or entity wishing to assist the individual.

At the onset, a person can be helped, there are times of need but there are times when a person is driven to a kind of madness because they are unable to control the messages received.

Alexander says schizophrenia actually occurs after the voices and messages drive a person into a psychotic state, not simply hearing these messages, this is not schizophrenia. Once a person is unable to reason with what is occurring, that is when schizophrenia begins.

There is no need for this to bother you because no matter when a person experiences it, by choice or by partial impairment of the body by some intention or neglect, this is for their learning.

Changes occur in the body that allow this to happen. Drugs are not the answer, no drug is the answer or cure all. The mind is the only thing to be changed, studied, learned, understood, and the only thing that needs change within it to heal the entire body and cure most earthly maladies.

Alexander says your world is obsessed with pills, by commercialism and insecurity, this will stop, and your healing will become evident when there is too much cost involved with the purchase and manufacture of pills that provide false hope and temporary relief.

Your doctors do not primarily focus on prevention and overall health, they fix a singular problem. Happiness does not come from a pill bottle. Happiness comes from within.

Alexander wants to know if you have a question?"

"To tell the truth, I'm not quite sure I understand his overall hypothesis concerning schizophrenia."

"My guide says he will rephrase in hopes it will provide more understanding. There are breaks in the energy body of what a person has around them, this allows so-called spiritual communication more easily, as most individuals would want, if they understood this.

But for those who only hear negative messages, this is because their mind and body are of a lower vibration, and that attracts the abundant number of lower beings, that exist around us all.

The majority of energy beings living in a human form have higher vibrations that do not allow a lower entity to approach them, or to have communication with them. Raise the vibration and hope can be seen for those with this illness."

"I'm sorry, but I just don't see the overall picture here, what am I missing?" Dr. Cline asked as he gazed at me with a blank look on his face.

Alexander was now sending more information, "My guide says many do not understand that they have a psychic gift and communication connection between worlds. This is something you want and that most who are aware of this ability hope to achieve.

Schizophrenics have no filter in place yet to sort through the information they receive, and their doctors are not aware of the world beyond this one, therefore, in a clinical setting, there is not much hope beyond a pill or isolation for these people who have gone mad by definition of your world.

He says there is hope for them if you come to understand the relation of all levels of spirit and body within one another. All is related; science separates and isolates each system; we are all one."

"What can I do to help my patients who have schizophrenia as a diagnosis?" His tone of voice seemed a little agitated.

"He says any level of healing will do wonders for them, but as with any health or spirit matter, energy does so much until a person returns to their old behavior and mentality. There must be a change in thinking, a new way of understanding.

If a person has the mental capacity for learning, as all do, then thought should be created to understand health and to learn more about the mind-body-spirit connection. There is much that can be learned, healed, accomplished by inner work, not outside stimulation.

Alexander says all can be accomplished with your mind, with your energy and the purest form of it. We are not alone and the communication these souls receive is evidence of that. They are still stuck in the realm of yours where the doctors are feebly trying to comprehend these 'problems' by years of medicine that does not confront the changes in humanity and their metaphysical abilities.

When you come to the point where you can measure and understand these, this is when a shift will occur. A change will happen. You can direct thought, healing, and energy towards this resolution to bring peace and calm to those who are undergoing that type of experience. They are not lost, living their life gives them the greatest satisfaction when they return to the spirit dimension.

My guide says there is not much that cannot be learned from this mental state compared to yours or any other. Positive physical and mental health are related, there must be something more that doctors can do, this is what they say and wish for, but little work is done to accept new ways of thinking. The label 'new age' creates a wall and barrier between doctors and thinkers in this field, but this is what will join them together. Many mental health problems will evaporate when this change is seen.

Many will receive help because our world will be acknowledged, people will have hope, not fear, because they can easily locate those who understand, these beings can have a higher spiritual level because of the communication if they could harness it for the use of humankind.

Alexander says they are not defective or broken by our standards. Man places many labels on their own kind which serve no purpose other than placing that person in negative energy. Often times the doctor visit makes worse the ailment or condition because of the labels associated with each 'problem.' There are no problems, people instantly become negative about things because of outside stimulation by doctor, society, pills, drugs, stigma. All unnecessary. If alone in the woods, this would not be experienced, and differences would not be seen or felt, a person can work through many things on this plane without intervention by 'unnecessary medicine.'

He says you can do this; you can plant the seed and help those eventually make the turn away from this type of doctrine. There are those who are open to it. You will not increase their psychosis or mental delirium; you will help them, and we can aid you in this. All humankind should help those in need, help those above and below your level because all need basic requirements to survive and each can help the next achieve."

Dr. Cline sat up in his chair and leaned forward toward me, "This guide of yours, he seems to have a low opinion of our medical profession. Is it his contention medical providers such as I, are nothing more than a bunch of feeble-minded drug pushers who have little regard for our patient's health?"

I surely didn't expect this, "No sir, my guide wasn't in any way suggesting that you are not a good doctor. He was merely providing you with..."

"We're done here," he said as he stood and retrieved an envelope from his desktop.

Walking over to his office door he opened it and then looked at me. I stood and headed for the open door as I feared I was about to get a scolding for being a psychic. Something I feel he truly didn't care for in our society.

He presented the envelope to me as I passed by and as I cleared the doorway, he closed the door behind me. As I pushed the down button for the main lobby, I glanced inside the envelope and there was the $150.00 dollars in cash as promised.

Once out on the street, no taxicab was waiting, but a genuinely nice doorman called for one, which I had to pay for the ride myself, but I was just glad to be home again.

*Note to Reader: Regarding 'Electroconvulsive Therapy' there is nothing being done by this. The effects reported by some recipients that state they are receiving healing, or their ailments have been cured are completely false. There is no healing being done that isn't already being done, even without the person aware of it, that goes on anyway but inside the mind. There may be a healing affect by the thought of the patient believing that healing will be done. It can be very damaging for any being to experience electricity outside of controlled methods that humans do not understand. There is much damage that has been done by this practice, though not as seemingly terrible as there has been in the past, much has improved. But death is still death no matter the method or no matter how 'humane' your world calls it. By this token, this treatment is still just as negative as any other that causes harm for health's sake. No reason that this should occur. There is nothing that the body cannot heal on its own if given the opportunity. There is no need to damage the body in this way. Tiny electrical pulses can cause thoughts to travel and can cause replacement of amputated limbs and can control replacements for them. Simulated heart attacks or brain attacks are not helpful as damage is still being done. Practitioners will not admit that the evidence is proof. There is much damage, but they may feel that benefit outweighs the positive that can truly be done outside of their terms or realm. There are some that can benefit from this but not in the way that the doctors perceive. There are times when electrical pulses are misfired in the brain, maintenance is necessary, though this can still have problems for other areas of the mind and brain. It takes a great effort from guides to present the body with enough energy to repair the unseen body with enough energy and healing to repair those things unseen. Much can be done even with a seemingly broken mind. 'Normal' on your plane is a very widely used term that has no clear definition. Oddities and abnormalities are not always needed to be fixed and tamped down; existence is good simply by existing. There is no need for constant repair and upgrades. Improving the mind and coming into new knowledge is important. It is important to know that this knowledge is not new to all, only to some, it is universal and has been around for all that have ever occupied your life space. There is much work to be done in order for all to understand this. As you have been reading there will come a time, we are working on this, where all of humankind is healed by thought and amplified energy. Energy is in all things; inanimate objects have energy or at the very least absorb it and act as sponges. There is no need for medicine internally or for electricity to be applied externally for any reason. What is painful and harmful in large doses is also painful and harmful in small doses, no matter what they perceive to be the benefit. There is no side effect from anything the Creator has ever intended for you to use to heal any level of your being.

Chapter Five

Once again, my friend, Winston Thomas who is a trance medium invited me over for another séance. This time I asked some of my long-standing clients to come along. This was held in his basement. We were given the option of receiving a 'Past Life' reading or a 'Future Life' reading. Winston's spirit guide who will be speaking through him is known as Dr. George Wilson.

Dr. Wilson: Yes, this is Dr. George Wilson. I am the spirit companion or what some my term guardian angel or control for this instrument. Greetings and salutations to this wonderful assemblage here tonight. It is my understanding that some may be interested in past or future life readings. I have searched through the records of those who are present here tonight.

At this time, I wish to give you each a choice, and I want you to simply see before you two doors. The door on the left will be the door to a past life. The door on your right will be the door that opens to your next human existence in the earth plane. I will give you your choice of choosing whether you wish to have discussed a past life or the life that you will live the next time you incarnate into the physical body of a human.

With that being said, are there any questions before we begin?

Group: "No."

Dr. Wilson: Alright, let me say there is a spiritual law that covers what can and cannot be brought forth. This pertains mainly to the timeline of a 'Future Life' reading. So, for example, if I were to say in the year 2040 you were going to be born, then when you reach a certain age in your present life, you may say, 'I've got to die in order to get over there in time to get everything ready for my next life.'

So, I will not give you certain dates when it concerns a 'Future Life' reading. I do not wish it to be in your subconscious mind. Everyone understands if you pick the door to your right, I will withhold the date because your subconscious mind will cause you unease and anxiety and a lot of needless effort in thought.

Yet, I will tell you that being in your subconscious mind, any information that is given to you while in the human form will be most challenging to erase after you have been reincarnated. That means you will remember what is said tonight during that 'future life.'

Now, for those who choose the 'Past Life' reading, dates will be given for the most part.

Does everyone understand?

Group: "Yes."

Dr. Wilson: Now, all the information given tonight will come from the Akashic Records. It might be called the Higher Hall of Records. It has many names, or it means many different things to many different people. It is the Higher Hall of Akashic Records when the future life is researched.

This is Dr. George Wilson; I will be working tonight, please feel free to ask questions at any time. Shall we begin with you Evelyn?

Evelyn: Oh yes, please do.

Dr. Wilson: Which door do you wish to open?

Evelyn: The left one please.

Dr. Wilson: Now then, you have had many lifetimes, so I simply chose this one at random. Your incarnation into this world was in the eastern region of what today is called Mongolia. It was during the time when Genghis Khan was the Emperor of the Mongol Empire.

You were one of his many daughters; born to one of his many concubines. Your mother was taken from her village that had been conquered by Genghis Khan's army. Your mother spent only one night with the Great Khan, against her will, and you were your mother's only child conceived from that union.

You were born in 1218, during the early spring. Your name was Lisui, and you had dark hair and eyes; you had your mothers features which she inherited from her southern Chinese lineage. You stood less than five feet yet had a strong constitution as your life was awfully hard for one such as you. Many of the women of your village looked down upon you and your mother as they felt your mother should have committed suicide after being defiled by what they felt was an infidel.

Because of your mother's reputation in the village there could be no arranged marriage for you. All you knew was hardship as you and your mother did your best to endure. Some relatives who lived in another village did help with food and clothing at times.

Your mother succumbed to death at the age of thirty-seven, which was a normal lifespan for lesser women of privilege of that time and place. You died at the age of seventeen; you can add that to your birth year to find the year of your passing.

Evelyn: Why did I die so young, was I murdered?

Dr. Wilson: Not murder, it was late summer, and you had walked over to a nearby village seeking work. Two drunken male villagers had come upon you on the roadway and were seeking to extract some sort of sexual favor from you. You bolted and ran quickly to the village. Due to their state of drunkenness, the men were not able to pursue you.

There was a covered horse enclosure and you dropped down behind it to conceal yourself as you were unaware that they were not searching for you.

Darkness came while you hid and rested; you suddenly felt a stinging pain to your right hand, it spooked you and you fled heading back to your village. Observing the small wound later your mother simply applied a mixture of mud and herbal roots and gave it no more thought.

The rodent that bit you did indeed have the rabies virus. It was transferred to you through its saliva. No symptoms appeared for thirteen days, yet on the fourteenth the symptoms began and five days later you crossed over after suffering what today would be called a severe convulsive seizure.

Do you have any other questions?

Evelyn: That was a pretty short lifetime. I lived only seventeen years.

Dr. Wilson: Yes, you yourself chose that harsh lifetime based partly on the length of time. In the prior life before this one we are speaking of, you failed to achieve a lesson from that prior life, so, you wanted to return quickly and achieve this one experience before moving on to another full lifetime venture you see.

The failure of the lesson came about from another individual whose free will interfered with your life path which was not programmed to occur. So, you were granted from a higher group of beings the right to return as you did.

This was a fast turnaround time for you. Most energy beings, or souls if you prefer, do not reincarnate again until they have spent some time in the Unseen World; reviewing and studying the life they just experienced and also preparing for their next embodiment.

As there is no time or space in the Unseen World as you experience it here on earth, let me give you an example. In earth time, the average time you would spend back in your true home dimension would be somewhere between 400 and 1500 years before incarnating into the earth plane once more; some do not return for several thousand years. You, my dear Evelyn, were given permission to reincarnate within a 44-year period, and you did achieve your return goal of a specific experience.

I do not wish to rush you, but there are others eagerly awaiting their turn dear one.

Evelyn: Oh, yes, thank you very much.

Dr. Wilson: Who would like to go next?

Austin: I'm ready.

Dr. Wilson: Very good, and which door do you wish to open?

Austin: I'd like a future life reading.

Dr. Wilson: Yes, the door to the right. Now, I have what I call my basic speech for future life readings. Some here tonight have already heard this, so, I will repeat it again for those who are new to this type of séance.

In your future life, the life that is already planned, the life that has been laid out, the life that you are working towards now; that you are obtaining knowledge and information and being guided towards. I shall explain for those who wish this knowledge.

Your Soul or Spirit, whatever word you desire to use is simply made up of intelligent energy; the essence of this energy is a part of that which many call God or Creator or 'Source of all Life.'

As an energy being, you are part of God, you are not male or female but may then choose to be either when you incarnate into this physical plane where you must take on the mantle of male or female. Your race, your nationality, your parents, to be rich or poor and much more are chosen by you before your birth into this world. That is the basic pattern used.

I would like to explain how it is arrived at a future existence, and it is the future life as programmed, so to speak, from your past experience. In many past lives you're being guided in a direction to be of future service in a coming life or experience. It is basically the same life; you are the same being, same soul.

So, let us begin. I will turn the page of the book and I will start with the very beginning of the time of birth, not the year.

You will be born at 4:57 in the afternoon and it will be on a Tuesday. Your family name will be Tobalatsi, and your first name will be Jylua. Your father's name will be Vujsc, and your mother's name will be Panlela.

You will be of the female sex, and you will have a twin sister named Kylia. Your family linage will be that of South American, in the area of what was once called Brazil. I tell you of your linage because you were not born on planet Earth, you will be born on a moon that orbits the planet you currently call Saturn.

Austin: Which moon will that be? Saturn has many moons as I recall.

Dr. Wilson: It is called Rhea. In your far distant future life, there will be many planets that have been inhabited not only by humans but also by those you now term as space aliens, and do not fear, those who are from other planets, other galaxies will not enslave your species or seek your annihilation. They will come in peace to offer assistance at a time when the earth is experiencing a great manmade apocalypse.

They will basically save you from yourselves; the greed, the mishandling of earth's resources, the overall fear and the warmongering will engulf your planet into a death spiral of which humankind will be unable to free itself. Their intervention will usher in a peace that your world will be so grateful for; those who survive will start anew as they blossom out into the universe with the assistance of these extraterrestrials.

Your home and work will be on this moon. You will not marry, nor will you have any children; yet you will have, what I will call for your understanding, a personal partnership with two other females, as this will be the norm of the place and time.

Your work will be that of a cargo loader. Loading mined crystals and minerals onto large spacecrafts, as you might call them, that take these natural resources to other planets lacking in such components. These will be very desired by other planets that use such elements for their technologies and power infrastructures.

You will use no machines to load this cargo as you will have mastered, what I will term for your understanding, the art of levitation. All will be done with your advanced mental capability. Not all will have this ability.

As I see it, Jylua will be 176 years old at the time of her crossing over into the Unseen World. Your death will be normal for that point in time.

Austin: What? How will I be able to live such a long life? Will I be bed ridden and weak minded?

Dr. Wilson: You will be sound of mind and body. In this advanced future there will be no need of Nursing Homes, Hospitals or Medical Centers as you have now. As a matter of fact, there will be no Doctors of any kind in this future existence.

Humankind will be using, what I will call for your understanding, Mind Energy Healing. Each individual will have the ability to heal themselves of any disease or condition which may present itself.

Healing will be done so by internalizing the force of nature and by the use of minerals. No synthetic medicines will be used. The body will be treated with high regard as to what will be placed into it and what will be done to honor and protect it during this forward-thinking time period. No more sedentary lifestyles or poor nutrition will be presented.

There will still be risk-takers and mishaps, as you term it, but they will not use the barbaric surgical practices used in your society of today. No invasive surgery will be required in this future existence. The mind will be utilized to its fullest capacity of 100%. Your mind will have complete control over the physical body to regenerate itself.
Austin: Thank you.

*Note to Reader: There is much that has been done to create an atmosphere that will have beings from off the planet received more readily. There are those that have had sightings that are unexplained, and this is being done in hopes that it will foster the ability for these people to welcome them and not assume that it is an attack on their earth. There is much that is being discussed as more and more living on the earth have witnessed unexplained events in the sky but there should be more done, and will be done, to prepare this into the minds of those who are less readily open and welcome to it. It is important that there be less doubt of the possibility; it is not important that all believe in sentient life but the ability to conceive the potential for other life is important. They need not believe that we are the singular race in the cosmos; this is an old habit that is dying slowly. There are those who have visions and experiences and as soon as they look at these events more critically, to go about the process of examining them deeper, they will see that this was not a random event or something that they can dismiss as a random event. More and more these discussions are taking place by those who would have before been uncomfortable brining this news to the open. There are many who share these beliefs, that share a knowing, that there are beings beyond that of the earth and can exist in the same manner of your physical existence here. It will take a time of great upheaval before they render themselves available in physical form, and directly available on the steps of any government building, in great numbers. At present, they will be coming to you once there is greater seemingly chaos, or events that cause disorder of those that would cause harm or seek to control their existence. It will take some time yet before they're physically witnessed on the ground by large numbers of humans on the earth. Waking to this knowledge is important for those who will be experiencing it. There are many who have always known there would be contact, and information shared between life on earth and that which does not come directly from it in the present form. There are others who are coming to this knowledge now and will experience it with greater ease when more share information between those that have known, and those that have only recently known. It is important to continue your patience for there are many who will need to be made aware of the possibility, simply because they have never conceived such a possibility, not simply because they do not believe, but because they have never considered that as a potential outcome. It is important to know that there are many who say that there will be violent entities, alien creatures who wish to do harm to the earth or enslave it. This is not true. The only entities that shall interact with any life on this planet, will be peaceful and of an evolved degree that will only allow sharing of information for the improvement of all that inhabit it at the time they disclose themselves. There is not a time when the earth will be enslaved by outside beings. There are some who wish to manipulate for their own good, just as there are many energy beings or those on the earth in human form, who have goals and motivations that are less than desirable. It is important to know that there is much done to create a peaceful intervention, so that no outside negative influence interferes with the earth. This is in the same manner that your own guide or spirit companion, the one who is with you at all times, is present and shields you when you ask and combines the vibration of your energy and physical bodies with their own energy which is readily available to protect you. Know that it is possible that there are outside influences that obscure facts and truths and whisper negative motivations to some that are in power, within your governments. It is only because they make themselves susceptible to it that this occurs. We do not offer assistance where none is wanted or asked for. The beings who have succumbed to this outside influence will be gone when these true beings make their presence known. There will be a peace in the aftermath, and they will help to usher in a new type of technology and beliefs for those who are present. Time is short for the waiting period which will take place; just know that there is work being done to expose those open to it in a more direct fashion than what was done a century ago. While many fear some global elitist faction is secretly meeting with aliens who desire more control, it is really only two groups of life forms controlling one another. One group is not made more powerful by another. Plans have not become more ruthless because of this union. Power that exists is permitted because a population willingly gives up its own power and control no matter who is the perceived boss, overlord, or person or thing holding the power. Deep within your planet earth there is another race. They too are considered alien, but it is not necessary to view them as adversaries. There is a great deal of talk and speculation of all race types, but like anything in existence, it will gravitate towards beings of similar vibration and frequency. Some take comfort in the knowledge of some specific being's existence and others are concerned they are, themselves, being controlled. What is more important is not who the controller is, but that there is any control being exerted in any particular fashion. More citizens look for a devious space alien to blame for situations and lack of love. There is not much more compassion or energy exerted when the controller is thought to be their own mind or another legitimate human being. Curiosity can be satisfied, but it is important to look beyond the type of being or entity at the source of any situation. It is not the being that should be shocking, it is not the type of being that is important. What is important is that an entire type of being allows this controller to manipulate any power over them, real or perceived. As some come and go from this planet, others have arrived and have remained. Don't see them as interfering. They, in a way, are no different than humans except that many races have come together in a unified plan or sense of purpose. Some factions of humans have done this, but many humans are still overly concerned with those who have different skin tones or origins: these things do not matter. Some alien beings are here for extrapolation of information, others maintain the energy systems of natural areas, others seek power and control. These are all present in your human form, these same desires. Often, ideas are made taboo or shrouded in mystery, or they are created in the public as being false so that the public dismisses them or relies on a new control source for some resource. Meanwhile, those in power or those who remain behind the proverbial curtain still practice these techniques. What is made popular in mainstream is to pacify, to contain, many ancient mystery school philosophies and practices, methods of communication and divination, are currently used by many popular figureheads; many more use them as a source of information, though they may not be a direct conduit.

There are alien races on your moon which orbits the earth. Though to be clear, they are not all observable. We have mentioned this difference in vibration previously, not all of your neighboring planets are void of life as you currently understand. There are beings present on moons and planets in your solar system. Though they are present, they are not actively engaged in your world in a physical sense, some dwell in energy form only; that is to say, they have no physical covering or body. Though, it is necessary to state that actions of any kind expressed in any manner radiate energy outward in all directions.

Dr. Wilson: Now, we need to move along, so who is ready to go next?

Loraine: I'll go next if no one objects?

Group: (no objections were forthcoming)

Dr. Wilson: Very well, which door do you choose?

Loraine: A past life please. The right door, ah, sorry, I meant to say the left door.

Dr. Wilson: Very well, as I open the left door, the door to a random past life, the date of birth will be 47 B.C. on August 22 as time was calculated in that era. The time of day was mid-afternoon.

Your name was Casinoel, and you were female. You had many brothers and sisters. You spoke an off dialect of Greek which was a result of Alexander-the-Great's earlier influence on the region. You lived close to the pyramids as you were Egyptian.

Your family would have been considered upper-middle class for the time owing to your father being an engraver of stone. He was employed by the royals and the kingdom to engrave and decorate their monuments, homes, and funeral tombs with hieroglyphs.

You knew of Cleopatra, yet never saw or crossed her path. You were married to the son of a man your father worked with. His name was Ahmes, and he became a scribe.

You would give birth to four children, all girls, but only one would survive to adulthood. You're crossing over to the Unseen World came on 25 A.D., September the 3rd just after midnight. Your passing was due to old age by way of pneumonia.

Do you have any questions?

Loraine: Did I not work or have some type of special skill?

Dr. Wilson: You were tasked with being the mother, wife, running the household and watching over the servants. This, I can assure you was more than a full-time assignment in that age.

Loraine: Yes, looking at it that way I'm sure that's true. Thank you.

Dr. Wilson: Alright, who will go next?

Walton: I would like the door to the right. A future life please.

Dr. Wilson: I must offer an apology at this time to you Walton. I am unable to provide that information. Would you care for a past life reading instead?

Walton: Ah, I'm not sure I understand. Is there some explanation as to why I cannot be told of a future life? I must admit I'm a little concerned and not sure how I should feel about this.

Dr. Wilson: There is no need for concern my dear fellow, you simply do not have a future life to live. You could say you have reached your final destination in this one area of your spiritual enlightenment. You are an ancient soul who has mastered the '7-Levels and Sub-levels of the World of Illusion.'

After this life you are presently living comes to a final conclusion, you will ascend to the next sublime undertaking of your journey to a higher limitlessness that shall open unto you as you endeavor ever forward; seeking to join once again with God.

With that being said, can I interest you in a past life reading?

Walton: Oh, okay, well…I'm not sure…uh, well yes, I guess I'll seek a past life.

Dr. Wilson: Very good, since you have had so many past lives let me go a long, long way back across the span of time. Back before your current age even can calculate or verify that energy beings walked upon this planet in the human form.

I understand many do not hold with that which is known as 'Atlantis.' Yet it was a real civilization of which you had several lifetimes throughout its history.

Let me say before I begin that the instruments used for radiocarbon dating in today's time period are extremely limited in true accuracy. Time is not about how it advances, or its linear movement; it is about change.

With that being said, the past life I have chosen to relate to you was some 207,491 B.C. as you count time, that is, if you were able to measure that far back in the existence of this planet. You were male, your name was 'Lzi Bj Movc Jkvvl' and you used telepathy to communicate, which was the norm at that time. Verbal communication was used only by a small minority; however, the majority were proficient and comfortable with using thought transference.

Married you were with no future plans for having children. Your wife's name was 'Po Dii K Jkvvl.' She was a scientist in the field of indigenous life forms as it would be called in your present time. Po Dii K had been tasked with finding solutions on how to deal more effectively with the aggressively large carnivore's that roamed freely outside the city walls.

Your career title was that of a 'protector of humanity.' You were stationed, as it were, near the entrance to a great walled city known then as Wjv-Oq: which meant 'Deliverers-of-Light.' Your post was inside a tower which contained an instrument that was used to repel large roaming creatures, that which today would be termed 'dinosaurs.' The apparatus utilized a large crystal and several smaller crystalized minerals that generated what would be similar to a laser weapon of today.

Creatures would approach the entrance to the city, as the walls were too high to scale, and it was your function to repel them using a non-lethal dosage of energy to send them away. You never used a fatal quantity of energy as Atlantean's were living, at that earlier time, in harmony with nature and with their fellow beings.

Walton: May I ask, were the Atlantean's more advanced than we are now?

Dr. Wilson: There was much in Atlantis that was technologically advanced compared to other civilizations of that time and those that immediately followed. They would be considered advanced by today's standards; still, some would view them as archaic, but it is because they used different methods for achieving the same results in many areas.

There was not a telephone system per se, there were devices which could amplify intention and messages but that was all initiated and received by others through the self. There was higher regard for the self, there was more unity within the group. Combined group determination could accomplish great things.

There were many crystalized and inorganic based technologies that powered their civilization. They had the ability for long distance transport by ground and air. There were limited abilities to be transported from place to place without the use of some device such as a vehicle. This would be some type of device similar to the 'science fiction fantasy' transporters of your movies and TV programs of today.

You could be in one place and be sent to another place without the need to self-travel hundreds of miles. The importance of all of this, what it hinged upon, was that many were capable of using more of their mind, and by measurement, if they were not using more, they were very gifted in using their mind in a way more than simply as a storage device for information, as is your custom now.

They were aware of what their minds could produce. The ability of the mind to impact physical objects, the power of their thoughts. It is very real and possible to produce an outcome based solely on the energy that you emanate from your being and send out into the world.

Many were aware of these, and many things became possible because all energy was directed upon it. All had independent lives outside the group but there was much more done as a group, as a whole, for the benefit of all of humanity as you would say. The ability to direct energy as many show you in 'science fiction fantasy,' these things were not fantasy, power came from the power of all.

Later, there were many destructive things that occurred in Atlantis, such as your researchers of today who created weapons out of initially good devices and medical discoveries; many things, nearly all things can be weaponized if that is the intention of a few.

As I see here you will cross over to the Unseen World at the age of 91. Your passing will be peaceful and uneventful.

Alright, my apology, but we need to move along.

Walton: This has been most interesting, thank you so very much.

*Note to Readers: The fundamental design of the '7-Levels and Sub-levels of the World-of-Illusion' is as follows; the physical world of matter was created so that energy beings from the spiritual dimension could come here, among other reasons, to basically experience firsthand, what they cannot experience in their home dimension. You can observe and learn by viewing and studying an ideal or concept; but to truly understand you need to be a part of that which you desire to understand. Observing a beautiful flower means very little until you experience the annihilation of the flower; to be able to see the unconditional love behind the creation of the flower gives it worth and meaning. The earth was created for those energy beings who need the true experience of a thing; in order to understand the true meaning of creation as it pertains to the balancing of positive and negative energy. The earth, and the universe it is a part of, are simply put, a holographic illusion designed to provide a place to experience the negative, or the so-called evil, that cannot be experienced in the positive categorical nature of the spiritual dimension. When you enter a human body, your true memory, that you are eternal and cannot perish, is temporarily concealed from you, so that you can then live the emotional, mental, and physical of the experiences you desire for your enlightenment. The negative now becomes very real. Once you return home, you then have a truer understanding of the nature of unconditional love. The earth is just one school among many; there are many other life forms within this illusional universe seeking the same in evolutionary consciousness.

Now, concerning the 7-Levels; in the physical world, that which is called earth, everyone lives on the same level. Right now, in your world, there are individuals who range from highly intelligent to those who are simple minded. All are living on the same level. In the spirit dimension, there is a separation. Like attracts Like. The spirit world contains 7 main levels, and each main level contains 7 sub-levels. As an example, say you are in the physical world, you are born, live your life, then grow old and die. Say you lived an average life, your soul would then return to the 3rd main level, sub-level number 5 in the spirit world proper. There are 7 sub-levels in the 3rd main level, and you went to the 5th sub-level of the 3rd main level. That is what your life on Earth brought you. Now, you are on the 3rd main level, sub-level 5 in the spirit dimension in an ethereal body. After dwelling there for a while, you show interest in rising above that situation. For example, say you grew through knowledge, teachings, and incarnations to where you raised your vibrations so you could qualify to advance. At that point, you would be ready to evolve to the 6th sub-level of the 3rd main level. When you desire and achieve success there, you could move into the 7th sub-level of the 3rd main level. When you master all on the 7th sub-level of the 3rd main level you then advance to the 4th main level, but you would start out on the 1st sub-level of the 4th main level. You would have to go through those 7 sub-levels before you graduated to the 5th main level. Out of the 7 main levels, anything below the 3rd main level is not desired. You want to progress out of the 1st and 2nd main levels as quickly as possible. Yet, there are souls who enjoy being there in a state of lower vibration; where they fight and conspire to debase themselves and those trapped with them. Many are there through their own free will for they enjoyed the animalistic chaos and mayhem they brought forth while in the human form. Energy beings on the sub-level above you are always encouraging you to improve and progress up to where they are. You would be doing the same for those beings who are on the sub-level below you. When you reach the 7th sub-level of the 7th main level you then ascend into what we will call the 'Original' Dimension. Now, for those who can comprehend this; the physical world, the earth, and the universe it dwells within, are basically a holographic representation which was created by higher evolved beings from the spirit dimension. The spirit dimension is also a holographic representation created by even higher enlightened beings from what, for a better understanding, we will simply call the original dimension. For example, in the physical world you need a human body for your soul, as many call it, to be able to exist there. In the spirit dimension you need an ethereal body for your soul to be able to reside and exist there. Once you enter the original dimension, you are now pure energy, you still retain your personal identity, yet you no longer need any covering to venture forth into the vastness of eternity as you progress ever closer to reuniting with God, the 'Source of all Life.'

*Note to Reader: Concerning the ethereal body; your ethereal double is more of an energy body, this is the you that exists beyond all other confines of physical reality and the other restrictions that you may place on mental and energy bodies in the human form. There is much to be learned about this but also learn that no matter what term is used to describe it, this, and many other terms and practices are all the same, they are accomplishing the same no matter what you call them. There is much distraction between groups who claim to be practicing specific arts or beliefs, these are all accomplishing the same as those who they seem to oppose or who call themselves different. An ethereal double is your energy body when you are not in physical form. You have the ability to leave your body, your physical body, and travel, grow and learn. It is also possible to leave your body and 'bi-locate' even while you are awake, and your body is functioning. The mind in the physical body has many abilities that are not researched, nor is it accepted as anything more than just novelty or daydreaming. The conscious and subconscious mind are powerful and to some degree can operate the body for a time while the energy body is absent, though connected to, the physical human form. You are able to experience your home, other situations, there is not a separate you, this 'other body' is your true body and is allowed to free itself from the physical form at various times. This is accomplished through deep meditation, by astral projection, this is what is taking place in these practices though they are all the same no matter what term you place on them.

*Note to Reader: Astral Projection is the complete elimination, through a focused, calm, and meditative state, of all senses and feelings that are only perceived or generated through the physical body. You completely disconnect but are able to safely return to your physical body. It is merely a term, astral, for that body which is your truest and highest self that inhabits your physical body at present. To project into the astral plane is only to experience all realms, or a specific dimension, through disconnecting from your physical body.

There is no specific astral realm. Often, this term is used by those who project but there is no specific astral realm. This is simply the term that for you could describe leaving this physical world. Though it is quite possible to experience other time periods and places or locations in this physical plane where the earth is located. The process is through meditation and awakening your entire energy body, your entire true self, this entire form of energy that inhabits this body. There is much that is located in the brain, but often this is where the perception of your world stops. The eyes are here, and there is much that is not considered for sensing or interpretation because it is with the physical eyes and the mind that the thinking becomes accustomed to being done. It is important to sense every area within the physical body, become aware of each part of it, and allow these new sensations to become aware of it. Intend to leave your physical body, shifting your awareness and creating a visual impression of yourself in your mind of this new location, will shift your ability of perception and controlling the present location of your body to the control of your thoughts, much as is experienced by those who are on the other side and helping you. It is imperative that you state or intend to have a specific purpose; this does not mean that you are not simply allowed to experience the world, your habitat, without the constraint of your physical body, but you should intend to do so. Do not simply sit and meditate and then become discouraged because nothing has happened or been experienced. Such as dreams, there are many things that happen, there are many where you project into an astral state of mind, where your true body leaves your physical body, and you travel your world or others. It is because the mind has not considered, in the physical form, these experiences to be important. It needs to become accustomed to these experiences and understanding that these are true experiences that you wish to recall and remember. Often this method of mind body separation is experienced but once the event has taken place there is no accurate recollection by the physical body. Training the mind to retain this information while you are in the physical body is important. You should be aware that there is information available to you, you can return to this world, your true home, at any point for knowledge and wisdom. It would be through the practice and focus of your thought and meditation and that it can be accomplished. Often the ability of those who attempt to develop this is short lived because they are not able to achieve extended periods of departure from the body. For many, once they realize that they are not simply thinking about another location but are able to move within it and truly perceive it, because they are there, they immediately return to their body because their focus and attention is not true to the level necessary for extended absences. This is why this disconnection is often experienced through sleep; this allows other areas of the body and mind to overcome the actual and perceived obstacles through the mind and other limitations that are true, and those that you simply perceive. It is through this dream-like state that in waking consciousness, the world can be experienced by you as well as other worlds. Simply stating that you are willing to do this will begin your journey. There is much that can be accomplished in terms of skills and abilities in your physical existence and some of these will also better equip you when you return to your true home once you discard your physical body. Others simply help with guidance and information and perspective while within this lifetime, there are no skills and talents that do not help you fully appreciate this lifetime, the true nature of existence, and the true experience of all creation, none are simply for a carnival-like fancy of entertainment.

Dr. Wilson: Alright, who would be next?
Amy: I guess I'm ready to give it a go. I'll take a chance and pick the door on the left.
Dr. Wilson: Very well, a past life reading; as I peer into the records, I wish to place you in the Kingdom of Portugal, living several miles outside the capital city of Lisbon during the time of the Inquisition within that country. The date of your birth was 1529. It was early evening. It was October the 8th.

You were female and your name was Bella Maria; you were named after your great grandmother, which was considered an honor. Your family name was Bramodamilo. You were from a mid-sized prosperous family, and you had a normal up-bringing for the most part. At age twelve, your father and another prominent man squabbled over the ownership of a parcel of land that separated their estates. This other individual became so angered, he reported to the catholic church that witchcraft had been used to curse his wife who had become bedridden from an unknown sickness.

The church investigated this allegation which your father denied. While questioning your father, one of the church investigators took notice of a birthmark on the back of your neck, which they stated was the mark of a witch.

After taking you into custody you were stripped of your clothing and examined for other signs or marks that would be supposedly found upon a witch or demonic creature. Other common blemishes led your captors to impose physical torture as they were not convinced of your pleadings of innocence. Under the agony of this type of questioning, you confessed quickly that you were indeed a witch.

The church investigators turned you over to the municipal authorities and the following day you were put to death by burning. Your father, fearing more reprisals withdrew all claim to the disputed parcel of land.

This incarnation was prearranged by you to be short and to end as it did. Do you have any questions?

Amy: Can you tell me the reason I would want such a short life as that?

Dr. Wilson: You had two reasons for that limited lifetime. Overall, you have lived in the human form more often as a male, rather than a female. So, you chose to be female to assist in balancing out your personal preference of equal lifetimes of male and female.

Just know, this is something unique to a minority of energy beings. Most are not concerned, as you are, as to how many lifetimes they have experienced based on which sex was employed. The majority of Energy Beings are more concerned with which sex would give them the best possible outcome in learning and experiencing the lessons they had chosen for themselves.

More importantly, for you, this short life span gave you the opportunity to experience a shocking demise, as it were, as compared to most of your other incarnations of which you crossed over to the Unseen World with relative ease, such as through disease or old age.

Amy: Thank you.

*Note to Reader: The vast majority of energy beings are removed from the human body seconds before any traumatic death is experienced. Your Master Teacher has already approved your release, and so other energy beings are directed to assist you in separating from that body. As you leave that body you were occupying, you will at that point feel no physical, mental, or emotional pain whatsoever as your human form is damaged or destroyed. Because your body's physical brain is still functioning, still has some life, it will react to the pain and trauma the human body is undergoing at that point in time. So, when you see someone who 'seems' to be dying a horrendous and excruciating death; it is simply the physical body itself, which is reacting to whatever type of damage is being inflicted upon it before it expires; screaming and crying out for help for example.

Dr. Wilson: Now, is there anyone who hasn't had a reading?

Scott: Yes, I'd like to know about a past life please.

Dr. Wilson: Very well then, this random lifetime chosen shows you were born, as I see here, in the year 34 A.D. It was March the 20th and you were of the female gender. Your name was Prisca, and you were born in Rome, Italy.

You had golden hair and green eyes which were not common attributes of the Mediterranean complexion of those inhabiting that area. You took your looks from your mother who came from the Nordic lands.

Your father, Aaron was Jewish yet converted to Christianity to please his wife, Freya, who herself was a recent convert. They kept this secret from the Roman authorities as Jews and Christians alike were looked down upon during this time period. Your father held lands and considerable wealth outside of Rome, which did not go unnoticed by those close to Claudius, who was Emperor of Rome during this time.

In your early years you were raised in Judaism yet became what some now would term a devout Christian as pertaining to your fundamental belief system. Roman soldiers apprehended you inside the catacombs as you were assisting runaway slaves who were trying to flee the city.

Emperor Claudius condemned you for admitting to and boasting that you were a Christian. You spent a short time in prison after your refusal to make an offering to the king of the roman god, Jupiter. After your release, you still refused to convert to the roman belief in polytheism. Torture was used and you were imprisoned for another short period before being put to death as the romans could not break your underlying spirit.

You were executed three days after your fifteenth birthday. Through addition you can find the time of your demise.

Scott: What was my reasoning for such a short life?

Dr. Wilson: You had been given a mission to undertake in that life. You fulfilled that mission by staying true to your newfound faith; even though it cost you your life.

Scott: Thanks.

Amy: May I ask a question about Scott's past life?

Dr. Wilson: Yes.

Amy: I was raised Catholic, and if I'm not mistaken, Prisca was a little virgin girl who was a martyr and later became a saint.

Dr. Wilson: There is truth to your statement, yes indeed.

Amy: Ah, those who pray to Saint Prisca, which was a life Scott lived, and he's not a saint now, how do those prayers effect Scott?

Dr. Wilson: For your understanding, there will be no effect toward Scott; as a human or as a soul being. For all intensive determinations, the name 'Saint,' as applied to individuals of any specific religion holds no inherent value, other than to those who have a belief or faith in the named religion.

Amy: So, if I pray to Saint Mary, the mother of Jesus, is she listening and going to assist me with my dilemma or whatever?

Dr. Wilson: That soul being that lived that human lifetime as 'Mary' has moved on to experiencing other embodiments for its own personal enlightenment.

Each soul, in the human form, is watched over by spirit beings who are assigned to it at birth. When they call out or pray for help or guidance those spirit beings respond. Doing what is or is not allowed to be done for their charge.

Amy: What of the Pope?

Dr. Wilson: The Pope in the beginning was to be the guide and teacher of those known as Christians. Through the ages, corruption has all but destroyed the basic foundation of this once great concept. The Pope of today is nothing more than a figurehead, just as your Presidents are, as those in the corporate shadows of greed and power pull the puppet strings.

Amy: Oh…thank you.

Dr. Wilson: As we close this séance, let me just say to all of you here tonight that you were born of humankind, an individual, and you shall live your life as an individual, and whether you accept it or not, you shall enter the Unseen World as an individual; required to answer, not to God, but to your true higher self for the individual acts you performed while in the physical body. You, and you alone, are the final judge and jury of the acts you bring forth while expressing your chosen lessons, and of the use of your free-will while incarnate.

This is Dr. George Wilson. God's blessings upon this delightful assembly.

*Note to Reader: Concerning 'True Prayer' this is a matter of your intent. Select your outcome; envision it as you would enjoy it coming to fruition. Ask that energy be sent so that it is done. This is the same manner by which healing or other energy is transferred. You can send energy to it. You can repeat your statement of intent in your mind as often as you wish. This will radiate out from your body and deliver the energy into the universe. The fact that your mind is power that constructs the universe around you, this is doing the same. Your energy emanates from all around you. Know that some things will not be interfered with and there are some that may ultimately change because of the energy directed by you and others towards it. It is only necessary to speak the positive outcome you wish. It is possible that you ask your guides questions and receive answers directly or in some physical manifestation on your plane. It is only necessary to have in your mind the vision of the completed outcome that you wish to achieve. The asking of prayers for others is as simple as asking for prayers or positive outcome for yourself, in some certain situations. Simply settle your thoughts on the outcome or action you would like to see and visualizing this energy leaving your body and affecting the universe for the positive development of this event, action, feeling, will contribute greatly to it. This act is done with all thoughts that you hold true, and visualization helps the physical body and the physical mind perceive the true nature of what is attempting to be created. It is not always necessary to visualize, simply settle on your intention, your desired actions, and outcomes. The energy will be released simply by your repetitive thought energy or words spoken. It matters not how this outcome is affected by your energy if it was never meant to be. There is much that relates to some general and basic plan, and goals can be met no matter what path you take, they can be received in many forms, so fear nothing of skewing your original purpose in this lifetime by altering an event through your power of thoughts and energy. There are some that will not be changed and others that can be changed. Realize that for some, no matter what energy you wish upon them, there will not be change until they are ready for this and accept it and desire it. It should be known that there are many who are positively impacted by your energy even though the desired outcome is not presently visible or measurable. There is power in numbers. There is great power in groups of spirits who wish the same positive outcome, though in some cases, it is not possible to intervene because the will of so many is that someone be saved or otherwise from some act or timeline of events. Simply see yourself as you wish the events to take place. Radiate love into the event; radiate the vision from your body into the world. Allow these things to be expressed by you and they will flow more easily into others when the situation is desired. Appreciation of those things which have manifested only serves the higher self as it is seen that you are not dabbling for the surface's sake, not addressing a cause or issue simply for vanity or other impermanent reasons. To appreciate an outcome or situation is to be able to rely on this in the future. Thoughts are no less

ignored simply because gratitude is not shared,
but the appreciation of such gifts is important. This
is much in the same way that one should appreciate
the senses and everything in their present world.
Allowing full appreciation allows deeper
understanding of the true nature of that which is
appreciated and the reasons and purposes for it.
You now know the reasons for your existence but
there are many intricacies of this. Appreciating
each aspect of yourself only shares into it the
greater energy and understanding that has come
with your full awareness of this. Appreciating
something, an aspect, an emotion, appreciating this
in another person only serves to amplify this in
yourself and within that person. Simply by your
perception it is amplified and through the energy
exchange process. It is important to learn all things
that relate to the senses and the body and allow
them to be experienced. Do not become a mind on
'autopilot' for this process may lead to deterioration
in these areas when attention is not paid to them.
The correct prayer is the one full of universal
positive creation, that which is done without vanity,
without attempting to change the events for
personal gain and selfish interests. When those
reasons are the motivations, the desired outcome
may be reached but there are other areas that will
need to be addressed. This is often why it may
appear that luck befalls many people only to have
one problem after another after another. They may
also give you the impression that their life is
running smoothly, and you may view them as being
truly fortunate. You are all fortunate, but there are
some who hide the strain that is present in their life

because of the 'ill-gotten reward' lessons for each
individual appear in many forms. Each has free
will and often the lesson or teaching situation is
tailored to that specific lifetime and specific instant.
Simply because you choose a different job than
what you first intended does not mean that you will
have missed on some opportunity or lesson. The
style can be changed so that it can still be
implemented. Some feel they are trapped, and this
is not the case. Free will dictates many things that
you do, many situations are still present because of
the purpose of your lifetime, but many events take
shape based on the decisions and actions and
energy of the person living that life. It is important
that if you are asking for the protection of another,
for the healing of the earth, that you simply send
that energy with your mind, with your thoughts,
your works, you can send this same energy as you
would send healing to any person, thing, object, or
situation. Healing energy is not the only type of
energy which is channeled by humankind. Know
that each emotion is energy and each emotion, the
energy within it, can be sent as you would healing
energy through you to another being. Anything can
be sent. The emotion, the action desired, the energy
associated with it in its truest form and purest form
can be channeled. It is important for all who will
read this to know that you are not required to enter
a state of trance in order to channel. Simply
meditate on the energy and send it from you. All
can channel; most are channels for their own energy
without being aware of it and therefore cause
actions and reactions without being aware of their

direct effect on their own lives. All can channel energy to others. All receive.

Chapter Six

A friend of mine, Drago Moffit, who I met at a local psychic fair does spiritual healing. His technique involves hands-on-healing, and crystals to balance the energy as it pertains to the mind-body-soul aspect of the whole human individual.

Drago had called me a few days ago about getting a reading. Exchanging the usual pleasantries, I welcomed him with a hug, and we settled down in my living room.

"Well, what would you like to ask Alexander?"

"I have been having trouble with my gallbladder, I have what the doctor calls 'chronic cholecystitis' and he is recommending I have a surgery called 'cholecystectomy' to remove my gallbladder altogether. I thought it wouldn't hurt to get some spiritual insight from your guide about my gallbladder condition and any spiritual implications from having it cut out."

"Well, let's see what he has to say. He's telling me the gallbladder is, in a sense, the area where outside information is stored inside the body.

Not in terms that the brain contains the body's information, but in a sense that the knowledge that you experience, and feel is stored there. Your emotions regarding that which occurs outside of you. There can be anger here, there can be resentment, being ignored, being invalid, not being suitable, not being thought good enough for a particular endeavor or function.

Alexander says there is an absence within the self, within the true being, that humankind continue to ignore this area. They continue to fill their lives with activities which do not serve their highest good, but they are pushed into them because they believe, by their upbringing, by the social programming in which they've been involved, that it is necessary for them to engage in these things.

He says this is not a veiled message to you by not giving you the activities or mindsets which they fill their time, it appears this way because there is no universal activity or thought which causes it. For different beings, the problems that cause this suffering will come in various forms, but the cause and its manifestation are all from the same root and is why the problem resides itself to the gallbladder.

Alexander says it is not necessary to remove it in any case. There will be some trauma in a life that may require certain areas to be removed because your current science and medicine do not recognize the body as the greatest and truest healer imaginable. They also do not recognize other areas of science and medicine which can aid the recruitment of other cells in the body in order to regenerate and heal certain areas of the body.

He says it is, again, not to shield you from this opportunity by not sharing it with you, but it must come from many individuals within this area of study before it will be widely accepted. It is also important for those who undergo these procedures, which are only necessary by current standards, in order to gain understanding of the impact they have on the body and the alternatives that are possible when another method is sought.

At no time during an aggravating illness is it necessary to remove from your body that which comes to it by way of birth. There are methods for removing tumors, you can be considered not born with these. It is not necessary to remove these growths also. What should be understood is that anything that occurs within the body is able to be repaired, remedied, healed, or manifested in another way by the mind, by the mind of many, by the use of diet as prevention and as cure.

Alexander says there are many aspects and elements on your world that can cure and reverse aliments which are considered fatal once contracted. It is not a method for you to understand all things on earth, but to understand that which plagues your body is by your cause and can also be remedied by your hand and mind.

The source of energy required to heal a mind or body is not to be done by one doctor in a lab coat prescribing various medications. The greatest doctor, medicine man, and healer reside within your mind, but the addition of the community, the addition of friends, neighbors, and relatives, can aid an individual who has ignored an injury, malady, or some imbalance long enough that it is not intruding dangerously into their life.

He says it is important to understand that the mind of one, the mind of a few, the mind of many can also impact the mind and body of one. You can aid and repair on behalf of an injured individual. Understand that if the being does not want the energy, the repair, they will not accept it, no matter if they are conscious or unconscious by your medical standards.

Ignoring the self, this is the typical answer for problems. It is not typical because we relay it to you often but in various forms this is what causes physical ailments and injuries for individuals.

It is more common now to practice surgery and the removal of organs which seem unimportant to the method of living in your world. Surgery was never available and then became more available, and now it is considered less invasive to remove an organ than it is to cure the mindset of an individual with positive and uplifting words and energy.

Alexander says it is a quick repair for many and it is popularized by the practitioners in the field, and then doubled by those who have had the procedure. What only a few are realizing is the inability of the body to regain its full operation and function in certain areas when they are ignored after a surgery; all surgery is invasive.

All surgery upsets balance and requires direction of healing activities. There is no healing method within surgery, surgery itself is an additional injury to the body. Trauma can be reversed but often trauma can be performed without additional harm to the body to correct it, or that the trauma has already created access for a repair. Even those with closed skin can be repaired by alternative means and measures.

Alexander says corrections can take place to the body without further harming your operation and function. There are practices that will come to many, which can heal and repair many traumatic and ongoing ailments without needing entry into the body to repair them, and with little more than energy direction and diet.

Exterior methods are slowly becoming available to the earth. It will be difficult to bring them to areas in which the regulated medical practice holds such a strong grip on the lives of human beings.

For those who have had surgery of any kind, it is not reason to fear or worry that you will not live at optimum health. It is, however, important to understand that an organ becomes diseased or imbalanced because of what negative energy, by mind or by diet, have impacted the organ.

Simply because you remove the collection point of your pain and suffering, does not mean that you are removing the source, you are not removing the true cause. If, for example, you had pain in your finger, you would not remove the finger, you would remove the weight which has been dropped on your finger and you would remove the hazard or element which currently causes a weight to be dropped onto your finger.

He says it is this healing process, the progression to the true source and nature and beyond, which will lead many to be repaired.
If you have had a surgery understand that this area that is now changed or removed will slowly return to the same imbalanced way of existence, or it will present in new areas of the body unless you change your mind, thoughts, expression and intake of energy, your diet; the source that caused the malady originally will need to be corrected.

For many, there will be ignorance on this part because the surgery may bring indescribable relief in comparison to the suffering they had undergone. Some will experience the change in other areas and will not have future instances because they have corrected the imbalance, for others, it will become an ongoing problem, often in this lifetime, but can lead to eventual presentation of energy imbalance in other lifetimes.

Alexander says focus on your ability to heal yourself. Do not examine yourself by comparing any aspect of your nature to that of another being. You are not capable of being compared to another being. You are too unique, each of you, to be categorized and compared, and treated, medically or otherwise, as a mass of beings that may or may not have a problem similar to another individual.

You can seek advice, you can see that others with similar problems have found remedies, but remember, it is the mind. You can take several medications which may help you or may unknowingly cause greater imbalance, but it is the mind, that which you do not see readily in other people, that is the source of change.

Address the aspects within yourself which you currently hide from others. Address that which makes you feel inferior. Acknowledge the existence of these elements. Do not fear showing your flaws or shortcomings into the nature of existence.

It is these things, the things that you call imperfections, it is what makes you unique. It is by addressing them that you grow and learn and take more from your experience here in this lifetime."

"My dear Evelyn, it would seem I have a choice to make. I shall think profoundly on what your guide has said. Go with god little one." He said heading for the door.

"Thank you, may god's blessings go with you."

Four months later I met up with Drago at another psychic fair. I asked what he had decided to do concerning his gallbladder. He gave me a sheepish grin as he lowered his head and said he chose the easy way; that of surgery.

I told him not to feel upset with himself, for we all have free will and can choose what we think is best for ourselves.

Chapter Seven

The temperature outside would drop down to 22 degrees tonight according to the weatherman. I was sharing an older duplex with a female friend of mine who was a tarot card reader. We occupied the left side and there was a young male couple who were living on the right side.

We shared all the expenses equally. My roommate worked at an upscale restaurant while I worked at a department store running a cash register.

The young boys said they both worked at a local fast-food restaurant, but my friend and I could hear through the thin walls that they also sold marijuana on the side. They had a lot of late-night visitors.

We paid them no mind, as they were very polite and even helpful to us at times. It was not for us to judge them for the path they had chosen in life.

I was checking my e-mail on my older model laptop and discovered I had received an e-mail from one of the dental hygiene workers from the dentist office I attend.

She said her name was Olivia Sullivan and that she wanted to see me for a reading. There was a phone number and a list of days and times I could reach her on.

On the first listed day and time I called and got her voice mail. I said who I was and gave her my phone number. That very night I received her call.

Answering, "Hello."

"Hi, this is Olivia Sullivan. I'm sorry I missed your earlier call. I was looking to book a reading with you when you have the time." Her voice was hurried, but pleasant.

"Well, I'm free tomorrow in the morning hours. I don't have anyone scheduled until later in the afternoon. What would be a good time for you?" I asked as I put on my reading glasses. I write names and times on my calendar.

"Would ten o'clock be, okay?" She asked.

"That sounds lovely, I'll see you then."

"Thanks, I'll be there." She hung up.

The next morning, she arrived a few minutes early. Knocking, I opened up the door and I did remember her from the dentist office.

She was slim, had short brown hair and brown eyes. Average build with a few extra pounds. She appeared to be around thirty I guessed, but she looked tired.

"Please, come in. Have a seat on my sofa. Can I get you anything to drink? I have water and green tea, and some cold Pepsi Cola if you prefer."

"Oh, thanks, but no thanks. I'm good." She said sitting down. She pulled a pack of cigarettes from her purse and was fishing around in her purse for a lighter I presumed.

"Oh honey, I'm sorry, but no smoking in the house please."

"Ah, sure, no sweat." She said as she got up and went outside.

About seven minutes later she returned, "I'm ready now. Oh, I'm a little short on cash this week, could I possibly pay you next week?"

"That would be fine. So, do you have a question you'd like to ask?"

"Naw...I'd rather your guide just tell me what he sees for me." She said as she started biting her fingernails on her right hand.

Alexander started right in, "Okay, let's see, my guide is telling me disabled individuals can move at a faster spiritual rate but do not necessarily move at a faster rate simply because they are disabled.

Just as every situation is experienced and the reverse is experienced, this may be another regular learning session for these souls. There is not necessarily more or less for them to know, only in different manners and more understanding because of the difficulties which are encountered because of the physical or mental impairment.

He says more than they progress quickly humankind will progress as they learn the lesson of kindness, love, and patience, as it relates to these individuals. There is much understanding that should be taken from these souls when they are present.

Alexander says no scoffing or dismissal as less capable, but the patience and love expressed to all humankind should be shared on to these individuals as they too are souls in a physical existence.

There is a higher frequency with them to ensure they're understanding these lessons since the physical sensations they experience may not be the same as able bodied individuals. There is extra guidance to help interpret and after this life, to go over and clearly understand what has taken place.

He says this may be the form taken in a life because of previous actions. There may be an understanding of them which can only be learned through the focused attention they now have through the absence of some ability that the majority of humans are given. They may not necessarily progress faster, they too can ignore, or miss their lessons or step off the path and must return to accomplish what was given to them as their assignments for that specific life.

Alexander says it is the absence or impairment that often gives them the focus and drive which can be missing from an able-bodied person. They may have less opportunity to be adrift from their mission because their focus is on less frivolous things since they are much more depending on others or must be more self-sufficient.

Blindness, as an example, has the ability to allow those experiencing it to become greater at experiencing other senses capable in the human body and to understand the subtle nuances in human interaction as well as abilities connected directly to the spirit dimension and communicating with it.

There is less interference from mindless action and are therefore less distracted on their way to their goals. This can allow them to progress quicker or accomplish these tasks quicker or easier. They are given a focus. These souls can return for this specific purpose, of being disabled, when in previous incarnations they had missed the opportunity to complete some specific task. Not true for all beings. They are great teachers in their own right.

Did that answer some question you might have had, or do you now have a question you'd like to ask?"

"I can dig what he's saying. I have two identical twin boys that are age four, Robby and Bobby, yeah, I know, their names sound corny, but at the time I thought it was so cool. The shocker is both were born blind at birth. Can you ask your guide why I got the double whammy?" She now had tears welling up in her bloodshot eyes.

"Alexander says that for you, this life is about paying off karmic debt that was incurred several lifetimes ago. Energy expressed, in what some might call undesirable, needs to be balanced.

Your two sons are young souls who were unable to navigate through this complicated world in completing their chosen lessons and experiences in previous lifetimes. Now they have returned to try again in bodies that are limited in scope and will provide them with less distraction.

He says you three are known to each other in the Unseen World and agreed upon this journey for the benefit of all concerned."

"Well shit, I guess I need to suck it up and stop feeling sorry for myself." She used several tissues from her purse.

"Is there anything else you'd like to ask?" I was starting to feel her pain and sorrow that was emanating from her vibrations.

"Yeah, how much karma would I get if I shot that bastard who got me pregnant and split?" She chuckled for a few seconds and then returned to sniffling.

"Ah, I'm not sure..."

"Sorry, I was just kidding around. Thanks for the info. I better get home before the boys drive my mother nuts."

She pulled herself together and headed out.

On my next dental appointment several months later, I asked about her and was told she had quit her job there and no one seemed to know anything else. I said a prayer for her, her two boys and her mother.

Chapter Eight

As I pulled into the parking lot of my apartment building, I noticed a familiar car. Standing outside my apartment was Belinda Montgomery, a new client of mine. She was in her late twenty's and had red hair and green eyes. A little on the heavy side, but average for the most part.

"Well, hello dear, is everything alright?" I asked as I unlocked my door.

"Oh Evelyn, I'm so sorry for just showing up like this. I know I should have called first, but I had so many things going on and I was in the neighborhood. So, I figured, what the hell, I'd take the chance to drop by and see if you were able to do a reading for me." She seemed almost out of breath as she rattled off that statement.

"It's okay, come on in. It's been a slow week for me to tell the truth. Let me change out of my work clothes. Please make yourself comfy on the couch and I'll be out in a jiffy."

Belinda settled in and relaxed. She declined my offer of refreshments.

I sat next to her on the couch and started doing some deep breathing to prepare for Alexander's entrance.

"Now then, my guide is here, what would you like to ask?"

"It's about my nine-year-old son, William. He keeps getting ear infections and the doctor wants to do surgery to put in drainage tubes. He's worried about the excessive use of antibiotics to clear the infections, so he wants to try surgery.

Surgery just scares me a little because William is so young. I just wanted to check in with your guide to see what is causing him to have so many ear infections. Is there something else I can do to help him?" She seemed sincerely concerned for her son.

"Okay, Alexander says you should be aware that you hold part responsibility for these infections. There is much you do not understand on your plane about your impact on William's energy.

He says there are actions you take that directly impact the energy body and physical body of William. Care should be taken to understand how energy is in all things and that energy can be positive and negative. There is energy in words and actions and those words can cause harm to the long-term healing and health of any living thing on your plane.

Alexander says there are things that can be done, healing, positive, loving energy, and similar that can rectify this situation. Please be patient, have understanding on things that matter. Care of a child is important until they can fully develop on their own for their spirits' sake. Damage can be done if they are not past certain milestones in their development that can take many years or even lifetimes to undo."

"So, does William need tubes in his ears?" She blurted out.

"My guide says all healing comes from within. There are things you can teach William to heal his own body, positive thought, prayer, meditation, and affirmations, such as, 'I have a healthy and complete body, my body heals on every level.'

There is nothing from the outside that is going to heal any ailment better than your mind. There are supplements that can be taken to curb the signs and symptoms of this ailment, until it is learned how to use the mind to stop this, and the actions of the mother have better effect on the child.

He says pain pills to mask the problem are not overly helpful as infection still exists. Natural antibiotic substances will clear up infection. Sleeping to allow drainage will successfully remove problems. There is nothing that can't be done on your plane by diet and mindful health coupled with the correct energy and actions directed on the correct and proper results.

So much wasted time and action. There should be less time spent on worrying about a problem and more time doing the things that human spirits can do to correct these problems. Action!"

"I'm not sure I understand…so what causes William's ear infections?" Belinda asks point blank.

"Alexander says there is an energy imbalance that a doctor is not going to experience or look for because this part of the body does not exist to them. There is clearing that can be done with positive thought and meditation. There are no quick fixes. Anything taken internally or placed in the arm by your medical professionals will only cause temporary relief. There will be no long-term satisfaction from any of these, please understand this.

There is nothing that YOU cannot accomplish because YOU are the ones who create and destroy with your minds. Destroying an ear infection is just as simple as destroying anything good that humans tend to ignore.

He says to build up immunity, there must be balance on all levels of human existence, not just physical. There must be balance, spirit is important and can present its problems as reflections into the physical body parts. You are not alone in thinking that more should be done, but medicine can only provide physical relief, it is treating the symptoms and signs that are in the physical body, when the true problem can be in the mind or higher levels of being that are not overly visible to most of the spirits having an existence there.

Please understand these, we know you do. Please make this right, many infections in the ear can cause problems later in life for balance, hearing, cognizance."

"I just don't understand what I should do." Belinda said as she threw her hands up.

"I think my guide is trying to explain this situation in a nice and positive way. He…"

She cut me off, "Please tell your guide I don't need some goody-goody crap. Just tell him to let me have it smack in the face…I can take it!" She cried out.

Alexander started sending information, and if he does, I give it out, "He says you are living in a negative energy environment with your husband and son. The arguing, yelling and physical abuse created by you and your spouse have impacted all three beings, and all are suffering from this toxic situation that has been created.

Mentally and emotionally the boy is not developed enough to withstand this level of negative energy, so it manifests itself as ear infections and is causing other underlying physical problems that will soon become evident if no positive action is taken to correct this situation.

He says you and your spouse may choose to use your free will to live in such a negative situation, but to force this upon your son, who is an innocent bystander, so to speak, will invoke a karmic liability for you and your spouse.

Alexander says take immediate action to correct this negative environment for the sake of the young boy or remove yourselves from it.

He wants to know if that's clear enough?"

"Yes, it is. That's all I need to know." Belinda left my apartment with a strong determination to take action.

I think guides try to say things in such a way that they want us to think and come to a conclusion about something on our own. To use our free will, because those in the spirit dimension are not allowed to live our life for us. They can only try to guide us in a positive direction concerning our chosen lessons and experiences.

As it has been said, 'there is no right, there is no wrong, just life lessons and experiences.'

*Note to Readers: As for 'Mind-Energy Healing' go before yourself and ask what you wish to do, see it being done. Do not wait for the universe to create it, create it for yourself. Create with the mind what you wish to see. This method is for all things, not in only work and health. Heal yourself with your mind. You have the ability within yourself to place your hands on your body and direct energy with your mind. This is not simply your own energy recycling, this is universal energy, that which exists all around you. Your body will use it, your body will convert it from a 'neutral' energy into that which will be used to your benefit, for your highest good.

You can take an active role in your healing instead of hoping for some outside cure and its side-effects to correct your health issues.

*A note from Evelyn Adams; for what it's worth, here is what Alexander told me to say, 'I call for the universal energy to activate, to bring forth positive healing in the way of rehabilitating, rejuvenating, regenerating energy. Let that energy fill every atom, every molecule, every cell in my body with positive healing, bringing my body to a state of wellness and wholeness. (*) I direct the universal energy to seek out and destroy any infection, any virus, any harmful bacteria. To flush those from my body, bringing my body to a state of balance, harmony, and perfection. These are my decrees, for I am one with God. So be it.'

If you have a certain illness or injury simply insert this into the above paragraph, and you may invoke this as often as you desire. (*) I direct the universal energy to bring healing energy to (whatever you are having trouble with). To bring it to a state of balance, harmony, and perfection.

Chapter Nine

I received a strange letter in the mail from a small group stating they were sponsored by a research association, that studied psychic and paranormal phenomena. They wanted to know if I would be willing to be a participant in one of their upcoming study's. The letter did not say what their topic of study would be.

The letterhead was from a university I will not name. The letter went on to say, I and the other participants would remain anonymous in their findings. Their main goal was to ask a specific question to see how many of the participants answers would match or be similar in context.

It said there would be twenty-five psychics from twenty-five different states that had been selected, and that none of us would know who the other twenty-four were.

If I gave my permission to be one of the participants, a five-man team would come and document my response to their question using video, audio, and other paranormal equipment.

Also, all twenty-five psychics would each be paid a stipend of $355.00 dollars for the one day of service rendered.

So, I thought about it for a couple of days, and asked Alexander what he thought about it. He simply said it was my choice to make, not his. I admit, the money sure was enticing as I was working for a nice restaurant as a hostess and could surely use some extra cash.

I called the number on the letter and spoke to a young sounding girl at the university and made arrangements for the day and time their team was available to come to my apartment.

Three weeks later, the five-man team turned out to only be two guys and a girl; they were your typical college looking individuals. Casually dressed and courteous. They arrived on the appointed day and time agreed upon. They were carrying all sorts of fancy looking equipment and thingamajigs I didn't recognize.

After introductions were made the team explained their basic functions; Troy was in charge of operating the cameras, sensors, meters, and things of that nature; while it was Dexter's responsibility to handle the contract, which I had to sign to get paid, and to record and document everything that happened during their visit.

Jana, it turns out was what they called a psychic 'fraud' investigator. It was her job to determine if I was genuine or a fake. I must say, that caught me by surprise.

Troy and Dexter set about setting up and sweeping through my apartment; using their gadgets to measure temperature, electromagnetic waves, and all kinds of other stuff I didn't quite understand.

Jana just sat next to me on the sofa; she would stretch her arms out toward me and run her hands around the outline of my body, but never actually touched me. She did this several times and then she would write in a little notebook, making sure I couldn't see what she had written.

"Are you trying to read my aura," I asked pleasantly.

Jana's reply was straight to the point, "I'm not permitted to have a conversation with the test subject. You can direct your questions to Dexter. He will be asking you the question that deals with this particular study."

"Oh, okay," I said as I took note of the 'test subject' remark. Glancing around my apartment, I watched as the two young men seemed to be finishing up.

They had me sit in a chair opposite from Troy who was manipulating an elaborate camera set up on a tripod. Dexter had positioned himself just to the left of Troy facing me.

"Are you ready to begin? Do you need to summon your spirit operative?" Dexter asked.

"Yes, I'm ready to start when you are," I said as I took in and released a deep breath which helped me to relax.

Dexter gave Troy the thumbs-up and he started the camera recording. "Let me state that this psychic probe will be dealing with what has been occurring nationwide concerning 'mass shootings.' Are we good to go?"

"Yes, I'm ready."

"Do you know the name of your main spirit entity that works with you? If not, just say no; we realize not all psychics are aware of their controllers name."

"All my information from the other side comes from my guide Alexander," I answered politely.

"Very good. Let's begin; regarding mass shootings, what does your guide Alexander have to convey to us concerning the spiritual interpretation behind this mainstream phenomena that affects our current society."

Alexander started sending his reply, "My guide wants to first explain the main reasons for mass shootings; but be aware not all mass shootings will fit this pattern, but the overall majority will, he says.

Many times, an Energy Being, or Soul if you prefer, will join up with other like-minded beings and plan out lifetimes that will intersect once they have incarnated into the physical world. They do so in order to encounter what cannot be experienced in the Unseen World; and on a larger scale, to balance out energy that has been blocked, so to speak, and that energy needs to be expressed in a positive manner before it seeks a negative pathway to express itself.

For example, these Energy Beings agree to come together, each taking on a particular role while in the human form, which will help them all grow in awareness and enlightenment, or to create a positive balance where too much negative energy has developed. They are all a part of the same soul group; for like attracts like.

Alexander says, in the following hypothetical situation he will be utilizing for our understanding, there will be twenty-seven energy beings involved in a pre-planned mass shooting event. The time and place have been selected; it will be an office building in a mid-sized city in a southern state. One energy being will be the designated shooter, eleven other energy beings will be designated as murder fatalities, and the remaining fifteen energy beings will be wounded in varying degrees without any casualties.

Alexander says after the plan has been acknowledged by a higher council of energy beings; it will now be implemented. The energy beings have all incarnated based on their various human ages, which they will be at the time of the event; their lives will be guided, so to speak, by their spirit companions bringing them all together so the event can then play out as planned in the Unseen World.

He says, as the termed traumatic mass shooting scene concludes; now comes the reaction of the first responders, the family, and friends of all involved, the community at large, and those exposed through the various media sources across the nation.

The desired effect sought by the Unseen World, for allowing this to occur, is the outpouring of compassion for their fellow human beings, and to express unconditional love toward individuals, that may not even be personally known to them.

This assists in balancing out negative energy that has been expressed through; hatred and anger, toward individuals and groups who are of a different race, nationality, religious belief, or sexual orientation; whether known or unknown to them.

Once the mass shooting has concluded; Alexander says it is now especially important to understand the shooter, those killed, and wounded are all simply actors performing upon the so-called stage of life. Look behind the named frightening act and see the true meaning; that of invoking unconditional love that is greatly needed in this nation.

He says, it is important to not judge or invoke hatred or rage toward the individual who carries out such a predetermined violent act as a mass shooter. The act of being a predetermined murderer and of being a predetermined victim of a murderer carry their own personal awareness and enlightenment for those involved. Let love be your first weapon, when threatened by fear, whether you comprehend the true nature of the act itself.

Alexander wants to know if you have another question."

"No." Dexter then stood next to Troy as they started reviewing some of the images captured on their fancy equipment.

I mentally asked Alexander what was taking place. He said they were trying to discern if their machines captured any measurements showing proof of his arrival and departure.

"Does anyone want something to drink? I have water, tea…some Pepsi Cola perhaps?" The boys were too busy playing with their gadgets to answer.

Jana said, "No thank you."

My curiosity was up so I asked Jana, "How did you come to hear about me?"

"I'm not at liberty to answer your questions." She stood and whispered something to Dexter and then left my apartment.

The boys finally stopped what they were doing and started packing up all their equipment.

"Is that it?" I asked looking at Dexter.

"Yep, that's it."

"Were you able to get any readings on your devices when Alexander arrived?" I asked.

"We're not at liberty to answer any questions at this time." Dexter said as he continued packing.

That 'not at liberty' line must be something the university taught them to say I guessed.

They soon departed and I never heard from them again. I wondered what the other psychics came up with about mass shootings. I never saw any documentaries on the subject or read anything on the internet about any university studies on mass shootings pertaining to psychics.

Oh well, maybe later on they will present something in written form or something to view on TV or the internet.

END*****

Really Annoying Dead People *Book #3*

Chapter One

As I was walking out to check my mailbox one evening, my neighbor, Greg Simson, who was sitting on his porch enjoying the cool breeze waved me over. He is around age fifty I would surmise and is of average height and build. Greg is aware of my psychic ability yet has never asked me about it or requested a reading.

Greg invited me to sit on his porch, which I must admit was a bit of a surprise since we usually just give waves or exchange greetings as we pass by. Sitting down and relaxing he offered me some pink lemonade, which I gracefully declined.

"Well Miss Adams, I guess you are a bit surprised at my little invitation to come chat with me." He said in a friendly way.

"It's never too late to make a new acquaintance, and please…call me Evelyn." I said as I felt there was some underlying reason for this casual invite.

"Oh…ah, please call me Greg. Well, as most folks around here know about your special gifts of the spirit, might I seek some guidance from your friend Alex, that is, if it's not any bother?"

I figured as much, since I felt Alexander drawing near as Greg started to speak, "Well Greg, I'd be happy to help however I can." My smile put him at ease.

"Well, I'd like to ask about 'cold sores.' My daughter, Penny, who is about to turn twenty-six seems to suffer these outbreaks quite a bit throughout the year. She gets embarrassed at times when these pop out. Is there anything your friend Alex can tell me about cold sores?"

"Alright, let me tune in…he says these sores or blisters are tiny annoyances. They cause fear and disruption for many people because of the guilt they have regarding the thoughts of others that this is always somehow earned or received because of unprotected sex. This is not true. This disruption in the skin is a manifestation of anger and the inability to manage one's health.

Alexander says, simply because it is not showing on the skin does not mean that this presentation is any less present in the body. It is always present in medical terms. Your ability to watch the words you paint your day with is an important feature of the human language system. It is important that your speech be done with you and your personality and your dreams and ambitions in mind.

He says too much of what is said or done is at the expense of the self and is done with the purpose of 'telling them what they want to hear' so that some unrighteous position or kind grace is earned. One thing that you can do is to determine what you want, what do you desire, this can be as important as acknowledging your higher self and working for a deeper understanding or as simply as granting your curiosity the opportunity to jump from an airplane with a parachute.

Alexander says the key in both situations is to honor the self. Do not speak to others that you wish to perform these acts when you do not. Do not speak to others that you wish to perform these acts with the intention that they will hold you in higher regard than previously, simply because of their association with the specified activity.

This is not necessarily passed from parent to child because of birth. This will not manifest in beings who follow this chain of human succession if their intention, their verbal communication, and their energy are all balanced and maintained in a manner that does not ignore the self in an attempt to attain some higher good, that, in consideration of the true nature of the earth plane, is not truly serving anything or anyone but the ego.

He says this can be related to the previous information, that when your ego is served too well, even the physical can succumb to unsightly marks on the body. External tumors and lesions can have many reasons for appearing. You are all aware that such marks may be disturbing or unsightly, but so are the masks and shields you wear that hide your true nature and your true feelings, so much so that they can cause harm to your physical body and nutrition.

The process is not a simple one to acknowledge this event and recover from it. There is no easy cure, other than to repair deficiencies in diets, to ignore that which is not for your highest good, and to complete activities, thoughts, and ideas that serve the self, the true self, not the ego mind.

First, for many, it will be a matter of learning the identity of the self and the ego, learning what voice commands the most attention and identifying what serves your greatest purpose. Currently, many do not understand ego; ego can be stated as the physical mind that protects and carries on your activities. It is not the unique you, the ego will crave more if left unattended and serves to protect the self in ways that may be considered building walls. The ego can be damaged and cause it to lash out because of the possible harm to its appearance. The ego is not who you are as a being on the highest level, it will exist with you always in some form, but not in the same manner.

Alexander says it is important to understand the manner in which the ego operates, while not all emotions are based in the ego, the ego, the protective self, can cause emotions and actions automatically if you do not function on any level within your mind other than auto-pilot. Living carelessly, not dangerously, but living without being engaged your ego can become more powerful than your true mind, your true self.

Because of this it is necessary to learn what living really is meant for in this lifetime. By that, we mean that you are not simply watching as a spectator, you are actively engaged in life, you discern emotion, action, and energy from that of others and yourself, you examine causes, you are learning. While this is not always the case for all people, most will feel the sensation of release when they determine the nature of their true being when compared to being driven by ego which serves, basically, to protect you and the material possessions which it gathers as insulation; primarily in a competitive way so that it is the best ego in comparison to the others it will encounter.

He says it is not enough to be aware that there is a drive within you that will operate no matter if you are blind to life or not but knowing that your body is operating without creative process, without learning, that is what should be more disconcerting to you. It is the moment you engage that others will learn from and with you, you are quite literally a lifeless zombie, as it were, when compared to others, when you are living only as the ego and not the higher self. Actively engage your world."

"So, she has some soul searching to do and to stand up for herself and her true beliefs and to not kiss ass to go along or get ahead is what I'm hearing." Greg stated.

"That's one way to see it." I spoke.

"Oh, sorry for the 'ass' word. I didn't mean to offend." Greg said softly.

"Trust me dear, I've heard much worse." We both chuckled.

Parting company, as he was excited to phone his daughter and discuss what had transpired, I headed home to watch some television. One of my favorite shows would be on soon, and what might that be? Why 'Psychic Detectives' of course.

Chapter Two

A young couple, Sara and Klem O'Rourke had phoned, and we set up an appointment for a reading. They were a young couple who looked to be in their mid-twenties if I had to guess.

Knocking, I invited them in and after some small talk we got down to the business at hand. They were both in different stages of depression over the loss of their five-month-old baby boy which they named Dexter.

To their shock he was found dead in his crib. The paramedics worked on Dexter at their apartment and continued their efforts in the back of the ambulance but to no avail. An autopsy was conducted by a pathologist and because no viable cause could be evidenced, Dexter's death was ruled to be a 'Crib Death' or that which is called 'Sudden Infant Death Syndrome,' where the cause is medically unknown.

Sara and Klem said they had read my book, 'Annoying Dead People' which spoke of a similar situation concerning 'crib death' and they were seeking information on why Dexter had chosen to leave their family in that way.

They said they were financially well off, both were in good health, and they were having no marital problems, to the contrary, they were so ecstatic with his arrival they were on cloud nine Sara said.

"Alright, let me tune in to Alexander, my guide, and see what he has to say about Dexter's early departure. He is saying that Dexter's short-lived lifespan had nothing to do with his chosen parents. His early departure was based on his last incarnation being cut short."

Klem asked, "What does his last lifetime have to do with this lifetime, our lifetime together?"

"Alexander says that in the previous lifetime to this one, the energy being you named Dexter was an elderly female whose lifespan was to be eighty-five years and five months in total duration.

Now, this energy being, your Dexter, who was in the form of an elderly female in this prior life was in the hospital and receiving medical treatments. There was an error or what you might call a medical mishap involving the wrong medication being administered to this elderly woman and it caused her to die five months prematurely.

Alexander says, because the early death was in no way caused by the energy being you named Dexter, that energy being then had the right, if it so chooses, to be reborn and live in a physical body for a period of five months, which it felt it was cheated out of, so that the energy being would then feel as though it got its full earth time experience of eighty-five years and five months that was originally planned for it to experience in this dimension."

Sara spoke up, "So Dexter had no intention of staying with us, after I carried him inside me for nine long months? Why was he allowed to do such a thing to us? The heartache we have felt has been a nightmare for us. Our whole lives have been turned upside down with his death."

I could hear the betrayal she felt in her words as the anger flushed forth. "Alexander says there is no blame to assign to the one you named Dexter, just as there is no blame for you or your husband toward each other. Because you are in the physical form, you will have trouble seeing the love that has been created by this situation.

He says as you learn and experience in this realm, you both will realize that forgiving yourselves and forgiving the one you named Dexter will lead you to a greater understanding of unconditional love for yourselves and for all of humanity.

Alexander says do not see this as a negative experience in your life, just view it as an experience and then move from it. No one comes to this realm, this planet earth to live a happy and carefree life with no lessons or experiences to encounter; otherwise, they would simply remain in the spirit dimension if that was their objective. You come here to face that which you yourself have chosen for your enlightenment and spiritual understanding.

He says that the energy being you named Dexter is a close spirit companion to you and your husband in the unseen world as you are all from the same soul group.

Nothing has transpired that was not already agreed upon before you or your husband were born. You three were the ones who proposed this situation to higher beings who gave their approval. Seek not to judge or blame especially when you do not have all the insight of a particular situation or event."

Sara just stared at me as in disbelief at what Alexander had said. Klem took Sara by the hand, and they headed for the door, "Thank you," Klem said as they left.

*Note to Readers: It is not necessary to pass judgment on another for many reasons. Your existence is only temporary, only you will judge your actions, and the actions of those involved may be for the experience that was brought forth for them. There is much strife on your planet but there is always a need for those in a human existence to learn to forgo violence and hatred when they have been wronged; just as there is a need for those in a human existence to learn to stop hatred and violent actions. This cannot be experienced on the levels of existence in the spirit dimension where you will return once your time in the human existence is complete. You can promote peace and make information available to alternatives, but there will only be peace where you decide to create it in your own environment. You cannot change others, only observe, and allow them to be. You should be peaceful first. This will radiate to those around you and throughout many levels of existence. Worrying about others or trying to bring them to your way of thinking should not haunt you or frustrate you. There are many who are simply not interested. Making information, an alternative viewpoint available to those on earth will allow it to be digested by those who are interested when the time is right for them. Many come to a lifetime here for nothing but strife, hatred, violence, and wrong deeds. There is no reason to judge them for they are experiencing just as you have, though their focus may be on different areas than what you are currently engaged. You too were once in their shoes so to speak.

Chapter Three

There was a curious letter I received in the mail, and it was addressed to me and for a return address there was no name, simply a post office box number, city, state, and zip code listed. The one-page letter inside was typewritten and not signed, but there was an ordinary envelop with the above-mentioned address on it and a first-class stamp was attached.

The typed letter merely read:

To: Evelyn Adams

Please be so kind as to explain, if you can, whether the existence of 'God' can be proven now, or in the future, in a scientific method that does not depend on any qualification pertaining to 'faith' or 'religious' belief.

Also, adding any qualifying information or hypotheses concerning the use of the word 'dimension(s)' as to its relevance to the above subject topic.

Thank You

Well, I must admit I found this a bit odd to say the very least. I studied on it for a few days and finally decided to ask Alexander if he could provide me with the unnamed architect of this letter. I wasn't sure if the individual who sent it was seriously seeking information or if it was just some kind of hoax.

Alexander said the individual was a Rabbi who was having a crisis of self-doubt pertaining to his personal beliefs as opposed to the teachings he received from the Jewish religion.

I decided to respond to his letter with the following information provided by Alexander:

Dear Sir/Madame,

Concerning your questions regarding can God be proven scientifically now or in the future and information pertaining to dimensions as related to God.

I must at this point presume that you are aware of my ability as a Medium. Therefore, this is what my guide Alexander has to say concerning your above-mentioned questions.

He says science, in the future, will prove many things. The existence of communication that exists beyond physical means will be proven; there will be many abilities that will be proven. The existence of the many dimensions that exist will be proven.

Alexander says the reason that these are not widely accepted now is because of the scientific methods to produce and measure them. There are many procedures that do not allow for these subjects to exist. There are many methods that do not allow for these matters to be measured, there are no acceptable means to prove any form of communication or energy transfer beyond that of what physically can be measured at this time.

He says there are not tools or measuring devices through this sort of ideology, that are currently in existence, that will produce accurate readings, or any readings of these occurrences. These things will be proven.

There will be many who arrive and speak on behalf of the Creator, but many will still interpret the information as they see fit for their present place on their spiritual journey in that specific lifetime.

Alexander says while the existence of a more unified and less structured spiritual guiding force, or religion, will emerge as the dominant force, there will still be many who restrict the Creator to some specific ideas or form. It is not for humankind to decide and deliver that message of their definition of the Creator to all; it is up to each individual to decide what is acceptable for him or her at their present place in their evolution. Though coming to this knowledge will aid all, will aid the individual, this is progress.

Alexander says there will be ideas surfacing in the scientific field that will lead others to the conclusion that there was not a random series of events that lead to the creation of the world or any other galaxy. The other life forms that will be encountered and discovered will shake many from the religions that have existed in the world for a great deal of time.

They will not believe that their God had created these other life forms. Some will still believe but will view them as demonic while others will claim that their God has created these entities. This is a slow and trying process for many who are aware of this knowledge already at this time.

He says to remember, simply because they are unaware in their physical form, they do know and have some knowledge of this, no matter their evolution once they return to their true existence. What is applied in this lifetime is aided by prior knowledge and the path set forth before your arrival, you can be of peace but have no knowledge of the Creator, but a better understanding of achieving your goals will be aided by this knowledge.

Nothing is gained by ignorance, but nothing lost in some areas. Stagnation will set in if learning is not made your purpose, anyone's purpose, but remaining the same often one does not lose ground, depending on the area being considered.

Alexander says it is to break free from control that is important. To see that the world is to be experienced, not experienced through the filter of what some specific group or entity expects you to believe or feel.

There will be scientific proof of other realms of existence, and this will lead many, through the channeling of information, this proven method, and this will lead them to the existence, the true existence of God. Your ability to communicate beyond your physical means must be proven by 'scientific methods' first. There are those working in less acceptable areas of science that will eventually push this to the forefront.

Concerning your use of the word 'dimension' as it pertains to God, Alexander says each area of planetary living has been located in such a region that each domain is watched over, tended to, and life and energy brought forth into it by a Creator for that specific realm of existence.

This is not to say that there cannot be more than one entity infusing power and direction into the life and plane of existence, but there is only one single being that is responsible for its ultimate direction no matter what other entities or life forms may inhabit it or cross from other dimensions to assist with that dimension's existence.

He says there is one Original Creator that then observes these Creators and can assist them. This is much the same way that many groups of people delegate power to accomplish a common good. No one person on your plane can watch a massive area or oversee the production of a complex event or complex item, this is the same for existence as you know it.

Alexander says there are many assigned to watch over your area, there is only one to direct and become responsible for its driving purpose, its mission, but then there is the Original Creator which is then responsible for all life and all dimensions.

I hope this gives you a better understanding in your quest for information.

Sincerely,
Evelyn Adams

There were no more letters forthcoming after I sent Alexanders reply.

Chapter Four

One of my regular clients, Tina Dundee, called and asked if I would read for her daughters' fiancé, a young man named Leon Marconi. Her daughter Sonya and Leon were living near a spiritualist camp in a neighboring state.

Leon was taking classes at the spiritualist camp to become a certified medium, Sonya was also taking classes to become a certified healer. Tina said they were coming for a visit soon and while they were in town, she was hoping they could stop in and get a reading from me.

I told her I'd be glad to have them come over for a reading, so we set up a time and date for us to meet. It would be another couple of weeks before their arrival.

(Two Weeks Later)

Tina called and said Leon and Sonya were on their way over. I was already prepared. They knocked at my apartment door and after introductions and pleasantries' we all settled down to the reason for their visit. They decided to have Leon ask his questions first, followed by Sonya's questions.

"I feel my guide Alexander's presence drawing near, so Leon, what is your first question?"

"During my time at the spiritualist camp, I've noticed some of my teachers and their guides have different takes on the same topics discussed in our mediumship development classes. I would like to ask for more clarification concerning the topic of ectoplasm; what it is, why does it exist and how can it benefit humanity?"

"Okay, Alexander says there is a great deal of energy and wisdom contained within ectoplasm and also within the ability to bring it forth into the physical existence so that it can be observed. It is the purpose of turning on lights, as you might say, that this material exists. You have a lamp in your home, the light turns on when you turn the switch on. The light bulb does not come on because of the switch, the light bulb turns on because of the electricity, because of the power from an outside source.

He says this can be compared to the way ectoplasm works in relation to the human body. There is much that is not seen, there is much that is not observed, but these things transpire no matter if observed or unobserved.

First, understand that there are many forms of ectoplasm, or many forms of the energy that create ectoplasm. The simplest method for understanding this is that there are many forms of water. Water exists in large oceans, it exists in rain drops, you can drink it, you clean with it, it exists as ice, it exists as tiny particles that you consider a gas.

Alexander says there are many forms and uses for this. You will learn this about ectoplasm. It is not simply the physical medium who brings ectoplasm forth that displays it, he or she is not the only person using or experiencing ectoplasm. Other forms of communication and healing also use ectoplasm. Other forms of involvement from the non-physical plane of existence to the physical plane of existence are done using ectoplasm and forms of this material.

It is necessary to understand that all things are energy, and ectoplasm is just such a form as this. It is necessary to understand that it is not a mystical concoction, it exists just as air, water, and soil, it is in an amount within the atmosphere, but it is only harnessed and channeled by those who seek to use it, and that is not many.

Alexander says it is necessary that you understand that there is energy all around you, channeled forms of energy can be said to be ectoplasm. It can become physical; it can interact with the physical. It can be directed by the mind. It intervenes when the non-physical being controlling it wishes it to intervene because some other authority has wished it to do so in the life of a being on the physical plane.

Ectoplasm is charged energy in the sense that a healer or any other channel is a 'go-between' or standard. You are the channel through which the energy passes. Ectoplasm is the intermediate by which charged energy passes. Think of an electrically charged plasma that has a physical presence of a thick fluid. All of these characteristics make up plasma, but they come from specific sources, the 'ALL' of existence, the entire world.

He says it is even easier if you consider ectoplasm, to understand it this way, that ectoplasm is not an extra material, it is not some other thing, it is not an additional thing in creation for the purpose of anyone or anything in particular. When you focus your intention, when you charge an area, when you deliver that intention, when you send the energy, you are sending, literally, a ball of ectoplasm which contains the intention, the energy, contains the thought or emotion. Ectoplasm is the bucket that carries your water from the well. Your bucket becomes full because you have focused such a desire within the well for the water to be present. You may see this in healing or other areas. There is so much channeled, so much created, so much focused, that the area where the energy is gathering becomes a substance you can call ectoplasm.

It too creates channels between physical and non-physical. When manipulated it can manipulate the physical. It can also be carried in forms that maintain their structure. This takes much practice and focus but it is something that can be created, for the purpose of delivering energy, for the purpose of containing energy.

The majority of control over ectoplasm is currently held by those in the non-physical. The primary awareness of ectoplasm in the physical is by physical mediumship and the production for a room of observers. It is important to know that so much more can be done with this, and it is the simple act of focusing and intending that it is created.

Alexander says it can lift; it can move the physical objects. This can become an extension of yourself. It can be another means of communication and channeling, not only between a medium and a spirit guide but between two or many beings in the physical existence.

If you wish to start working with ectoplasm it is important to understand that there is a great deal of energy that will come from you and will be brought through you by your spirit guides. It is important to understand that the tree grows strong because of water, sun, and nutrition in the earth. This too is true of those wishing to produce ectoplasm.

Understand that in a very real sense, before charged or made to be physical, ectoplasm is pure energy in a very raw sense. It has yet to become with some purpose, it is only existing as energy. Be patient and it will grow with you. A regular schedule should be developed and maintained in order to produce this physical manifestation. Your desire and motivations should be evaluated. You can go forward into the light or step out of it, but it is ultimately your choice."

"That was very enlightening, may I now ask about how is mediumship influenced, if at all, by our 'sinus cavities?' The teachers at the camp don't seem to have a lot to say on this particular subject." Leon stated.

"Very well, Alexander says these areas are intensely sensitive to energies. It is also important to know that the energy and light from the sun directly affects these areas. These were placed within the physical body in these areas because of their ability to be in the sun as it relates to the sleep and waking cycles of a person and therefore receive more energy through these areas because they are in direct light while the person is waking. It is important to say that these areas are receptors and antennas. They are not simply a method of filtering your breathing air. They serve the function of a reservoir of energy while the skill is needing it for interpretation or as a full reserve to experience the sensations and to use the qualities of a particular skill that has been developed in a medium or person that is able to sense and perceive beyond that of which is widely acceptable on your plane.

He says they do not receive information that is harmful, though they are able to interpret the energy of others and may act as a warning. Negative energy and information are not supplanted in these areas, and you do not need to worry about harm. You cannot be harmed in these areas.

That is why it is important to know that when you experience certain energy or emotions, that is to say, when your mind experiences them, they are not yours. You often can experience the energy, vibration, or emotional state of those near you, as well as those at a distance, those not directly in your presence because of an ability to connect through the many forms of energy and medium skills and healing.

Alexander says it is important to notice their placement, they are directly over the brain and are direct receptors, as are the eyes, of that which is being seen and experienced by the body. On a much deeper level they interpret data and energy much more than what is on the surface and visible to the eyes. These areas are unaffected by hate and anger, they are only able to sense them. They are able to sense many things and often bring this energy in the form of an emotional or physical response process within the brain.

Please know that there is much focus that should be paid to these areas. Many parts of the body were only discovered prior to many beliefs held by current society but current society has not reexamined much of the body in order to understand its purpose and function by today's methods and interpretations. Today's understanding is still that of prior misunderstanding.

He says these areas serve the same purpose as many might consider the antennae of insects. They can be filled with energy by that of spirit; we can bring energy and gas, and chemicals, to these areas for your development, to balance the body, to develop an ability in you. To bring about a deeper level of trance. Often there will be a sensation in these areas as though one has experienced a sun burn or has been in the sun though they were only in an apartment or dwelling. This experience is because of the energy that was used and is similar to that energy that is delivered by the sun.

There is much manipulation here, not for negative or personal gains, but there is much here that the human existence does not know and takes for granted, and therefore much intervention is needed by those with the knowledge, those in the spirit realm, to balance and correct these areas.

Alexander says it is possible at times that these areas succumb to sickness because of sensory overload within a body or existence that has not yet adjusted to the sensory perceptions of these areas. It is also simply just a matter of physical imbalance that causes these areas to be irritated and filed with mucus. In most cases these areas being infected do not impact your ability to conduct your usual routine, your practice and utilization of your skills, only when they restrict, prevent, or change your breathing, which also changes the blood flow and rhythm of the body; that is when these areas can be impacted.

Many can experience some degree of all those possible interferences that have been mentioned and never suffer a need for rest from spirit while resting the physical body in order to recuperate. When you do experience the need for rest it is important that your use of mediumship abilities do not interfere with your physical rest and wellbeing. Simply because the skills and qualities and senses that you are using do not appear physical, they still impact the body in much the same way as any physical activity.

Alexander says they can change the energy levels in the body, and this may pose problems when healing is required or rebalancing to allow health to return to the body. As chakras dispense energy, one could say they serve as miniature heart centers for the manner in which they spread and dispense the energy through the body as the heart does with blood; that is the manner in which your sinus cavities, those contained within the structure of the skull, spread the energy to the brain and pass messages back and forth from internal to external and vice versa.

He says do not worry that an infection has made these areas less able to interpret data or less functional. There is little that is stopped in an energetic process because of physical mucus. Some energy will always flow through any physical form and much more energy can be supplied if it is something that is hampered by a physical passing through in order to reach an area.

The breath is what should be focused on when one is concerned if their health may contribute to their communication or other skill negatively. The breath has the most direct impact on your physical health. Diet is second, but as the natural process are concerned, the breath affects many rhythms and cycles, all must breathe, no matter their diet or other variables, the breath is always required, and respiration is the beginning process of the cycle within the body that regulates many things. These things being in top physical order should dictate your use of your perceptions, skills, senses, and other abilities when considering actions to take while you may be in an imbalanced stage of physical or energetic health.

Alexander says sinus cavities can be cleaned using water, they can also be aided by hands on healing, the healing of mind, or the healing of distance healing. These also serve to balance the areas and empty them from any cause of inflammation and empty them from any excessive substance. Much of a person's perception of another is by sending and receiving information that is expressed through these areas. It is not always the expression, the physical outward view of the emotion that a person perceives in another that makes them react in a certain manner or behavior, it is the energy being expressed through these areas in that one person that are being received and interpreted by the viewer that have the greatest impact.

Much is connected within the human body and within the human head. There is much that is known about the body and how all processes relate to one another. There is less known at this time about all ducts, glands, and connectedness and passageways are all interrelated within the skull, the brain, and the head. There are many physical secretions that use these areas but there is much for energetic exchange within these forms.

He says expression on many levels and receiving information takes place within these areas. It is only by experiencing the exchange that occurs between all senses, their merging through connectedness in these passageways, that an experience is truly felt. The true nature may be missed because it is only felt by what is directly and immediately available to the degree that a person is aware of their senses. Most often these are only the physical sense. Records are maintained of these experiences so that they may be understood later should they have been missed while in the physical existence.

Alexander says do not use any drying substance on the glands or ducts within these areas or within the body. Let excess be expressed naturally when there is an imbalance. The excess must be passed in order for balance to again be achieved. Balance cannot be forced, though much is not done by medicine to balance, it only masks. Masking these problems does not help them to alleviate the imbalance in the body. It is true, the body must now work physically more in order to bring forth a change because it is now working through tougher conditions, not just walking up hill, but now scaling a mountain because of the medicinal interference.

It is possible to take a natural plant substance to prevent further infection, however, if there was balance in fluids within the body, balance within the diet, these substances would not have to be taken and an infection would not be a concern. In that situation the fluids could pass freely if other areas of balance were maintained. There is also fluid exchange to and from the body with these cavities; energy is exchanged which also gives the impression of fluid exchange because of it. Dryness occurs because of this. Fluid, water, it is important to maintain a high quantity of this with regularity, within the body."

"Thank you, this has been most revealing in offering a clearer understanding of the subject matter." Leon said smiling like a child who had just been given a new toy to play with, his excitement even got me smiling and happy that the information Alexander had passed on would help him on his journey of self-discovery.

"Any more questions you'd like to ask?"

"Oh no, I'm good, but I know Sonya has a couple of questions about the healing arts she is seeking answers on." He looked toward his fiancé as he spoke.

"Very well, so, what would you like to ask dear?" I said gazing at Sonya who I could tell was a bit nervous.

"As my main focus is on healing and herbal medicines, I would like to ask about the spiritual ramifications of seasonal allergies if that is alright?" Sonya seemed to blush a little.

"Why, yes indeed, let me see what Alexander has to say on that subject…he says seasonal allergies are to allow you to know your body, to know what you are missing, to know what you are needing, to know what is missing from your current actions that remove you so far from nature and its care and ability to survive with it rather than control it.

Allergies are not a punishment, you have them now because even living in remote areas, living with fewer neighbors, living with the trees, you put a pane of glass between you and the outside world. You put a factory between you and your food. You do not need to isolate yourself from all that occurs around you. There is nothing in nature that you should fear. It is not a scary place to dwell, and, contrary to popular belief, you do not have to have something wrong with you in order to sustain your entire existence relying solely on what nature can provide to you when you care for it.

Alexander says it is a matter of death of the true individual that we have observed you reclaim your right to be inside. You were unusually welcoming to this idea of controlling your environment. It is not simply for comfort that you do these things. Fear drives many actions. Though there are only a few who experience the fear of these items it is the ability of the populations of earth to not follow what is true for their own self, to follow a path simply because the path exists, this is what translates to such isolation on a wide scale.

It is a message to open up and allow yourself to experience. Drop the expectations and quick dismissal of ideas, subjects, persons, places, and things. Examine them and welcome them in and decide for yourself what it is that you need, not simply what you believe you need because someone else has told you from birth what it is that you need.

He says ensure that you are not simply doing the opposite of the tide because you wish to rebel. Ensure that your rebellion against the tide is truly for you, that it is your belief, not one placed there by mechanism of society and other involvements. It is obvious for many at the time that there are other answers, they simply do not know where to look or where to turn. Welcoming all possibilities is the only true method of education and experience.

Too many roadblocks are placed on you by your own mind and your own mind allowing others to control it. They may not have a devious plan in mind when they make comments or attempt to impart a particular belief onto you, but your willful tolerance at all costs is a simple nod that this is what you desire. You may complain later, you may complain and feel wronged later; later does not mean too late for action. Later is simply a term to describe 'after now.'

Alexander says at any point 'after now' you can make a new decision, answer old questions differently. Do not allow answers to be set in stone simply because they existed as answers previously.

Allergies are not to cause you harm, they are to draw your attention. You are not living in a world in which control of any kind is necessary or at all

possible for the entire duration of your visit. Do
not worry. Know that there is a difference between
living with, for, against, under. Chastising others
who have not reached a specific conclusion is not
beneficial to anyone and will not allow you to
change at a greater rate, nor will it bring them to
your meaning simply because you have belittled
their ideas. Calmly, not calamity.

"Interesting." Sonya said bashfully.

"Do you have another question?" I asked.

"Yes, anything on genetic traits that are passed
from parents to children please."

"Sure, Alexander says there are many things that
can come from the blending of genetic material of
two beings that come together for the purpose of
creating the human form. It is highly dependent on
what the being within the human body hopes to
accomplish within the lifetime. There are many
aspects that were predetermined. It is not always,
but often necessary that races are born to the same
races. There are some slight differences, but this
will usually be the case. Often it was necessary to
make distinctions because in earlier version of the
physical existence it was necessary for the family to
be bonded to the new being. Bearing some
alternate resemblance, no matter what benefit may
have come from it, would have not had the correct
impact no matter what outcome was necessary.

He says it is important to understand that general
appearance will be manifested this way for the
purpose of creating similarities, but there is no
requirement that all offspring resemble the parents,
and it can be changed and altered. There are family
structures that are aligned or misaligned and the

genetic traits and perceptions of the family and within the family can play important roles in these areas. Even subtle changes or nuances can cause problems for those who are not readily open to some outside influence. It is important to know that not everything you do is impacted by your physical existence and there is much that comes from outside your body that changes your impression of it. It is not your unhappiness that changes your outlook of yourself. If you were only to be left alone on this plane, you would find yourself to be the most beautiful being in existence. This is not because you are the only being, but because you would have no outside words or comparisons being made by others or you comparing yourself to others or to some arbitrary expectation of what beauty can be or should be.

Alexander says there are many aspects, nearly triple the amount of potential genetic options, that are determined by a team working from without before your arrival here. It is important to also say now that the items that are said to be genetic, personality, and even some disorders, these are not genetic, but it is simply the being acting out and manifesting what it is constantly subjected to in terms of expected behavior and what is tolerated.

Often a being will be said to have some type of personality disorder, this is not truly a disorder. The offspring will also associate with it and will appear to have genetically inherited this trait, but it is simply the offspring mimicking and continuing behavior that has been perpetuated. Often these are not conscious decisions, but it is the only known path, so it is followed.

He says there is much more that is decided by you or on your behalf before your arrival. Items such as eye color may not be important, or they can be incredibly important. There are many aspects that can be trivial to a being's existence, or they can be the very item that every other moment depends upon. It is important to say that there are many things that are decided for the being that also impact the family and these are not the fault of the family, they were not deficient, they are simply now experiencing something that they chose to engage in with the new offspring.

Handicaps and physical deformities are not simply for the being experiencing them within that seemingly broken body. It is not the fault of the sperm or the egg, nor even is it necessarily what the mother or father engaged in during gestation, though the acts towards the fetus carry weight and energy and these to follow the same cause and effect pattern of the rest of the universe.

Alexander says there are no universal answers in this area. Some beings rely heavily upon the physical engineering that takes place within the womb while others are manipulated for the benefit of the being who will inhabit the body. There is not a universal answer nor are the advantages or disadvantages in either case. One situation is not superior or inferior to another."

"Your guide has been most helpful. Thank you." Sonya said as she smiled and then looked to Leon for closure.

"Yes, thank you and Alexander for the information, Tina was right on the money about your ability." He spoke.

"Well, you two have a lovely day and say hi to Tina for me."

They headed for the door. The following week Tina dropped by and gave me $60.00 dollars for her daughter and fiancé's readings. We had a pleasurable chat before she had to depart.

Chapter Five

Getting off at the bus stop, which was just one block over, I arrived at a small-town middle school that contained less than two-hundred students on average; I was there in response to a resumé I had mailed in for the position of 'substitute teacher' that I saw in the want ads section of the local newspaper.

Making my way to the main office I was directed to wait in a small side room. A short time later a nice man who identified himself as Russell Livingston, school principal, came in and conducted my interview.

"The function of a substitute teacher here mainly consists of keeping the class orderly and assisting students with any questions they might have from the homework assignment left by their regular teacher. I see by your resumé you do not have any prior experience in the teaching field, would that be a correct statement?" He said directly.

"Yes sir, that would be correct." I answered while trying to sound confident.

"Not to say you need that kind of experience, you see, because you will not be teaching, simply watching and giving a helping hand should students ask for it." Russell said candidly.

"Yes, I understand completely." I wanted to give the impression I could handle the duties at hand.

"The only drawback I see at this time, is that the class we need a substitute teacher for, is for eighth graders, which are around the age group of 13 to 14 years of age, and some of those boys, and even some of the girls can be pretty rambunctious, not to mention tall and strong. Ah, can you follow what I'm getting at?"

He looked at me as if to size up my understanding of what he just said, which I must admit I didn't have a clue, "I'm not sure…"

"Ms. Adams, let me be blunt, are you even five feet tall? Soaking wet I bet you don't weigh a hundred and twenty pounds." Russell said trying not to sound ill-mannered.

I was still not sure of his intent until Alexander popped in and mentally said, 'Smaller older people sometimes have trouble dealing with larger younger people who are experiencing puberty.' Then the lightbulb went off. "Oh, dear me, I gotcha now. I see your point sir."

"I would really like to hire you, but I just can't take the risk that you might get hurt. When some of these teenagers go off it can take several male teachers to restore order."

"You're so right, I hadn't even thought about that part of the job. Thank you so much for your time and being so frank with me. I do appreciate it sir." I said standing up.

Russell was kind enough to walk me to the bus stop and even said he'd wait with me until the bus came. After some small talk about the weather and the like, he made his true intentions known.

"I must admit Ms. Adams I have heard of you and your ability to commune with the unseen forces. My wife has several friends who come over once a week to play cards and two of her friends talk about getting readings from you.

I know my wife doesn't put much stock in fortune telling, but I'm of a different mindset than my wife. You see, back when I was a young man, my aunt was always having visions, and many came true. So, I have always had an open mind when it comes to such things as the occult, and I was wondering if I could come see you for a reading sometime?"

"Why yes, I'd be happy to read for you." I gave him my phone number just in time as the bus was approaching. Even if I didn't get the job, sometimes spirit brings people together for other reasons.

(Two Days Later)

Russell arrived at the appointed time at my home so after greetings and whatnot we got down to business as it were.

"Now then, what would you like to know?" I asked as Alexander was now present.

"There is a big school conference at the state capital I will be attending next month, and I was looking for ideas concerning changes that might be made to our current educational system." Russell said.

"Alright, my guide Alexander says true learning does not take place in a classroom. So many of your current classrooms fail to produce anything beyond the emphasis of memorization and recalling simply to produce test results. There is not much gained simply by memorization of facts.

He says, yes, there should be a basic curriculum in the early years, yet as students' progress there should be the permission to study what the student finds useful, what the being is called to, what the being finds interesting. As for high school and college, there is nothing more than a sheet of paper being churned out by various institutions in order that you become more civilized and easily assimilated into the work force.

Alexander says understand, not all areas of study are in a deliberate way leading you to a vast summation of nothingness. It is important that a doctor, your medical doctors, be well-versed in the human body so that they too become well trained and practiced in their methods. You do not want a return to barbaric practices simply because someone has said your school system is not worth the effort.

The problem with all forms of study is that there is no emphasis on how to think, on how to bring in new ideas. All ideas are learned, you learn what has been done previously, you learn to follow rules and regulations, and you learn to simply continue what has been done. There is no emphasis on how to bring new ideas into being. There is so much time between the inception of an idea and the manner in which it can be finally implemented in society because of so many clinging to the ways that have come before them.

He says your institutions are placing their emphasis on the production of test scores. All institutions. There are many that have connections for higher job placement, but it is what you are learning to do, learning to be placed within a job, no matter if you are the leader in that job, or connected to some high level of society, or you are a person thought to be in a lower form of work, you are being prepared for jobs.

The ones who are less successful in jobs is often not because they aren't trying, but they are not interested. There is no complete route, as it would seem, that is readily available to those who do not wish to pursue the current establishment in terms of advancing a paper certification for the attainment of a job in the work force.

Alexander says those who fight, and resist learning are simply not ready to learn by the ways and means currently offered, and that is the problem, there is no alternative for many beings, there is no alternative, nor are they aware of an alternative. Parents and guardians currently send their children to the buildings that they attended simply because they believe they must do what was done before them.

He says it is quite possible for a being to learn all that is needed in order to live a happy and productive life, and after a specified time, they could attend a school of structured learning if they wished to pursue a more technical and advanced area. Even more widely stated and easily understood is that all things can be gained by your surroundings, too much there is knowledge regarded as power and those with the knowledge to not have the kind nature to share with those who wish to learn.

It is easier to place that concern in the hands of others. It is possible for you to learn what is necessary in life and then to attend a study and practice center to show you the skills and lessons needed to enhance your life or to be productive in some manner or form. It would suffice to say that you could attend these areas when you are not present in the mind and ready to learn at the time the structure was given, or if there simply were no methods for you to learn.

Alexander says when education is allowed to develop in the individual, at the individual's pace, in the areas the individual wishes them to take place, this is when there is a success. A basic understanding of the world is helpful, but it should be noted that the basic understanding of the world is often not taught by schools, it is taught by interaction and studying the world. What is taught is how to interact within society and in what manner you should be thinking. This provides no alternative to other practices. You are taught how to play by the rules, you are not taught the true nature, which is that laws that exist in nature are true, all others were created by man and will not provide you with the building blocks you need.

Manmade laws are temporary. There is no law created by man that will stand the test of time. Laws great and small are this way, one day murder is legal, the next day murder is illegal, the next day it is legal in certain circumstances or by certain authorities.

You are not taught these things in a learning environment. You are taught about events but not the true nature of events. We do not mean to say that reality is being shielded from you but only that there is not a deeper understanding of the events that took place. So much is removed from the situation to be stuffed into books to be later passed on to those who could care less, this is not a proper method of education. Study what you love, and what you desire, not simply what you wish to have added to your stack of papers so that you can be fulfilled in some other way. When the knowledge is gained that you truly desire and that which will benefit you and others, the appeal will not be important. This is true as you learn about the world or learn medical practice, or some other technology. Anything you want to learn is at your fingertips, but all learning takes place in the mind.

Alexander says there is no universal method for teaching and learning, and as with most areas, this is where the conflict comes into being. There are widespread practices being carried out that only a few benefit from. The progress that they can see is arbitrary, the grading method is not concrete, all is left to interpretation. What you need is for your mind to be open and to study as you will. This does not mean that you cannot benefit from such higher education and learning, but often those who have problems are simply not meant for this system, and because there is only one widespread system, there will always be problems and complications. You can go beyond school, you can learn because you desire to, not simply because you are being made to so that you can be successful by some long-term means. It is important to understand for yourself what it means to be successful.

He says success in study does not mean that you have to sit for hours at a time memorizing facts. For some, this is necessary, for others it will not be. Do not be ashamed if you do not fit the criteria that is currently set forth. You will find your path and you will find your way. This is not simply an excuse for you to abandon all hope of education or that you should not learn.

Simply, you should be willing to learn and understand a great deal, but less emphasis should be placed on learning in the manner in which it is currently conducted or forced. True education comes when the mind is willing, and many now feel that once their higher education is complete, that they simply never need to open their mind again. This is also untrue. It is important, that until you leave your physical existence permanently, and even beyond, your true purpose, your universal purpose at all times, is to learn, grow, acquire knowledge, have new experiences, not cling to a repetitious patter for all of your days.

Do you have another question?" I asked.

"Yes...so, what can we learn here?"

"Alexander says there is a manifestation of energy here not present in other realms for the purpose of education. There is a generation of energy that takes place here through the interaction and complete volume of learning experiences taking place. There is not much accomplished by reading if you cannot physically grasp the subject. Quite literally then it is necessary for you to engage in actions for the purpose of experiencing these emotions firsthand and realizing their benefit or detrimental impact on you and others who encounter them.

It is important to realize that no matter your time spent here on this planet, in duration or what you fill it with, it shall be beneficial to you and others, tenfold, in comparison to that of learning in other areas where you shall reside.

He says the important aspects here are many. It is not simply love, compassion, not just these emotions. The understanding that these emotions are in each action and no matter your view, no matter the perceived action you take, these are the motivations in all actions, or the lack of their presence.

It is important to understand your position and how it impacts others around you, by this we mean that no matter what you do you are always an example. No matter your action or reaction, your energy is a guide for others around you, for only moments they may see you, for years they may accompany you, but it is the group energy that is important and the energy of the individual, on a large and small scale.

Alexander says you have the ability to impact several and several also have this same potential. It is important to know that all reactions spread out from the point of action just as a drop of water in a large lake. All points of action have an impact larger than what many perceive. Many feel that they are alone and isolated, even for these beings this is not true. You may examine your mind to find the cause for these feelings but even your actions, even when you feel there is no benefit, no purpose, no one watching, they are serving as a guidepost for many others.

It is important to understand that no matter the method you chose to learn any subject learning always takes place when it is desired, and study follows. The means do not justify the degree of learning; the intent of the individual is what determines the level of learning. It is important for you to know that there are many who do not seem to evaluate themselves and their actions, this is not necessarily a sign of a highly developed being or one who has a great deal of development left to take place before self-evaluation.

He says it is not for every individual to have introspection on this plane, to evaluate things deeply as they happen or nearly immediately after, there are many who will evaluate at a later time. Also, do not feel that you are burdened, not burdened, highly evolved, or less evolved than someone who is communicating with spirit guides, receiving extrasensory messages, or any other related skill.

These skills are simply a matter of practice and development. They do share information when they are truly working within their element, but often this can be compared to the skill of an athlete; they are an excellent athlete, this does not mean that they are exceptional in all areas of their life, though it also does not mean that they are not.

Alexander says peace and understanding, while these are objectives, while they are attainable, it is important to work through the necessary motivations and energy in order to achieve it. Nothing done by force will be granted, learning these emotions and how they relate, and how all beings are connected through these emotions; it is important to learn.

It is often very obvious your connection to all life when you are not in a physical body, but also it is often impossible to determine your beginning and your end. In a physical body you are defined as one being by the regular senses, while you should realize your greater connection, it is not important for development. Do not rely on higher powers or higher alternatives in order to live fully in this life. Do not hope for some higher purpose or power to nudge you before you grant yourself the happiness and peace that you deserve.

He says while these may sound like lofty ideas that are out of reach for many, the smallest emotion within your body that creates conflict is your true self telling you that you are not living in accordance with your self-balance, to your true plan, and it will invite you to correct these actions. This previous statement is true and is important to say before we include, as in many areas, that not all paths include the same events for all beings, not all paths include the same type of events for all beings.

A person may seem to be on a terribly negative path full of hate and anger, but it is possible that they are living the life that is in balance with themselves and their true self. While this is far from the truth in most cases, the external manifestation is often a mirror, or a window into the hate within the self, it should be used to illustrate the method by which all can live.

There are not specific tasks that should be done. There are not lessons in this manner. There are lessons within many actions, the energy within them is what is important. The resonating energy within all things is what is important. It is possible for two separate individuals, one living in an industrialized society, and the other living in a mud hut, to undergo the same level of lessons and personal development and growth.

Alexander says while one may have encountered these situations on a grassy plain, the other experienced them within the confines of the concrete city. Different energy will express uniquely to the individuals engaged in the activity. Often the groups with which you associate are groups that you have on the non-physical plane. If these beings were not known to you prior to your birth into this plane, they may have come to you because of the similar energy, similar life path.

While you may not associate with them entirely on the non-physical plane you may have decided to do so immediately before your presence here as a method of understanding the skills and lessons that were to present themselves to you. You may experience different lessons within the same being and they within you.

There are not present lessons that are determined and assigned to specific areas. The only aspect that is often expected, though there is much effort to spread the energy types, is that those with similar plans, similar histories, they will gather and congregate. What is not often grouped together is which beings within a group are interested in maintaining their current state and which beings are interested in opening to new ideas, new aspects, new developments, new understandings.

He says while you may initially group together out of physical attributes, it will be after any understanding and development is actualized, that you group based on what you hope to achieve, rather than physical attainment or physical attributes.

Hoping for a harder life to bring you greater joy is not a difficult idea to maintain, but it is not a hard life, there are not obstacles that are difficult. There are experiences to have. Often there would be no understanding if you believed you were living in a game, in a temporary situation. You are not given things to test your physical mettle by some exterior being, these are tasks that you have assigned yourself prior to your enlistment as a physical human being.

Life is not as hard as what many make it. Learning is not difficult; it is the process of expectation on outcome that proves difficult for some when their outcome does not match their expectation. You cannot know the outcome; you would not be learning in the same manner within the physical if you knew all aspects. Your physical and non-physical bodies are connected, and, in this life, they are dependent on each other, just as your need for knowledge and development and your need to be partially veiled from the future and previous cycles are dependent on one another.

Life will go on, no matter your beliefs now, there will be change in the future. Your purpose as a being, your true higher self, it is the singular purpose. Develop, grow; when you grow, we all grow."

"That is very interesting, but how can we as a society help to develop our children?" Russell asked.

"Alexander says if you allow young, impressionable minds to be given daily doses of violence and aggression through television, the internet and that which they view on personal cell phones; do not look surprised when they grow up to be aggressive and violent adults. The lack of parental control is just one of the leading causes of the chaos you experience in your present society.

They have come into this life to follow 'their' chosen path, not the path of the parents or society at large. Educate your young in the following spiritual truths; teach them to live a moral life, to assist those who have less, to be of service to others who are in true need, to work for the higher good of all humanity, and above all to love all life unconditionally."

"Wow, much to think about. Thank you, Ms. Adams."

"You're very welcome."

Chapter Six

My car, an older model Geo Metro, green two-door had stopped running properly so I took it to a friend's garage for repairs.

Alan Jones, who simply went by 'A.J.' was an average guy in his late forties. Thinning sandy-colored hair and a nice round potbelly. He was the owner of a small garage and a client of mine. Sometimes if the repairs didn't cost that much, he'd let me pay by giving him a reading or two. So that worked out for me and my basic budget.

Luckily, it was just a hose that was leaking so A.J. replaced it and we set a time for him to come over for a reading that evening after he closed up shop.

I saw A.J. pull up to the street curb so I met him at my apartment door. He was interested in Alzheimer's as his mother, a lovely woman in her early sixties had just been diagnosed with stage four Alzheimer's.

"Evelyn, anything your guide can tell me about this disease would be helpful." A.J. started off with.

"Very well, he says there is a need for knowing on your plane, the cause of many things, but there are many who seek answers outside the root cause realm. All things that manifest as physical are not physical in nature. Only treating the physical does not cure the problem, does not improve it, and does not prevent it from recurring. It is necessary to examine the whole self, the full being as it exists on many layers, levels, and even planes of existence.

There is a call for many to focus on these things, examine that which currently exist to major medicinal outlets. There is more in sunshine, water, and air, than in all of the medicine bottles combined as produced by your pharmaceutical industries. Alzheimer's is a call to self, it is necessary to focus much attention on the self, many diseases are this way, while all do not call attention to the same area in each person they occur within, it is important to state that all disease is not universal, some basic elements are universal, some attributes do manifest universally.

He says it is important to know also, specifically in diseases of the mind, that many are present on this plane with this presentation in order to call the attention of the groups or individuals they are coming in contact with as they live their life day to day. While all are learning lessons, this soul often has subjected themselves to this particular set of protocols for the specific operation that is at hand for those they will come into contact with.

This is not true for all diseases, but know, we are all connected, there are no lost moments, but many diseases of the mind are through the testing and trials of those they come into contact with, such as medical personnel, family, many others. The mind does not disappear; it is possible for these individuals to express themselves in this true nature, their true identity, out of their physical plane. You may reside in this plane without the physical, though you may not yet easily interact with it, they appear trapped when the mind becomes lost and unable to identify; it would appear as a system overload.

Alexander says these beings should be taught the ability to express, communicate, and exist as their true self without the attachment to their physical self. Many do this without knowing, through their dreams; they are naturally leaving their physical being and visiting various places, learning lessons, living in classrooms as you may call it. There is often nothing that can be done because this is something that is chosen prior to entering into the particular lifetime. The individual is not at a loss. Even years into the process they can communicate without it, it is the process of learning beyond the physical self that is important.

Even in this physical existence it is necessary to learn of your true being and true self and learn to express and use it. Simply being in a physical existence does not require you to use only physical means and methods. Learning your true identity, learning your ability, please know that simply forgetting things, a lack of memory, is not cause for concern in these areas. It is not a punishment. No disease is punishment.

Alexander says this particular set of circumstances presents itself as a learning tool and aid; it is often not presented as a set of preventable circumstances. When used in this way it is a steppingstone to learning the true identity of all involved. There are many who view the extrasensory abilities of communication as science fiction or only of divine intervention, these situations are not the case. When you receive communication, even after years of ignoring it has taken place, you can return the sender's call, as you might say.

If you can remember back to childhood when you may have done this regularly, and a being in their forties may now receive the same information or communicate with seemingly unseen beings, you can return their call, return their message. There is no punishment in this phase of learning. Diseases of the mind often associate with self-identity; this is the area to focus. Often what is heard or discussed by the receiver as hallucinations are not hallucinations or incorrect by any means, but physical terms it may seem incorrect, but they are true experiences. Often times these experiences, even under the medication that may induce them, are used as learning and classroom sessions where education on previous, present, and future is taking place.

He says often times when a person is exiting such a medically induced state, it is not easy to return to physical thought and being and perception, this is why many types of odd comments and experiences are reported from your dentist's office. They are finally completely able to exist for moments without sense of physical self and returning to it is as if the infant has returned and requires self-educating time in order to learn how to operate again in the physical body.

It is not necessary to understand all things but know that those things which you do not understand are all often related and not as different as your medicine would have you believe. Each disease is not as different as the definition. Often diseases that impact a specific area, but by seemingly different means, these are all related, they are all the same, and are all caused or occurring for the same reason. It is necessary to have a belief of yourself and focus less on the physical, this is true for those who have never before accepted the thought of life beyond the self in physical existence and how it exists simultaneously with the nonphysical, for many it would be as if the current life and their manifestation of heaven are concurrently existing.

Probably the simplest of existence terms in relation to the self is the tremor or deficiency of the mind. It is important to use certain areas, or like muscle they will atrophy. Complications of the mind or what appear as disorders are by this manner, they are underused, they are not used correctly, or they are a call to these deficiencies. It is not a matter of use it or lose it as you might say, it is a matter of you using it for the great destiny which you can achieve, no matter what life returns to this physical plane for lessons, all can achieve monumental accomplishments in line with their ultimate goals, and achieve more than planned, they can change their life course, if they wish to do so. If they wish to grow beyond."

*Note to Readers: Are pharmaceutical companies not releasing 'cures' for certain diseases for profit?

The method in which they suppress treatment is not necessarily as direct as what many think. They hold much information, but they suppress that which is readily available to you because there is no monetary gain in that which they do not sell and control. If, in your lifetime, you feel compelled to take their medication, you are supporting their claim that you are not able to survive and live a healthy and active life without their existence. It is important to know that there is nothing that comes from an industrialized production that you cannot also readily obtain from the world around you, as one single individual, you have much more within your power to remedy and prevent illnesses than that of medicine which comes from a box. We understand that there is often some temporary relief necessary because of your schedule and the methods in which you spend your time earning a rightful place in the career world. Consider the impact on your body as it works to suppress your natural response to an imbalance. Importantly, why do you work under such conditions that prevent you from healing and securing your health within your home before you must return to the toil and labor? There is a great deal of misleading information available to you about prospective 'natural cures.' There is much on the shelf in the market that purports 'natural' and nature connections and is therefore suited to the needs and desires of those seeking such a remedy. This is not beneficial to you to take these self-assigned labels as accurate nor are they beneficial. The essence of the source of the medication is lost once it is synthesized in a laboratory. It is important for you to understand that. There is a great deal which cannot be recreated for health benefit and including the same ingredients on the label will not allow this essence to manifest in your body simply because you have swallowed a capsule.

Health should first be addressed not by a corrective pill or invasive action, no matter what disease you are currently embedded and no matter what cure is unknown to you by any means. It is important to know that any ailment that does not involve trauma can be overcome or prevented by the mind and by daily living practices that support your body and aid in its functions. There is a great deal that is offered in the market that does not support these goals and, in fact, is a direct conflict. Important is nothing that is done instantly for the sake of health. As with all areas of life, that which is not corrected or addressed will return to you once it grows beyond the level which you can ignore. It is not necessary for quick relief, you must balance aspects of your life that allow harmony to exist between all areas, your health directly impacts all areas, and it is important that without that support you know that all other areas will suffer. It can be done, what you desire, without the use of pills or procedures, but there is much time and dedication needed in these areas. Other practices such as healing and the properties within nature are important and can assist in your healing and maintaining equilibrium. This should be your focus. The potential problem exists that you will not find a suitable remedy to meet your needs simply because you are focusing on an area that requires other attention and a differing remedy from what you seek. It is important to bring all things in line and balance when concerning health. One aspect of being cannot be healed or changed without impacting all parts.

Libraries exist with cures and remedies, but all manifestations take place in your mind and must be addressed. The malady is calling attention to your imbalance, your dis-ease. Misinformation exists on the safety of such a process, that the process of relying on the mind, relying on that which exists without society, that these are dangerous to you, that the clarity of these substances and processes cannot be trusted. It is important to see that what they speak in a method of discrediting other sources is very much true and prevalent in the methods they prefer you to use for any treatment. You cannot depend on that which is created by man in an attempt to copy nature. Nature can be relied upon, that which is brought through man can be trusted. These are subtle differences in English but important labels in source that demand attention as this is what your health hinges upon.

When there is trauma, it is important to say that there is more at work than a mere injury that breaks bones or damages organs. While it is important to you to correct these things the question to address is the reason this action has taken place. Just as ailments in the body presenting as disruption, what has happened in this life for this disruption to take place in this way? It is important to understand the balance of medicine and that which can impact your survival. If you are to survive, you will survive, if you are to suffer, you will suffer, if you are to leave this plane and move to the next, you will. There is no amount of magic potion that will aid your intervention between the divine and your will. It is important to understand that your true being has options beyond that of the physical and there may be times at which you decide to exit a physical existence of your own choosing. This is not important, what is important is that it is not necessary to ignore medicine. You may break a finger or an arm, you may have a cast to correct this problem. Do not simply carry out the mantra the medicine is unnecessary, that is the practice of medicine, simply based on what has been said thus far. As with all things you shall be the one that makes the decision concerning your life, there is no right or wrong answer, only cause and effect. What you choose for you may not be the correct choice for others. It is important to understand that there are not universal answers. Nothing is unique and yet it is all unique simultaneously. Ignoring bleeding or any other injury does not make it less important or lessen the potential lethal outcome, it is important to carefully select the manner in which you care for this injury with regard to selection of medication and treatment and the reason for that selection as well as focusing on what has happened to bring this event into the physical plane. So much is focused on recovery of the physical that any other aspect to human existence is ignored simply so the physical will survive. Survival and balance after trauma are only the beginning.

A.J. asks, "So Evelyn, what can be done to treat Alzheimer's?"

"Let's see, Alexander says learning the true identity of the self. Learning and using your ability and harnessing the ability that your physical and non-physical self provides you. Many use this plane simply to exist, to experience physical sensations, but they are limiting themselves by routine. Expect more of similar nature problems to exist for mankind. Many are on a learning path themselves, they are aware on various levels, and even without conscious knowledge, achieve lessons and goals, and learning that is carried forward. Many are stuck, literally, in a rut or whirlpool that will not let them escape.

Even when considered advanced by your physical measurements a person can learn new things. There is a group thing acceptance of many ideas and the acceptance that they are true. Age does not limit, indicate, prevent, achieve, allow, or deny any type of action. There are many who are less than five years of age who have greater understanding than those in their forties to nineties and so on. There are many who are in rest and nursing homes that are left by the side of society's road simply because that's what they have believed will occur at such an age or at such a juncture in their life.

He says they are simply fulfilling what the mind has dwelt upon for so long. Even now, even after much damage may have occurred to the physical container, even after much manifestation has occurred by the limits placed on the mind through various acceptance of ideas, there is still much they can do. Speaking to them about these things, speaking and communicating in non-physical terms and methods can achieve these things. They are not lost simply because their physical is in what appears to be a downward spiral. Lost is nothing. Time will be the investment and the return is the

true lifetime lesson and achievement by all
parties involved."

"Well, so much to check into and think on, but
thanks Evelyn."

"Oh, thank you for fixing my car, it runs great."
A.J. headed off to relieve his sister who was home
watching their mother.

Chapter Seven

I stopped by my old friend, Patsy Smith's house. She was receiving home hospice care for 'Congestive Heart Failure' disease. Patsy was given a diagnosis of four to six months to live, and therefore was considering the 'Medical Aid in Dying for the Terminally Ill Act' which is legal in her state.

After visiting with Patsy and saying our farewells, her daughter Hanna approached me outside of her bedroom and asked if she and her brother, David could come over to my place for a reading that very night, which I gladly agreed too.

Hanna and David stopped by, Hanna did all the talking as we shared some cold Pepsi Cola and a bag of corn chips. After a short trip down memory lane concerning her mother, we settled in for their reading.

"Alright, what would you like to discuss as I can now feel my guide Alexander's presence?" I said breathing deeply.

David looked at Hanna, "You're the one who wanted a reading, so, go ahead, ask her for Christ's sake." David seemed put off by the whole visit.

Hanna flashed a mean look at her brother, "I will, and don't jinx the message with your negative shit either."

"Whatever...just hurry up." David was not in a pleasant mood to say the least. I was wondering why he even came, over the years his mother and sister had many readings from me, but he never asked for even one.

"Sorry Evelyn for the way David's acting, but he's all for mama ending her life early to avoid the pain, and I'm okay with it if that's what she wants to do. But I just want to know what those on the other side of life think about Euthanasia?"

"Okay, my guide says there is a drive by many to end life and find the means to justify this action. There are just as many who willfully involve themselves in the life of another to prevent that life from ending. It is important that no life can be ended before the spirit has agreed to leave, if done at a predetermined time, or done so in line with a lesson to be completed, or done in line with your highest plan, only that you had agreed so previously.

Alexander says it is not important the means, but there should be a method for determining the level of happiness or mood of the being trapped within a physical body if they are otherwise able to communicate. There are many who will give up, but there are many who will fear this just as they fear the actions in their lives that precipitate other events which they fear. They will no more engage in ending their life by this method than by the hangman's noose if it were readily available for pain and suffering or for any other reason.

It is not important to justify an action that does not readily involve you but that if one chooses to end a life and is intent on it; there is nothing to be done beyond ensuring safe passage. It is important to understand that there is no right or wrong answer or decision in life and the measuring of actions in this way is done so by human terms. This is a very rudimentary way to view the world when it is merely just cause and effect.

He says this is not wrong or immoral, they are all decisions with which you can base your future actions, gain knowledge, and experience, and engage with others. There is much pain and suffering experienced by the hand of another which is often disguised as that pain which is caused by a disease. Know that much pain or dis-ease in a body is calling attention to the body system or area.

Pain, a great deal of pain, is in the same way working to call your attention, your management ability of your physical body, to this area. There are many who may not feel the drive to carry forward through the pain, but if an exit is attempted before a predetermined time, know that all actions will still take place that were necessary for any level of development of another, or even the being making the voluntary exit.

Alexander says lessons pushed off or not experienced are not held back for all time, they are not ignored, some change forms, others are delayed, but they will still come to pass in the physical, the future physical, or in the energy body once you return to your non-physical home.

Medicine in many forms ignores the true nature of the being. In the form of pure pain that cannot be reversed by medical means, the method of communicating with the true body, meditation, directing focus on the self where it was previously ignored. These are the things that need to take place.

He says there is much disharmony in the person who is experiencing long-term pain that is not managed. Even in physical beings who are pushing their pain aside through various efforts, it is merely masking an issue by hiding the physical manifestation of some idea, method, action, thought, or other energy or physical or non-physical attachment which needs attention or releasing.

There is not good, there is not bad, there is only action. One action leads to another action, leads to another action, and so on. Actions cause energy and emotion and reaction. This is what is done. What you experience may be necessary for your development. The mystery of your physical existence is knowing and not knowing when change should occur and when it should stay the same; to know when there is a higher being interfering for your highest good, and when there is an experience brought on simply for you to change and take action within.

No matter the purpose, no matter if you rise to an occasion or simply experience, or change course entirely, this is an experience. Experience each moment; as each moment, past, present, and future, are the greatest moments. Emphasis should never be placed on one of these over another. The past is your teacher, the present your classroom and the future are your ability to create anew."

"Maybe mama should rethink her decision?" Hanna said looking to David.

"Maybe you should mind your own business and leave mama to die as she sees fit. Just remember sis, free will is each person's choice." David popped off with a wicked grin.

"Thanks Evelyn." Hanna said pointing toward the door.

"You're welcome dear." I said softly.

As David led the way-out Hanna shoved him from behind and said "Smartass."

Chapter Eight

Asher Spillman and Cora Santiago were both Seniors at the local High School just eight blocks down from my apartment. Asher was the 17-year-old son of a steady client of mine who I had met before on several occasions. He and his girlfriend Cora were starting up a local 'ghost hunting' group with five other friends as a summer out-of-school adventure.

They came around one cool summer's eve and knocked on my door. After inviting them in they expressed interest in a reading. They said they had already purchased all types of devices for their investigation of the paranormal and had been reading up on and viewing YouTube videos on the subject matter. They wanted to ask some questions to add to their knowledge base, as it were.

"Alright, what questions do you have for my guide Alexander?" I started the ball rolling as Asher and Cora had been talking non-stop about the paranormal. You know how young minds prattle on when something new holds their interest.

Asher asked, "Ghost's or Spirits who are stuck here on the earth, who haunt, can they move on?"

"Alexander says yes, though not all choose to experience it. Some are here much later than we expected them and much later than they originally anticipated. It is of the utmost importance that they return, there is no gain in attachment to the physical plane. It can all be gone and lost in an instant. It is just a tool by which we all learn while in this phase of development.

Many wish to increase their so-called power and the method in which they conduct themselves is through the power of fear. All things are energy, energy and actions are combined and energy is how they survive. While not all are through attachment, many will fear what comes next for them.

Alexander says this is not fear with true cause. This is fear by what has been gained and learned on your current plane. What you experience as fear in regard to these areas is manmade. Fear should prevent you from falling off a cliff but not from experiencing the majestic view it has to offer. Proper adjustment to all things in life, though what is proper for one is not proper for another. It is important to know that all things are temporary.

Even those thoughts and ideals that you take with you to the next lifetime; they can be changed in an instant. It is possible for you to change your mind; it is possible for all to change their mind. What was once a conviction can be changed and new ideals held true for that spirit. All things are temporary. Fear is not an incredibly useful emotion in regard to what is unseen and what will be experienced later. Your future, what anyone experiences beyond the present moment, it is an experience. It is not a frightening mystery."

Cora chimed in with the next question, "Can we help ghosts that are haunting to move on?"

"My guide says there is no time for the entity to be concerned with what type of information you have to bring to it. There is no direct offer of assistance or energy that can be afforded in all cases

and result in the ability to move the spirit
forward. All in existence have the ability to change
their mind but all must do so willingly of their own
accord.

It is important to understand that in all phases,
on all levels, that which is similar seeks out similar.
It is also true that if energy is formed into an area,
that energy in some way or fashion, will be used.
Remembering these things, you can know what is
there with you in a specific case.

Alexander says if it is similar to you, it may
provide some insight to know that you are of no
harm. If it is dissimilar, you may be feeding the
entity the very life-energy it needs. While nothing
you do may guarantee anything move from one
dimension to the next, you do not necessarily need
to feed it. Any wild animal will return to you if you
continue to supply a food source; if you remove a
food source the animal will not return.

He says it is important to know that you are very
capable of changing your vibration, you are
capable, all are capable of changing their vibration,
and you can make yourself dissimilar. You can be
of love and peace of your own accord, it does not
always require the other party to change and asking
another soul to change is like telling the water to
freeze without a true mechanism to do so, except in
the case of the soul, you cannot act upon it no
matter your mechanism. Whatever you enact upon
it will be experienced of its own accord.

You know these things; many know these things.
It is not the easy-way-out to say that you should
simply change yourself, but no spirit, ghost, or
person or anything ever created in any space shall

ever change unless it chooses to do so. No matter what their state of being, rocks shall not change they shall only experience the energy enacted upon them.

Alexander says you specifically can use your skill to gain insight into their mysteries and each specific situation will be unique and specific to that situation. It is not important to know when exactly these situations began, possibly each entity will give you an indication why it is present or what it desires.

Some harbor so much hate and anger that they wish nothing for what once held them to this place. It would take much effort, passive, and peaceful effort to return their thinking to what it once was at the time of their release from their physical body. Patience and protection on your part is necessary."

"What is taking place for what is called possession or being possessed?" Asher asked.

"Alexander says a wearing down of one's own personal defense system. There are many things that can contribute to this. Mostly outside factors that a person brings to themselves by actions and endeavors that are less than admirable. There are things you can do to prevent this. There are many things on your plane which people claim to not understand but all is within their grasp to change or experience.

There are many who experience possession by actions of themselves or by actions of others. There are only so many ways to experience it but there are only certain ways to rid oneself of this experience. Positive thought, action, and energy must be applied, and changes made to a person's path, by their own accord, so that this possession by other forces or by the energy of low energy experiences or objects on your lifetime can be realized. There is much that can be done to tear a person down if they begin down this path and experience things that they believe they cannot handle because their defense system is weakened or down in some manner.

He says experiencing certain things in life wears one down and can make them more susceptible to outside influence than others and this can be possession. There is not a Hollywood version of this that is accurate. There are many in churches that believe that they can undo this. They can, but their rite is only strong because of their energy associated with it, not necessarily because they are of a certain belief system.

There is nothing that can harm a person that you are not already able to stop or prevent. Right action will accompany and attract right energy and similar energy. If you are available and open to negative impressions from outside forces or entities this is what you will experience. There are no demons to cast out, only influence to be broken."

"Please share information on the reason or purpose for what appears to be 'evil' entities scratching or harming a person." Cora now asks.

"My guide says this is an energy that is feeding off of the energy associated with or within an area. Much can be done to stop this activity if the energy associated with an area, or the energy created in the area is changed. Negative energy is not stronger it is simply easier to create and more pervasive than energy at a higher vibration.

While there is no rank-and-file structure that means more power for anyone, a higher vibration is the goal of many, but like a pyramid, there are greater numbers on the bottom than there are at the top because many are still on their way to an understanding. There is much that will overcome this if there is thought, and energy directed towards the entity causing the problem.

Alexander says often times the human receiving the physical harm is carrying some energy or emotion or previous experience that the entity resonates with. Normally you will not see a person of a higher vibration even approached by anything thought of as evil because they do not resonate with it. Like attracts like, those with similar beliefs find each other in the physical form and the same is true for those who are not in a human body. Those that find an area or a spirit or human in line with their beliefs will associate with it.

The energy used to create the physical harmful act is only present because of the energy being expressed in the area, associated with the area, and most importantly, the energy in the body of the human that the act is being carried out upon. Express, receive, and experience love at all times."

Asher now asks, "What are 'shadow' people?"

"He says shadow people are an extension of energy on your plane. There is much that they do to extract energy to allow their existence to take place. There is much that every entity does to absorb energy, and this is most easily absorbed through energy of a heightened emotional state. It is important to know that any emotional state can express energy but that energy which in some situations is most often or most easily expressed is of anger, hate, rage, and other forms of discord.

Alexander says it is also important to consider the types of energy you emanate and the energy of the entity that is manifesting as a dark figure. Simply because it appears as a shadow does not mean that it is negative. It only absorbs and gravitates to the energy in which it is in harmony with.

There are some who are only able to manifest in your plane in the manner of apparition. They are not more or less skilled in their lifetimes, but they can be found in areas where the energy and discord are great. Even where energy is not evident in a physical expression of discord, they can be present because of discord of thought and mind.

A person may experience great discomfort or confusion of the mind and not share it with the surroundings and those around him. There is much done to the body to alleviate these types of energy build ups but the repetitive nature or the inability to make change to allow a permanent shift is often too great and this energy is expressed into the environment because of their pattern of thought or behavior.

He says simply because it is dark it is not darker in motives it is simply manifesting in the manner in which it is able. More will see them because of the mind shift that is taking place for many. Many are also slowly coming to their ability and using it, the ability to see what is not readily visible in the spectrum of light and color that most humans and physical forms can see.

Though there is also much that they have simply chosen to ignore or even dismiss as trivial and nonexistent. It is important to know that those that emanate a shadow-like existence cannot ultimately control anything on the physical plane. They too can emanate energy and their presence can be seen but they do not contain the power to alter anything on the physical plane.

Alexander says their purpose is often one personally set by them, and many are not aware of their crossing over or that they should have. There are some areas where planes bend or energy from time is left in an area. These are also expressed in these ways because it is a form that is muted in energy and can only be expressed in this way. To remedy these energy areas, simply direct the attention of your guides to it. You may also send this entity and the energy the message that it is important to move from the area as their presence is not needed.

Some will respect this information, though many will not receive it when they are only able to produce or exist in the shadowy form that is seen. It can interact with you but not in a detrimental way. Sending love to any entity or form of life has the greatest impact on the existence of the sender and the receiver. Important updates will come regarding the manifestations that can be seen. More figures of notoriety will acknowledge and examine them."

"So, any more questions?" I asked.

"Not for now, if we have more can we come back?" Asher asked.

"Sure thing. Always glad to help." I said as they departed.

Chapter Nine

Albert Kraus is a paleoanthropologist, one who studies human evolution and came over from Germany many years ago to continue his research at a midsized university.

Not long after his arrival here in America he fell in love and married a friend of mine, Nikki Wagner. Nikki has been interested in the New Age movement and has tried, from time to time to get Albert interested too, but to no avail. His scientific mindset doesn't resonate, as she puts it to anything that can't be proven scientifically.

Yet, after years of marriage she got Albert to agree to come visit a psychic, me, and ask any questions he has on his mind concerning his research. She feels he agreed to come only to, as she put it, to shut her up once and for all.

When they arrived, he seemed in an okay mood as she told me he had decided to take it somewhat seriously.

"So, Albert, what would you like to seek information on?" I asked pleasantly.

"What race started the presence of humans on this planet?"

"My guide, Alexander says root races are that which founded the human existence. Some of these are brought forth now in this plane after having reincarnated in other times and have learned from their experiences. These can be experiences which will cause them to be a greater catalyst in this time or to be for a higher good.

Many do not realize their previous experience and many simply go about their lifetime not knowing, though always being drawn to that which will accomplish a greater and higher good for those that they are coming in contact with. A root person may simply be a being who is no more advanced than you but has made the effort and changes in order to bring back something higher than their self to the next lifetime they encounter.

Alexander says these beings are often at a higher vibrational level and experience the world in a different way. Often more open to emotions and often experiencing great trauma or distress in a life to bring about change and to create a karmic payoff of previous actions. There are more beings as part of root races than there are new spirits, but not all have progressed to new heights. Some will take many lifetimes before their work is done."

"At this time, I would like to ask about these so-called 'star or indigo' children my wife keeps talking to me about." He said with a grin on his face as he looked at his wife.

"Alexander says these are not a typical root race. These individuals are part of a separate wave of spirits that are involving themselves in the progress of the earth. These could be called a subset to the normal set of spirits that create the human populace. They have a mission all their own that is in conjunction with the rest of humanity, but they will complete separate tasks with different energy, bringing about various conclusions to old ways that are still being held by many.

Old ways need to change and serve as an example or even a building block for the future, but there are many dogmatic ways that should be dropped because they served only personal interests and to fuel conflict on many levels. There is much to say on this right now if you are prepared."

"Yes, please continue." Albert said.

"There is an interworking within this group that allows them, with greater ease and fashion, to communicate with our world, between each other, and to see within or experience the energy of another entity on your plane. Many are prepared for this before they enter your world, though through free will, they may not fully develop.

He says they are no different from any other spirit coming to your plane in this respect. There is a time in which they will come to pass and will no longer be needed, look at them as a booster. They will not fully engulf humanity or overtake it, but they are a separate race, if you will, that will push the envelope as you would call it. They are more open by their physical design to experience many things and understand them on new levels and bring about change and motivate people to do the same. Though they may not take seemingly great actions, with all beings too, the example they set through interest and universal kindness, and other truths they bring, they will motivate by example.

Alexander says they will come to know many in their time though they are not all currently coming in such a great flux as they once were. There is a new wave already entering and a time for them to rise and increase in numbers is underway. There will be a great surge of energy that will sway the energy in, on, and around the earth in new ways, and though beings of higher energy contribute to this, special races, or classes of beings, like star children or indigo children you might call, have the ability to reawaken this dormant energy in others.

You might equate them to a special team or special group coming in to assist those already involved; they will leave when their section of contribution is complete. They have already completed much and many who experience abrupt deaths can be concluded that they were of these special classes and have completed their work. Their work may not always be on a grand scale, only to motivate one person they come in contact with can become the greatest responsibility that one spirit coming to your plane may experience.

He says there are no small tasks as they all culminate in greater activity and perception for and of the human race by comparison within themselves and by other forms of life existent on your plane and in others. The ability to communicate and interact with other planes and dimensions is coming very soon. The ability for people to openly acknowledge alleged aliens on your plane is not coming as soon as we will hope.

Alexander says many will communicate with them and acknowledge them but there will still be many who refuse though the evidence is mounting, and these beings will help in greater ways. There will come a time when many different races live together on one planet since all are for the highest good. Though many will still live on their respective planets as many subtle differences in energy make it more harmonious to live among one's own kind.

There is a great healing taking place and there are many spirits working towards this with many types of energy and beings. All can work towards this, and many special classes of entities are being brought forth and are coming into age now to accept and produce it. Be watchful, some special classes may be easily swayed from their path because of the openness with which they experience the world. They may be easily rocked from their path and easily entangled in spiritual matters which do not matter or physical presence and materials which have no purpose for their life.

He says be watchful and you can see these beings. Often great conflict can come to a person because they are a special class who was brought into a specific area. There may be great conflict with one person compared to the mindset of an entire large group of people. This person's mere existence in this seemingly conflicted group is enough to bring the energy around of a few to new ideas and world thinking for the positive of everyone involved on any plane.

Though this is not always true; much conflict can also be the result of ego clash. Many ideas in history have been thought of as ludicrous, but many of these have benefited the human race and may be brought about by those in special positions. It will take time, as it has in the past, but many new ideas will soon be accepted by many. There is not much openness with certain ideas now. Trust that there are far greater in favor of these new ideas than what is currently popularly believed or portrayed."

Nikki interjected, "See, you learn something new every day my love."

"If you say so my dear. For now, what more could be said of root races?" Albert said looking back at me.

"Well, Alexander says these are classes of people that come in waves and generations. As was said, each person may have a mission and goals to accomplish but an overall group that begins to enter the world has a higher purpose. Each may be seen as a new age when they enter. There are always higher goods to be done but these spirits enter the world with much more to work in as a catalyst for previous generations already on the planet.

They can begin seeding the planet with new ideas, new terms, learning and understanding the past and bringing it along to the new ways. Each may also bring subtle physical differences which may not seem visible, these are sublet changes in the evolution of man, in part because of man's control over his physical realm, and others seen from your plane as needed improvements to come with the coming age and changes that will be experienced.

You can see this as marked time periods throughout history when there were major thought shifts, major developments in the society of man and the views expressed by them. It is needed to be known that there are some changes that take millions of years, all improving the human experience or making it more worth-while to those who decide to venture into it. Classes of people often do not understand those who came before them and as much as this is a learning process for those who are present, this is also a learning for those who are coming in. To learn from the old or accept it. To experience it, to break free from it and to push on with the new for the better of the humans in this existence.

Alexander says there are many who have outside influences from other races. These are called 'gemantrai.' These are a combination or by-product of two or more species of existence mixing at any one time. These are not merely intermingling of animals as you might use that as an example.

There are also changes and additions of DNA by other species to attempt to improve and contribute for the higher good of humanity."

"Isn't gemantrai the name of a book?" Albert inquired.

"This is the name so chosen to bring forth the information of spiritual beings and those that people call aliens. This term has many meanings."

"Thank you so much Evelyn." Nikki said as she stared at her husband.

"Ah...yes...thank you for the information. It was most intriguing." Albert said as he stood to leave.

"You're very welcome, have a blessed day."
My gut feeling was Albert didn't 'truly' think much about what Alexander had to say. Oh well, maybe a seed was planted and something of value will grow forth. To each his own as they say.

Chapter Ten

A most unusual request came my way. My mailman, Roberto Rossi, who knows of my psychic skills knocked at my door under the guise of dropping off my mail. After a brief exchange of appreciation and small talk he told me the following story.

Roberto's daughter, Rosa and her so-called fiancé Noah Burke had been arguing over the concept of marriage in the 21st century. Rosa for marriage and its traditions and Noah against the notion of any contractual bindings of marriage.

Rosa and Noah wanted me to be the deciding vote in their dispute as to yes for marriage or no to marriage.

I explained to Roberto I could not and would not make any judgement concerning two adults who had free will to make up their own minds as to marry or not marry. I told him each person must follow their own path and no one else has the right to interfere with their chosen decision. He said he would pass on my message to Rosa and Noah.

Yet, to my surprise Rosa and Noah showed up at my home that night and said they would like a reading not seeking a yes or no answer from my guide, but just information on the spiritual standpoint of the institution of marriage itself as a viable concept.

After a bit of refection, with the above understanding I agreed to their request for a reading. I could tell from Rosa's demeanor she felt she had the upper hand in all of this, as I could sense Noah was nervous and felt he was going to be pushed in a direction he didn't want to go.

"Very well, my guide Alexander says this is an institution that survives out of guilt, pressure, insecurity, and longing for external stimulation though you are ignoring many other opportunities internally and externally. There is much about this institution about ownership. It was born in a sense that it has always been done but there is much concern about the possession of one being or another and the treatment of beings as property.

Recently, in a wide scope, this has become celebrated, it is incorporated so heavily in society that control is celebrated and those who do not engage in it are mocked or shunned for choosing a different path or ignoring this concept entirely. The right to enforce your partner to abstain from any other activity with another being, sexual or otherwise, is the problem.

Alexander says there are many who agree this is an ancient practice and assumes that those in a partnership will not find true happiness or meaning until a marriage is executed. Many fear being alone, many fear abandonment, just as putting a small band-aid on a severe trauma patient does little for the patient, involving yourself in the prospect of marriage does not truly address your discrepancies in personality, or that which causes you to be afraid, it slows them, masks them, they will appear, they will be addressed, perhaps in this lifetime, perhaps many lifetimes from now, perhaps outside of a physical body entirely.

There are many who involve themselves in happiness with another person and often times this partner can occupy their space for the majority of a lifetime, but there is much that is done to pressure or control a partner with expectations. While one partner may not realize this is being done, the other partner is growing, both should be growing and changing and activating all possibilities in this lifetime.

He says marriage should not be viewed as a requirement. Marriage should not be viewed as some everlasting prospect which holds you to the earth with any sense of accomplishment, that you would lack any good deed because you are married or not married. The celebration of mutual unions can be had, should be had, should be celebrated, or addressed by any means thought necessary.

However, do not assume that because you have agreed to join your physical existence together that your paths in life will also follow the same road. Also realize that the mutual coming together for the child, there is much that should be done to achieve a union for this purpose. It is not required from every being, but for many it is simply bringing new life, for others it is bringing new life and raising the new being with the same individual, and for others it is a matter entirely different.

Alexander says all beings, to some degree, in some area seek a sense of permanence. The very nature of all things around you shows you that all things in life are very impermanent. This is not a detriment to your environment. This is not something you should fear or worry over; it simply is in existence in this manner. Fearing change is a simple statement, but many do fear it in some area. They build physical and non-physical barriers and habitats to protect themselves from learning what is truly within their own being.

Change should be welcomed, change and temporary permanence, perhaps a better method for describing the situation, should not be judged so harshly. For many, they will not take the advice or adhere to the societal pressure or demand and more conflict is created because of this. Independence can be achieved in both realms, but more anger, hate, and rage are being done because this institution is so engrained in society. You can see that there are many unions, detrimental and positive, that exist without marital, religious, or government sanction.

He says the possible union, the possible benefit, the potential for hate and dissolution of a union is just as possible no matter the term associated with it. There is simply a method needed to create control measures. Many things are done in many societies simply because they have been done before. There is no real examination of the benefit, purpose, or use of the act. Marriage is about equality and mutual understanding. Two people or many people can mutually benefit one another without control, but perhaps the control is what they desired to experience in this lifetime. The essence of any institution on the earth plane is that it should be evaluated for each individual.

Coming to terms with the temporary state of all things in life and learning to allow the energy of the human experience ebb and flow without constant fear, judgment, and acting outlandishly because of these things. There are many actions, emotions, people, and experiences that are meant to be seen as permanent in your lifetime, there are many things that are not permanent. Clinging to your desires when the world around you, the people around you are changing, this does not help you.

Alexander says build your home and your resiliency within your mind, within yourself. You should not desire to be, alone or not alone, you should desire what you feel is truly for you and for your learning. There are often not widespread and general statements that apply to all situations and all people. The rules, laws, acts, practices, and statements expressed on the human plane are often simply for learning but often attempt to entrench the greatest number of minds into similarity that one being can forget that objecting, publicly or privately, or simply following a different path without calling attention to it, that being forgets it can be done.

This is allowed; it is permitted. You do not enter a pool to stand motionless; you enter to make waves, to enable cause and effect. You enter life to experience it. Perhaps to make as much energetic changes as possible, perhaps to be as independent as possible. What is or is not for you now may or may not have been part of your history or future.

He says the essence of experience is to engage in it fully; to not ignore your emotions, to learn and engage and to free your mind from what others attempt to store in it. You are a fully aware being capable of all things great and small, the rules, laws, and practices that make many feel restrained can be lived without. That which is declared absolutely wrong, morally incorrect; it will exist, and lessons achieved with or without suffocating practices and methods for attempting to corral those seen as loose ends or those who want to fight any apparent system that attempt to impart the most similar and easily digestible thinking to the greatest number."

"What?!" Rosa shrieked as she stood up.

"Holy shit." Noah said as he let out a big sigh of relief.

Somehow, I think Noah felt vindicated by what Alexander had to say on the subject of marriage. Rosa on the other hand went ballistic.

Rosa screamed, "This is just a bunch of horseshit!" She turned and looked down at Noah who was still sitting on the sofa, "Did you pay her to say that?! Did you?!"

"I never…" Noah was cut off.

"You are a lying piece of shit!" She screeched as she headed for the door.

"Baby…Rosa, I never paid nobody nothing. I had no idea what her guide was gonna say, really…" Noah stood up.

She stopped at the door and turned, "If you loved me! If you cared for me at all…you would man up and do right by me!"

"But baby, you said whatever her guide…" Noah started to plead.

Rosa left, slamming the door behind her.

Noah now turned to me, his mouth was open, and a look of disbelief came over his flushed face as he finally spoke, "She won't get far, I have her car keys." He said dryly. Making his way to the door, he disappeared into the night.

When Roberto came by with the mail the following afternoon, I asked if all was well with Rosa and Noah. He said it would be better if we did not speak of it again.

Chapter Eleven

My dear friend Armond Polanski writes for a blog that investigates and reports its findings on conspiracy theories. He came by for a reading to seek information on several topics.

"Well, my old friend, it has been a while since our last reading." I commented as he entered my apartment.

"Yes, too long. I've been traveling abroad and now have returned to the states. It's good to be back home again." Armond said as he made himself at home on my sofa.

"So, what would you like to ask?" I was ready to get started.

"Concerning government control or altering of the weather; what impact does it have?"

"Alright, Alexander says there is no detriment to you personally, however, there is a harsh impact to the environment when it becomes super-heated or the depositing of foreign substances are inhaled by people, or are deposited into the environment. There is no clear need for this to happen. There is not a drawback to experiencing the process of the environment as it is designed to take place.

There is no merit in altering weather, for no natural process involving the weather, ever changes form. There is the constant flow of energy and changing it or adapting it forcefully to your desires can have catastrophic effects on the environment surrounding it. There is a need to study further the reasons for this and if it is to continue, to study the energy and chemicals used to provide this. So long as there is not an impact that negatively alters the balance of other areas, this is possible to be acceptable.

Alexander says creating suitable environments for food growth in starving areas can be acceptable, but remember, you are not dependent on these variables as you have established them. Should some level of government imbalance itself and stop these flights or methods, or society crumble, the environment will not sustain itself in this method.

It is important to know that on a much grander scale; there is much that can alter patterns globally by continued use of rain generating material. Weather cannot simply be directed upon an isolated area. It is important to know that no matter how direct you attempt to control it; these actions still spill into many other areas. Other areas may not need this outcome, no matter how fruitful it may appear to be. There is much that the natural process of nature and the weather do to balance and regulate itself.

He says it is not necessary for you, mankind, to alter the deserts to create farmland. The methods of farming should also be addressed but creating that farmland in the Sahara Desert for example, this is not always a positive outcome. There are other methods and means. Also remember that what your desired quality of living may be, it may not be true for those who live in that region. There is no need to alter environments to the standards of those in other countries.

It is helpful to give the tools and resources for fresh water and other basic necessities, but it is not necessary to mechanically change the process by which food is grown on a global scale. Natural methods of all production of food and creating a suitable environment are best left untouched. It is important to maintain balance. There is no need for these alterations to take place. They are not benefiting your world on a global scale. Much of these actions are taken for global market and commercial reasons. Others are based on commercial reasons through military efforts, the ability to control resources and provide or negate security and the like.

Alexander says the so-called chem trails in the sky are not falling in your area to infiltrate you negatively. In other areas they are because this process is not thoroughly monitored and maintained in all regions as it is in others. Some of these alterations are for what appears to be for the greatest good of all. Occasionally bringing rain, but there are others where the greatest good is not in mind, and these only serve as demonstrations of the power and ability of these programs.

There have been catastrophic weather events that were the direct result of testing such power or alterations, which has taken place that was not intended by their using the machine or chemicals. It is important to know that no major shift in the earth and its surface or substructures will be changed or halted by the spraying of any chemical. No matter what damage has been done it will be righted. Nature will fix all once it is left alone without man's interference or once the vibration is raised to such a level that immediate action is necessary.

Patience, this will all meet the minds of many and more will observe these truths rather than seeing them as actions and stories of the fringe minority who they view should not be trusted. These stories, the true accuracies, will be known by many."

"Concerning the Space Shuttle's last mission; were there any hidden agendas there?" Armond asks.

"My guide says there are methods and means that aren't openly being shared at this time. There are developments in these areas, as most areas, which are not shared or openly discussed for fear of secrecy between nations being violated. There is concern that other citizenry will not respond to capabilities and methods in the same manner as all should.

There are some that wish to prosper from this financially. There is an opportunity for this to be done by private companies and those with knowing. Their government will still have the method of reaching space without needing outside assistance from other agencies or other countries. It is important to know that the government space program can travel much farther than what it has shared in the past. There is no alternative intent outside of personal financial gain and the ability to maintain, what they consider, to be national security.

He says it is in the interest to be established on the moon or other planets before other nations so that the areas can be secured on the controlling party's behalf. It is important to say that you should look to the stars and the planets, and you will see evidence of this and so many other things that are attempting to be concealed. Take your mind away from that which is not lasting and look beyond the surface of the planet, there are many amazing things beyond your solar system and should be explored.

Many beings have attempted to contact the populations of earth, and many have contacted the governments in various forms. Many do not listen; many have only seen the request to stop violence as a method of control. We do not conspire to take your ability to control your individual self from you. We do however wish that your will not be imposed on the masses of your own kind or on that of others.

It is important to practice autonomy. Practice faith in others. Patience is a virtue that is needed. Make small changes now and there will be others who receive the ideas at a later time. Not all will come forward; many will come forward once there is someone who makes their beliefs public. Once it is known in public that there are greater levels of secrecy being kept in all areas of government and bureaucracy there will be more who side with the true information and those who bring it.

Alexander says there is a method now for releasing information that is contrary to belief, that which the government releases in a method so that the true story, though contrary to many fabrications given early, does not upset or cause a stirring of emotions. There is a bombardment of information that causes one to look deeply and closely at nothing. An individual must clearly associate with the specific item in order to fully understand and appreciate it. There are not many who receive their information from outside popular outlets, which, through some intent, but also some political meandering, spread their news in such a manner that bombards a mind.

Some do so to compete with other sources, some do so with pure intent that nothing be truly inspected. An individual inquest must be made to every story that an individual finds important. There are seldom unbiased reports. There are seldom true stories. There is always a skewed vision that is placed over a story so that it is received better than before or so that news outlets can compete against themselves.

He says the story of space is similar. There are future plans, there are plans to go farther, and this will be achieved because a new drive will be developed. It is not possible by current calculations and methods to achieve any goal beyond your moon using current technological methods. The motive is to generate the resources to do so. Often there is nothing more than a denial of some area only to have outside funds come to the front so that others don't have to continue to bear the expense. This is true in this case but there are still government conditions that will be met and flights that will be manned and used without the public knowing of this information. Interest will be stirred. All revolutions in technology are driven by your dollar or the ability to market a new resource; this will drive this area too.

There is a method to their madness, but no truth is immediately evident because of their need for security. Peace will come at a greater advance if they should choose to remove those resources that are combative or ones that they consider to be for defense. All feel the pain of war, there is no need to create it or defend against it. Trial and error will lead to the creation of a new system of exploration beyond your solar system.

Alexander says it will take much time but there will be new fusion technology that will allow exploration into the immediate area from your current planet. It is important that these new developments be utilized with the good of all considered; no warring faction should be permitted to rule new areas. Unity through being human, through common ideas. It is not necessary to change the will of others, only allow those to come to it in their own time. Protect those who are unable to see the brutal nature of some no matter who they are."

"Is population control a true problem on this planet or is it just another control measure used to further government's hidden agendas?" Armond asks.

"My guide says population control is not an issue in the sense that the earth is being overrun by rampant births with no room for them to cohabit successfully. There is much talk about this subject in terms of fear and security of each nation, as though the birthrate is going to continue to soar to rates that overrun the national food supply and medical authorities. It is important to know that specifically these two areas should be addressed for all people.

Medication that is the true evolution of medicine to incorporate the non-physical body, and the food supply brought in line with more traditional and historically used production methods. The current process of farming and medication administration is not sustainable without causing more harm and more damage. The detriment to those who eat this food and use these medical products is not aiding them in a manner which is sustaining to any level of their being.

He says in the best cases they are merely putting neutral substances into their bodies which do not cause harm of any kind. There are vast sections of land that are uninhabited on your planet. It is not necessary to seek out other worlds simply to have more room to expand. It is important that the living, specifically the sheltering methods, how they are currently conducted is also not sustainable.

Many should not live in the manner in which they do. This does not mean the slum lords of large cities. This is the manner in which they are far removed from the earth and that which they take from it. To learn where and how to sustain yourself without dependence on another, that is to say some dependence is necessary, but the complete and total method of ignoring the processes involved in food production and acquisition, and the method by which homes are constructed and how the land is made to live around your homes, rather than all of these aspects being in harmony with each area of your existence. This must change. Many of these methods will not be readily followed because there is no commercial application to live in harmony with the tallest tree in the forest or in harmony with creatures that live in the deepest depths of the vast oceans.

Alexander says daily there is not consideration of these things but there are signs that make it available to all to know that they are not working in a proper direction. It is also true that no one will come to these terms unless they bring their own mind to it willingly. It is a challenge for many to live with the earth. It is not an extreme view to live in harmony, you will not revert to dirt floors and unsanitary conditions, but the method for many physical beings to be present on this plane at once, these new but old methods must be implemented or there will be greater health problems and fewer resources to sustain the population growth.

It is also important to say that no matter the human impact on the earth, the earth will always survive, the earth will strike balance, and the earth is quite capable of purging and acquiring energy. The earth does not ignore its own signs such as beings in a physical body. You can do harm to your physical body, there will be signs that you need to change, and repair can be made quickly if you follow these indications and your true self speaking to you.

He says the earth can be harmed but is aware of the harm and will correct it. It may not be immediately evident the corrective action taking place, but there is always balance to the earth. Left to its own devices, without human interference, the earth will heal and repair and maintain balance.

The earth can exist without you, but the earth is here for you, to live with and support one another.

It is by harmony and balance; it is not a resource to always be bent to your will alone for the sake of profit. It can provide everything."

"I'm very grateful for your time Evelyn, this has helped me to have a better understanding on these topics that I will be discussing in my future blog's." Armond said as he prepared to leave.

"Thank you for your kind words, I'm sure Alexander is more than happy to help in any way possible. Please, stop by anytime." I spoke.

Armond left $30.00 dollars on my coffee table as he moseyed off.

Chapter Twelve

*Note to Readers: The next two chapters occurred after the Coronavirus Pandemic reached a point where the state, of which I currently reside put in place the 'shelter-in-place' order and six-feet distancing.

So, to comply, I stopped allowing my clients to come to my home. I currently share a triple wide mobile home with two other retired ladies in a mobile home park. We each have our own bedroom and share the common areas, each paying 1/3rd of the rent and utilities.

This works well as I retired early last year, age sixty-two, to focus on my mediumship. Now, due to the coronavirus pandemic I only do readings over my cell phone for my longtime clients at no charge, due to so many being laid off from their jobs, and the health crisis that has affected them and their friends, families and loved ones.

I received an early morning call from Carter McDougall, the son of a long-time client of mine. He was attending a large university studying to become a Medical Research Scientist, but as the university closed due to the coronavirus, Carter decided to use the time to work on his thesis which deals with improving global human health; and to my surprise, he told me he is also a Holistic Healer and a Reiki Master practitioner.

There were several questions dealing with vaccines, epidemics, and pandemics that he was seeking information from a spiritual point of view to include in his thesis.

After getting myself settled, "So, Carter, where would you like to start?"

"I'd like to begin with your spiritual perspective on the Human Immunodeficiency Virus that causes the Acquired Immunodeficiency Syndrome which at last count infected over 65 million people and has killed over 25 million globally since 1981. Specifically, the impact the epidemic, or I should say pandemic has had on Africa."

Boy, I was surely scratching my head on what I just heard over the phone, Alexander may know what he was asking, but I didn't have a clue. "Carter, I just want to say you're talking to an old lady who never made it to college. So, whatever you just said went right over my head." I heard a slight chuckle on the other end of the cell.

"Sorry, I'm accustomed to talking to other university students and professors, please forgive my wordy statement. To rephrase, I'm just seeking what the spiritual take on HIV and AIDS is for Africa, as that region is one of my main areas of concern for my thesis."

"Well, let's see, Alexander says there was and is a need for the individuals who live there to experience much of the energy that was and is taking place. There is a need for others to learn how to help others. There is ancestral fighting and other collaborations taking place which need to be placed secondary to human existence on a much larger scale.

Alexander says the need for peace is not a mission simply to have for the sake of selling books and newspapers and making others feel good about their work or missions there. The added benefits, the overarching goal of peace and the way in which it carries over and spills out into other events, this is the purpose.

There are many who have never known hunger, these entities now dwell in very opposite conditions than to what they were familiar to in past lives, but this is by their choosing and for their benefit.

He says it is not for the judgment of anyone that this epidemic has taken place in this region. There are many from the same soul being group who have been brought into this area and it is necessary for the progress and growth and understanding of the group that it exists here.

Know that this is not universal truth regarding AIDS and HIV, there is not the same reasoning in every instance, but the turmoil found here is the regions method for expanding and developing. Expressing energy that needs to be released is the method by which the violence is brought about. There will be greater motivations for alternative means as the current infants develop into adulthood.

Alexander says society as we now know it will not survive in its current state in this region, by far, the most tragic events have yet to pass. They will move and grow beyond them, but the worst is yet to come for those in this area.

This region is not a battle for all world nations to interfere, as with all areas of development, any method of peace by force will not allow peace to prevail for any considerable amount of time.

Eliminating what is seen as a negative energy or entity will not prevent its existence in the future if it is not experienced now as it should be.

He says there are many who wish to help in this area, and there should be none who should be prevented from assisting but consider the means by which you provide aid. Are your methods personally driven? Are your means and methods supportive of all who live there no matter their beliefs? Are you attempting to change those who dwell there?

Alexander says while there are no correct or incorrect answers it is very important that you realize, in all aspects of life, not every battle will directly impact you, and if you involve yourself, you should not expect change to occur by what you feel is correct. What is correct for you in your life is not necessarily correct for all. This does not make anything false simply because it is different but know that your universe and perception of it is not the same as others you encounter.

He asks, where shall the children go? This is the question and often the concern is how the children will be raised in this area. The concern is not to be discounted because of the area but consider for a moment your concerns and ponder internally if your concerns for your own children, or the children in your country, if these concerns are legitimate or if they are simply concerning because you have nothing more tragic or seemingly detrimental to fear because you live in a less violent area.

Wondering to yourself is not a sign that you are crazy, introspection is important. It is important to carry out this personal investigation before carrying forward, charging forward, into a new realm with an outside idea. This does not mean that we are telling you to keep your ideas to yourself because they involve another region. We are not saying this in the least bit but consider carefully what it is that you are concerned for; careful evaluation is needed, do not have a quick reaction simply because 'something must be done.'

Alexander says wondering to yourself about any event or action is important. There are no right or wrong decisions, only cause and effect, often the regret you have about a decision can be lessened when you follow your true path, not one that has been decided for you by others, and it can be lessened when you have carefully considered to not intervene. It is not important to always share your idea; it is not important to always conceal your idea. Be patient with the world, be patient with yourself.

Offer help but do so unconditionally. Do not offer help with restriction. Do not offer help on the condition that anyone change their behavior. This can be seen in battles where medical aid is offered to the opposing forces troops. While this is a basic metaphor and some instances this did not happen, or it happened to a greater degree, it is important to decide to act in this manner.

But simply because you are changing your mind, or carrying out this act, it does not prove long-term success if you do not internally agree with the action. Just as peace by forceful means will not truly create peace. Often the greatest change comes in death or by the absence of a being in a region due to death. This is a very real and true possibility and should not be discounted because, for many, it is the only way true change will come.

Alexander says peace for all time is not a flowery garden in which a select group of humans wish to reside in their minds simply because the world is too harsh. They are idealists who are able to create peace within themselves, others can follow this. As the greater number of people can impact the individual, so can the individual impact a greater number of people. He does not feel that there is any loss simply because there is less hate in the world within an individual.

What is meant by this, is that there are many groups who wish for peace but want conditional peace or peace only for their kind. They wish for peace but also aim to do harm to others who oppose their views. Peace for all time is a realization that all methods and means are of importance and all life is valuable, not simply those who share your world views.

He says there are as many opinions on the living of life as there are grains of sand, blades of grass, and drops of water in the ocean. It is not a decision by the few or many to control a party of the opposing side. It is important to understand that there is no need for control. Many will grow beyond this and at a point in your civilization there will be a reverse within the community.

Alexander says if you shall describe this now as few carrying about amicability, and many being self-centered, soon there will be few who are worried about the self and property and many worried about the manner in which a greater good for the self and the group can be accomplished.

Soon the realization within more beings will come to pass that there are not many long-term possessions or ideals that are held here. Nothing which can be held in the physical world is something that passes with you throughout time. Often it is these things, the money, property, control, these things are only temporary, but they are what drive beings to carry out specific actions in an attempt to gain more of it or them.

Mashing all beings together in a world is the greatest method of teaching teamwork. There is so much isolation. Isolation by country, language, color, race, religion, economy. You do not need to stand in lines hugging one another all day but it is important to know that lines drawn on a map and other arbitrary factors do not impart wisdom to those around you. It is not more in the Creator's good grace to help only those within your fair city or your block, or within your group of friends because you were all the same and segregated within your tiny little world.

He says this is not to say that you must branch out, but isolation because there are differing factors of existence, this simply must go. You must, as a people, learn to contribute to many areas of life for your own benefit and contributing to the life of another's world for peace in your own life.

The mechanized nature of society will change. This is not to say that industry will go back in time and there will be horses instead of your current method of travel, but there will be changes in which the focus of industry is less on making profit for the sake of profit, and more about creating useful items and practices for the benefit of many who can use them.

Profiting from villages who do not have clean water is not a plan that anyone should be formulating in the present. The manner in which the clean water is delivered, and the waste carried away is a concern for us all. Survival is important, but it is not always required and not always necessary that all survive in the same way."

"It's a good thing I brought my recorder, your guide just said a mouthful." Carter said as he laughed.

"So very true, Alexander can dish it out when asked for." I said grinning, "So Carter, what's your next question?"

"These soul groups your guide refers to, as they come into this area, are they aware of their so-called mission concerning the balancing of energy?"

"Alexander says the amount of knowledge contained within your true self is not able to be put into calculable numbers. There is even greater levels and measurable amounts of information available to you and it resides outside of you but your connection to it is always in place as you wish to use it. You will not realize the true nature of things for this specific lifetime when you are constantly concerned with actions and events of previous lifetimes. There will be some who have greater recollection of what has transpired for them or what will take place but often this will need to be provided to you by a spirit or non-physical being.

This is done so that you are focused on this lifetime and not concerned with what may or may not have happened several centuries ago. There are many things that you will or will not do in this lifetime based on previous lifetimes but the manner in which you drank milk in a previous lifetime or your interactions on a daily basis are not important.

He says many times there is greater knowledge available within you concerning this lifetime and regarding previous lifetimes but like any unused or ignored aspect of being it will slowly live in smaller and smaller quantities, that is, it is not at the front of your mind where you are consistently retrieving and accessing it, so it becomes less dominant in your mind.

Often dreams are snippets of previous information. While dreams can also be actual events, travel, and communication in spirit while you are sleeping, they are also events that you see only with your mind, they can also be the creation of your mind. There is no singular aspect of a dream or its nature, but they can all be discerned if you begin to recollect them and use them and exercise your mind so that they are seen as important, not something of fanciful whimsy which you'll have no interest in after 45 minutes of being awake and beginning to engage in your daily activities.

Alexander says what is important is that you understand that there is nothing hidden from you. All is available to you. Understand that there may be sensitivities regarding specific incidents or events, but you are not shielded because we do not wish for you to know. There is much that beings will convince themselves of, much that they believe is important to them and is the make it or break it answer for them in this lifetime or any lifetime. With many questions and answers, simply wait a few days, even waiting several hours, your answer will come to you, or you will see how insignificant your conundrum really is once you are beyond the heat of the moment. Not that any one thing is insignificant, but when you quiet your mind, you will see the answers around you or in your mind.

He says you are all precious beings living precious moments, it is not to be worried over that you were a 'have or have not' in this lifetime or in any other. No matter if you were murdered, if you murdered another, or if you saved several children from drowning, all events are equally important, you are no better or worse because you spent your life sailing, spent your life in a cave, or spent your life lost. All things are for your benefit and therefore the benefit of all in existence.

You can access anything you wish, if it cannot be displayed to you or explained to you it will be stated so, the reasoning often given. You must also understand that if certain events are explained to you which must take place for some other purpose, some greater purpose, a purpose which may impact several people, you may not be shown something which could alter a path towards this event, but this is not always true. You will always have the freedom to choose, you will live on a timeline of your choosing no matter what anyone believes they have for you.

The exception to this statement; any prescribed events or situations or lessons, or emotions which you wanted to experience as part of your existence will manifest. It is not a god-force placing these events on you, it is your own doing by free will or by your choice prior to entry here. Because you created these events, you are the creator, in the moment or prior to physical existence, you have created what has been presented to you. You are capable of all things and are involved in what you are capable of experiencing.

Alexander says it is the trust you need in yourself; this is what is most often missing. The confidence, not to say that you are supreme, but to understand that you are worthy, you are capable, you do not need to place responsibility in the hands of another being, physical or non-physical. You do not need to reside yourself to inaction because you believe some other being will unfold the events in your favor. You are the ruler. You are the controller. You are the designer. Have faith in yourself above all things and above all others.

Any questions on what he just said?" I asked to make sure all was clear to Carter.

"No. I would now like to seek his spiritual take on the use of vaccines and the impact they have on global health, especially as they concern pandemics."

"Very well, Alexander says most vaccines do not harm the body in the sense that it tears down your physical nature. It is the harm that there is anything entering the system at all that is not created with the intent to uplift or uphold the human being. This is very much a contrary statement, opposite to the nature of what a vaccine is and what it is given for but understand that simply because you want to be healthy does not mean that others want you to be healthy. Simply because you are a good person does not mean that others are good people.

He says there is much more at stake than simply the freedom to refuse. There are greater lessons at work, you should consider very carefully what it is you would like to do and for what reason you would like to refuse. Do not simply do anything in your life because others are doing it, arrive at your own conclusions.

Alexander says concerning the AIDS and HIV you mentioned earlier, it has been almost 40 years and still no vaccine has been developed to prevent this syndrome or virus by your medical or scientific researchers."

"Ah, yes indeed, that is a very true statement." Carter said.

"So, have you another question?" I asked.

"I would now like to ask about our current pandemic, that of the Coronavirus or what some are calling COVID-19 virus that is the top concern of the World Health Organization and the Centers for Disease Control among other agencies. What is the spiritual take on this pandemic?"

"Let's see, Alexander says to begin with, there is much fear in our world for disease of any kind. There is always a desire by many to help, but there is also a desire by many to use any incident such as this to amplify the panic and use it to drive other actions as a means of controlling populations and driving money from one pocket to the next. In any epidemic or pandemic there is fear but most of this is brought on by outside sources, meaning that you do not personally be afraid, you are told to be afraid, often directly or indirectly, but many are just as open to any emotion. They wait to feel any specific emotion or concern until they are told to feel that emotion.

He says this does not mean that your associates or the news media outlets are saying, 'It is time for you to feel XYZ about this event.' It is the repetitive nature of that which you introduce into your mind which allows your own feelings to become these outside feelings. You are experiencing them as your own because you have allowed your mind to be concentrated in these areas and you have become filled with this view so that it is now also yours. In this way there are many emotions, worries, fears, and other aspects that are amplified because a single source shares the message and more minds are snared by it, rather than considering the impact it may or may not have on their own life and the reality that it may, in no way, bear any weight in their personal life.

Alexander says it is important to consider all possibilities and no matter your source it is one viewpoint or many viewpoints, but there is always a differing viewpoint. The important matter is not for you to take any viewpoint and establish it as your own. Only your perception will hold value for you. Only what you see and believe for yourself as accurate will carry true meaning for you.

He says as for the coronavirus it is spreading at a disturbing rate, as some would say, due in part at

the many different ways countries are trying to
contain its spread. It is important to know that
those who experience this will have had prior
knowledge that this event would take place. It is a
matter of experience and development from a
spiritual point of view that many will have
gruesome experiences with this outbreak.

Alexander says our fears are not going to
subside until we power on our mind and use it to
distinguish between the various levels of deception
that are presented by various leaders and media
platforms."

"Will a vaccine address the coronavirus
pandemic in the future, such as in the way we try to
prevent the flu virus each year?" Carter asks.

"Alexander says these are not requirements for
sustaining life of any kind on this planet. There is
no vaccine necessary. Many attempt to intervene in
life and many will still fall ill and succumb to many
diseases no matter what preventive measures are
taken. It is not a matter of protecting the physical-
by-physical means. If it is to happen it will come to
pass. If you wish to protect yourself, use your
nutrition to protect your physical, not quick actions
which carry no weight.

He says use the strength of your mind to protect
your body. Release that which is not for you and
engage fully in that which brings to the surface your
true being. Do not live-in fear. We repeat these
messages often because they are the root of many
questions and answers and social arrangements in
your world. We are after the same knowledge that
you seek on a daily basis. We wish to help you
grow, growing does not mean living the life of

another, taking on the emotions of another. The tree may use the nutrients of previous trees in much the same way that you may consider the generations before you, but like the tree, what you create will be unique only to you."

"So, in a nutshell, what is your guide saying?" Carter asked.

"Well, in a nutshell, Alexander says that the coronavirus is just a larger version of any other disaster, whether manmade or natural, that those on this planet face. Forest fires, erupting volcanoes, tsunamis, tornados, flash floods, epidemics, hurricanes, wars, genocide, and the list goes on and on.

He says much of these events are orchestrated by a group of higher evolved beings, in conjunction with certain soul groups, who agree to participate of their own free will, in order to bring about lessons and experiences for those in the human form. These lessons and experiences are designed to teach unconditional love on many different levels.

Because humankind resists overall positive change in favor of fear, greed, and power, higher evolved beings who oversee this realm, create so-called opportunities to bring out the true unconditional love 'energy beings' in the human form are capable of expressing, and much needed change becomes possible in advancing humanity and spiritual awareness.

Therefore, those who experience the coronavirus, concerning just being sick or also succumbing to death, already agreed before their birth into this world to play their part in bringing about this tremendous global lesson for humanity."

"Thank you, Ms. Adams, and my personal gratitude to your guide, Alexander."

"You're welcome." Carter clicked off.

Chapter Thirteen

Baxter Wellington, who is a client of mine requested a phone reading for his father Randol Wellington. I agreed and his father called at the prearranged time. Randol is a financial analyst who is contracted by a state government in the northeastern part of the country.

Randol was not the type to chit-chat as I found that out after answering my cell.

"Hello…"

"As the coronavirus pandemic creates chaos and fluctuations in the stock markets, how will that affect the 'Dollar' being the World Reserve Currency in the future?" Randol asked straight away.

"Ah…okay, let me see what my guide Alexander can reveal about that…he says there are many schemes devised for the disruption and the continuity of daily life in the United States. It is important to say that the dollar is not the strongest currency in terms of reliability and economic production. There is a great deception by those in authority to maintain this myth to the American people, and even those that report on it, that it is the strongest and most reliable currency.

He says there is a method for calculating the structure of industry and its reliability within each economic area. These means and methods do not depend on currency and are more substantial and more accurate in determining the stronger government, stronger economy, stronger production, and the long-term sustainability of a value.

Alexander says the U.S. currency will be affected by the coronavirus pandemic, but that it will be just one cause, while there are many who are going to devalue the dollar by other means and actions. It will not be their intent, but the profit margin within their companies is more important to them. There will be more devaluing and therefore the dollar will eventually become worthless as time goes on.

What is also taking place on this same timeline is that others are realizing that this is not a true method for determining value and it distracts us all form the true meaning and effort associated with each product. The economy is often an arbitrary and abstract thought for many. It is simply the relation of your dollar and what it is able to purchase for you at the market once you have produced some amount of work in order to obtain the dollar.

He says there will be a time when Marshall Law is declared but this will not be a widespread problem, this will be very isolated and conducted with the segregation of the media. This is more difficult to do today since there are so many outlets for media and methods for communication between people in various regions.

Yes, it was done previously by your government that there would intentionally be no reporting on a subject simply because no information was given or because instructions were given to the media to not broadcast on a topic. Ever more is the media relying on the government for information, they do not wish to experience problems in their future by not complying. There are deeper interests than what is being reported and not reported.

Alexander says the overall financial aspect of the coronavirus pandemic will not be reported to the American people to offset fear and panic in the population. There will be a degradation of society in the future just as many have seen in science-fiction movies of Hollywood. This is not a negative impact on culture and society, but so much of what you do is a facade, and has you so removed from the very nature of the world, that it will happen simply because there is not enough in terms of tent poles to keep the tent up which was built on a solid foundation but is now controlled for ludicrous resources."

"Well, did that answer your…?"

"Thank you." Randol Wellington clicked off.

"Wha…ah…okay then." I clicked off as I shook my head in disbelief. Even the living can be annoying sometimes.

END*****

Parting Words:

Divine Love, Wisdom and Energy are given freely to humankind from the Universal Consciousness through the experiencing of hatred, war, racism, disease, sexism, bigotry, molestation, suicide, natural disasters, rape, torture, abortion, pandemics, murder, and the like, for they are great lessons to realize in your search for spiritual awareness and enlightenment on your journey back to God.

Evelyn Adams

Printed in Great Britain
by Amazon